HOW TO
INVEST TODAY

HOW TO INVEST TODAY

A BEGINNER'S GUIDE TO THE WORLD OF INVESTMENTS

EDITED BY

LAWRENCE LYNN

WITH CHAPTERS BY

KENNETH G. ALTVATER • GEORGE S. ECKHARDT JR.

CHARLES L. FAHY • ROBERT FRATER

JAMES GALBRAITH • OTTO GLASER

JOHN R. MARKLE • CHARLES SMITH

HENRY HOLT AND COMPANY • NEW YORK

Henry Holt and Company, Inc.
Publishers since 1866
115 West 18th Street
New York, New York 10011

Henry Holt® is a registered
trademark of Henry Holt and Company, Inc.

Library of Congress Cataloging-in-Publication Data
How to invest today: a beginner's guide to the world of investments /
edited by Lawrence Lynn with chapters by Kenneth G. Altvater . . . [et al.].
p.   cm.
Includes index.
1. Finance, Personal.   2. Investments.   3. Securities.   4. Estate planning.
5. Mutual funds.   I. Lynn, Lawrence.   II. Altvater, Kenneth G.
HG179.H633   1995
332.6—dc20   95-10838
                                                                    CIP

ISBN 0-8050-3733-0

Henry Holt books are available for special
promotions and premiums. For details contact:
Director, Special Markets.

First Edition—1995

Designed by Ann Gold

Printed in the United States of America
All first editions are printed on acid-free paper. ∞

1   3   5   7   9   10   6   8   4   2

CONTENTS

FOREWORD

Many times during the past two decades I sought a book on investment alternatives suitable for the novice. I always failed to find anything that would serve. There was no single, concise, reader-friendly book profiling everything from stocks and bonds to estate planning to real estate.

So I decided to assemble a team of experts and put such a book together myself. You are holding the results—a complete explanatory guide, using a minimum of jargon, that will start you out on a satisfying investment career. Everything is here to help the newcomer learn the terms, plan a portfolio, and review the many types of fixed- and variable-income investments. We have even included a chapter on the most common mistakes made by fledgling investors. If you are new to investing, this is the book for you.

Inevitably, thanks need to be offered to the many individuals who helped discuss, assess, revise, and contest the subjects covered here. To my respected colleagues who contributed full chapters, I salute a job well done, genially and comprehensively. For their ideas and constructive criticism, the list is long of those who read and reread sections, offering suggestions and encouragement. Those who deserve special mention are: Bert Bandini; Brian Berg; Bob Bradford; John and Janet Bubb; David Castle; David Clarke; Richard Davis; Renate Donovan; Larry Englander; Dixon Foss; Alice Faye Hamilton; Rebecca Galbraith; John Graf; William Green; Marion Brice Griffey; Roger Heuman; Dr. Andrew Kurkjian; Dr. Erik Kwok; Brian Lesch; Tom Lisenby; James Malone; David Matthison; Temple Moore; John Osborne; Alliana Poe; Guy Robertson; Ben Ronn; Greg and Sylvia Savage; Norman Shugar; John and Jan Turley; Mike Turner; and Don Zimmerman. Any residual errors found in this book are entirely attributable to me and in spite of all these wonderful helpers. I am also grateful for the background (and sometimes foreground) efforts extended freely by Dr. Michael Doran, my agent at Southern Literary Agency, as we all strove to make an exemplary contribution to the investment literature.

Last, and of course most important, I owe a vast debt to my wife, Dori, for her patient understanding and fortitude in aiding me with the seemingly never-ending task of editing and correcting the manuscript. Her sharp eye was as valuable as her good spirits throughout it all. I'm glad that I will never know if I could have put things together without her; certainly it wouldn't have been half the fun.

—Lawrence Lynn
May 1, 1995

ABOUT THE CONTRIBUTORS

DR. LAWRENCE LYNN, author of several chapters and general editor, studied chemical engineering at Texas A & M University and Columbia University. During a career in product and process development he worked at Celanese and at General Foods, then in management, first as Vice President of Riviana Foods and later as President and Chief Executive Officer at Pine-O-Pine Company in Houston. His expertise in investing led to a second career as a broker at Merrill Lynch and Drexel Burnham Lambert. He retired from Drexel as Senior Vice President, Investments, in 1984. At present he works as an investment consultant and writer. He is co-author of *Your Vision: All About Modern Eye Care* (1994) and dozens of articles on a wide range of subjects.

KENNETH G. ALTVATER graduated cum laude in economics from the University of Texas. He began his career in sales, administration, and training with American General Corporation, later entering banking and rising to Senior Vice President and Trust Officer with Southern National Bank and River Oaks Trust Company. He is now President of Allocation Company, which provides contract plan administration for qualified contribution plans. He has recently been appointed as an independent fiduciary for two large employee benefit plans in Texas at the request of the United States Department of Labor.

GEORGE S. ECKHARDT JR. received his undergraduate degree in business administration from The Citadel. After service as a career army officer, he entered brokerage with Merrill Lynch in 1972. Since then he has become certified in financial planning, particularly as it applies to retirement and estate planning. He is a member of the Charles E. Merrill Circle, a group of the most highly respected financial consultants at Merrill Lynch.

CHARLES L. FAHY was born and reared in South America, where he received his early education. He majored in international affairs and finance at the University of Georgia. After brief service in the United States Army he entered investment brokering, first with E. F. Hutton and subsequently with Oppenheimer and Company in Houston, where he is now a Senior Vice President in the special accounts branch of Phillips, Fahy, and Rockwell. He is also the moderator of the television program *Money Talks,* and a regular writer on investing; he is the author of the recent book *The Streetwise Investor* (1994).

ROBERT FRATER, a cum laude business administration graduate of the University of Wisconsin, Stout, entered marketing with George Hormel and moved on to management with Southern Timber Growers. Switching to finance, he worked first with the Association for Financial Planning in Houston, and later as Vice President and a principal stockholder of Houston Asset Management. He is currently Chairman and Chief Executive Officer of Redevco, an urban redevelopment and preservation organization. He has testified before the United States Congress on behalf of pro-consumer real estate legislation, and is regularly quoted in *Money* and many other public and professional publications.

DR. JAMES GALBRAITH received his undergraduate education at the University of Toronto and went on to graduate studies at the University of Idaho, specializing in geology and chemistry. He has two decades' experience in international resource analysis behind him, and is currently an independent consulting geostatistician in Houston specializing in the development of computer software and the financial analysis of the energy industry. His original research has appeared in many professional journals, including the *Journal of Geochemical Exploration, Ground Water Journal,* and *The Analyst,* and in publications of the United States Department of Energy and the Brazilian Geological Congress.

OTTO GLASER is an accounting graduate of the University of Houston. After two years of military service and four with Radoff Brothers, he changed careers and entered investment brokering in 1961. He was a senior broker with Merrill Lynch and at present is a Vice President with A. G. Edwards in Houston. His central investment interest and expertise lies in fixed-income investments, with which he has successfully guided many clients with considerable portfolios.

JOHN MARKLE graduated in business administration from Michigan State University. After working in hotel management he entered brokerage with E. F. Hutton, moved on to Prudential-Bache, and finally to Merrill Lynch, where he is now a Vice President in Houston's Westlake office. He is a technical analysis expert known for his skill in point and figure charting.

DR. CHARLES SMITH did his undergraduate work in business administration at McNeese State University, after which he entered graduate training at Louisiana State University, New Orleans, and then at Texas A & M University. He is currently a tenured associate professor at the University of Houston, Downtown, and coordinator of its program in real estate studies. His research findings have appeared in many professional journals, such as the *Journal of Real Estate Appraisal, Journal of Real Estate Research,* and *Journal of Property Management.* He also serves on request as a real estate expert witness and as a real estate consultant.

1
PREREQUISITES FOR
SUCCESSFUL INVESTING

LAWRENCE LYNN

The beginning investor usually comes to his task with no small sense of skepticism about what lies ahead. Through inheritance, or the decision to begin putting aside income instead of spending it, money is in hand that can be put to good use. There it is, waiting in savings or checking accounts, in a safe-deposit box, or tucked under the mattress. But for what should it be used? What investments are "best"? Which are "safe"? The problem is one of ignorance—unfamiliarity with a lot of unfamiliar concepts and terms. The new investor knows that putting money into interplanetary ore importing is probably not a good idea. Past that, all is dim.

So this is where we start: by laying out the fundamentals of what investment is all about.

THE BASIC REQUIREMENTS

There are four basic components of successful investing. These are: (1) time; (2) starting capital; (3) knowledge and skill; and (4) determination.

For a young person, time seems limitless. There is time for work, time for fun, time to waste. If one has decades of life ahead, a sizable estate might be accumulated by just sticking with a well-grounded plan. Blunders and disasters can be shrugged off as dues to be paid along the way. This is not the case for someone past fifty. Like it or not, in Nature's scheme of things, time is running short. Make a serious error now and there could well not be enough years left to begin again.

Starting capital is a more forgiving consideration. It really doesn't take much to start an investment program, no matter what one's income. In the daily flow of needs and wants, a determined individual with a small income can still set aside immediate gratification and build up a savings account. It takes fortitude and a strong sense that long-term results are worth sacrifices, but it can be done. In fact, the deferral of current pleasures so that capital can be amassed was, and is, one of the cardinal virtues believed in by the determined immigrants from whom many of us spring. Obviously, the larger the income, the greater the opportunities for savings and investment.

Knowledge and skill, ability to navigate through the world of investments (or merely some part of that world), are essential so that available capital can be used to best advantage. Although it is a good idea to be solidly grounded in at least the fundamentals, it is not necessary for an investor to keep in close touch with the minutiae of investment. A good broker can handle that for you.

The key is to find a broker who is not simply out to earn maximum income for himself and his brokerage firm. That can be tough, since brokers have profitability quotas that their firms expect them to fill. A shamelessly ironic old joke in brokerage firm circles is that it is best to make "errors of *commission*"—fee-producing commissions, that is—"than errors of *omission*." More than a few brokers, when under the gun, will move clients' investments around just to derive income from the transactions, so beware.

The final prerequisite for success in investment is determination. Without this, no serious results can be achieved. A financial program needs constant monitoring and adjustment, record-keeping, and review. There is a tendency among those who work for a salary to do the work, go home, and go to sleep. Investments demand better attention than this; the vagaries of economic cycles can destroy an entire investment plan, and a portfolio with it.

Time, starting capital, knowledge and skill, determination—

there they are, the elements guiding an investment program. The next step is to determine reasonable objectives.

Some investors set the size of an estate and work toward it; others want to assure a retirement income above and beyond problematic payments from Social Security and a corporate pension plan, fund the college education of a couple of children, or make major purchases such as a vacation home or a boat. Reaching any goal involves making value judgments and striking a balance between seeking further growth of your wealth and spending what you get.

INVESTMENT PLANNING

Conventional wisdom in investment holds that there are a half-dozen zones of investment planning. These are: (1) liquidity and temporary safety of principal; (2) higher current yield; (3) tax exemption and avoidance; (4) growth of principal; (5) the prudent man rule; and (6) speculation. These zones are not mutually exclusive; in fact, most seasoned investors find themselves involved in each, frequently all at the same time. It's a matter of mixing and matching as opportunity and common sense dictate, and as your objectives warrant. Here's an explanation of each zone.

1. Liquidity. "Liquidity" is a term borrowed from earth systems studies, specifically the water cycle. Atmospheric condensation of water produces rainfall, after which water percolates through and over the earth's surface until it evaporates and returns to the atmosphere. Left alone, this process goes on smoothly and eternally. In finance, liquidity means being able to put capital to use easily at any time.

There is a certain psychological benefit obtained by having the power of money on call, but money is really only of help to you if that power is converted into effort. Moreover, not using money is foolish for two reasons: it can be stolen, and over time all currencies inevitably become devalued. The forces of an economy produce more years of inflation than deflation, so a currency commonly loses value at from 2 to 5 percent yearly. "Pure liquidity"—money in your hand—should therefore be kept to a minimum.

A better alternative, while maintaining good liquidity, is to bank the money. Some bank checking accounts and all savings accounts provide interest income, albeit always crafted at less than the anticipated rate of inflation so as to make the institution a profit for holding your money (in addition to lending it out for interest returns). Time penalty deposits, such as certificates of deposit, where slightly higher interest rates are promised if you do not withdraw the money for a contracted period of time, offer a mildly better deal—unless inflation becomes rampant. During the late 1970s, for example, in the last years of the Carter administration, inflation reached 15 percent *per year.* It was a good time not to hover over cash, bank accounts, or certificates of deposit as their value wisped away to nothing in a hurry.

Ordinarily, it is best to harbor a minimum of your money in bank accounts. Put most of the money to which you want quick possible access into a mix of passbook savings accounts, money market accounts, and certificates of deposit. United States Treasury bills, notes, and bonds, and bonds issued by the top corporations of the United States, such as General Electric or Du Pont, provide a slightly better interest rate. True, there is a fee for buying and selling such issues, but the cost is quite small.

2. Higher Current Yield. "Higher current yield" implies a stream of income at a better profit than can be achieved by leaving money in the basic money havens. The available vehicles provide this with the trade-off of varying degrees of risk.

Corporate bonds are a corporation's promise to repay you your invested money plus a defined interest amount after a specified time. Most bonds have rates that tag closely to expected rates of inflation, but under certain conditions some may produce higher yields. For example, combinations of bonds in unit investment trust certificates or bond mutual funds have generated returns of 12 percent or even slightly higher. You can consider entities specializing in mortgage investments, some of them guaranteed by the Government National Mortgage Association (GNMA).

If you are bold enough to accept still higher risk levels in an active account, and are willing to put in the time and effort it requires to monitor and control an account more attentively, you might get into optioning stocks or bonds.

An "option" is the right of the option holder to either buy or sell a specified quantity of a security at a set price within a specified time. If buying, you hope that the price will continue to rise beyond the price at which you agreed to buy, giving you a profit. If selling, you hope that the price will have peaked and that any decline after the sale will be the problem of the new owner. A "covered option" means that you already own enough of the security to match the number of shares offered, without having to buy more to match your promise if the demand reaches that point. This is a relatively low-risk situation. An "uncovered option" is riskier, since you don't already have enough stock purchased to meet full demand, and you may have to make up the gap with higher-priced purchases if you get called on it.

The trick here is to spot a trend early enough to anticipate both the motion of price and what measures must be taken to cover promises. The rate of return for successful option work can be an annual profit of over 25 percent, but at the cost of meticulous attentiveness to what is going on.

Finally, you can get into real estate. Conventional wisdom holds that this is a high-risk area, but investments in land, and the minerals and structures under and on the land, can be quite profitable if their value is rising or if you can put to work whatever earning potential they have through rents or creative industry. There is a lot more to real estate investment than watching numbers, for value here is a function of local and regional economic trends, potential accessibility, and altering conditions of demand. It is usually a good idea either to be personally familiar with the site and situation of the real estate you are considering or to contract the advice of a real estate investment specialist. The legendary stories of naive Midwesterners who invested in property that turned out to be on the bottom of Lake Okeechobee in Florida and immigrants who were unscrupulously sold rights to tolls from New York's Brooklyn Bridge, are actually founded in unfortunate fact. So think hard before putting down your money.

3. Tax Exemption and Avoidance. Most of us have ambivalent feelings about taxes. We know that they are necessary to keep government services going, but we hate to pay for them—particularly if we aren't using them much or at all. It is especially galling to be a hard-working taxpayer whenever instances of government waste, theft, or sheer folly turn up in the morning newspapers. For those who want to put in the effort, however, the oxymoronic characteristic structure of taxation philosophy—trying to take your money yet making it possible for you to slip part of the noose by using loopholes—makes it possible to reduce payments to a more satisfying level than would at first seem likely. This was a particularly urgent matter when the highest tax brackets cost the taxpayer as much as 70 percent of his annual income, less so but still appealing now that the maximum is down to 39.6 percent.

The oldest stalwart device with which to duck taxes is municipal bonds, since they are exempt from federal income taxes. Many states exempt them, too, if the bonds were issued by a city in the state of your residence. Governments provide this loophole so that people will be inclined to support municipalities, the alternative being the unpleasant matter of raising property taxes.

With municipal bonds you protect new income generated by the bonds, but what about a shelter for income from sources such as salaries, stock dividends and interest, or stock capital gains? At one time it was possible to find tax shelters in ventures such as cattle-feeding projects, petroleum exploration and drilling, and some equipment leasing. In a time when governments large and small are scrambling to counteract budget deficit problems, new tax laws have done away with many such avenues.

The guarded exception is real estate, which can still be made to provide good tax savings under the right conditions. Mortgages are allowed in excess of initial equity in many real estate projects, and income tax deductions against interest paid on a home are helpful. This stems from the IRS code allowing all such interest to be deducted from *taxable* income. How much reward can flow from such real estate investments? There are as many ways to structure real estate deals as there are deals. A broader sense of the possibilities is provided in chapter 7.

4. Growth of Principal. A young person in a middle income bracket just starting out doesn't usually need to worry about matters such as added current income or tax shelters. Starting an investment nest egg, and nurturing it, are the main concerns.

A fundamental here is the individual's willingness to sacrifice some immediate gratification (through spending) and some liquidity (through holding onto cash) and invest. Part of your net worth should be put into vehicles that will grow, warding off the effects of inflation while their value itself increases. Buying rare coins or stamps, jewelry, racehorses, or art objects is not a good way to proceed since, aside from extremely rare cases, such purchases do not increase in value anywhere near the rate of currency devaluation. They also have a nasty propensity to be suddenly devalued, as was the case with a notoriously overrated Van Gogh painting some years ago that ruined an unwary Japanese investor.

Obtaining an interest in healthy, burgeoning corporations is a much better investment approach. Not bonds, a company's debt securities, which are usually safe but not particularly dynamic, but stock in the company itself. You can buy "preferred stock" (PFD), which provides a fixed return out of the company's annual profits, or "common stock," which pays out however much is left after bonds, bank loans, and preferred stock equity are honored. Stocks are freely traded in the various stock exchanges around the world, the most important of which are in New York, London, and Tokyo, and to invest, all you need is money.

Canny investment in and tracking of common stocks is the best way to attain financial growth. How much growth is possible? A random walk on common stock investments would have led you to gains of 9 or 10 percent per year for most of the past century. It is possible to double this degree of profit if you are deliberate and work at it. That ought to be an attractive idea considering what achieving a 20 percent annual growth means for personal security. No one but a Hollywood star or a cocaine trafficker can get income raises like that year after year.

5. Prudent Man Rule. Under some circumstances, such as making absolutely certain that an elderly person can count on a trust's consistent, un-risk-laden investment income for life, the so-called "prudent man rule" of the local lawmaking authority is your investment guide. This guide is usually very specific, and that's a good thing, since any damages to an estate taint the estate manager, sometimes through imprisonment and fines.

Most estate managers work hard to be even more conservative than a "prudent man." They seek out the most conservative, stodgy corporations for preferred stock purchases and put most of their faith in different bonds. Investment like this will mean a gradual wasting away of capital, but virtually no risk of losing big parts of the estate.

6. Speculation. Speculation is essentially a carefully considered risk. You decide to "take a flier" on an investment that may pay out wonderfully but for which there is moderate to great risk. The rule here is never to risk more than you can afford to lose. How much that is depends on how bold and how old you are. If you are young, have an adequate income and the expectation of job security, pay raises, and the like, you are probably at a point where you can do some speculating with a portion of your estate. If you are elderly and retired on a modest, fixed income, the reverse is the case.

Speculation is not the same thing as wagering on a spin of the roulette wheel if you put on your thinking cap and don't let wild promises overcome overt warning signs. You can increase the odds in your favor by assembling information on the investment area—how it works, how successful past performance has been, who generated the best results. Shy away from anyone who comes on like a used-car salesman, trying to push emotional buttons and offering a special deal if you put in your money *now*, before you've thought much about it. Chasing rainbows is not what investing ought to be about.

SOME TYPICAL SMALL INVESTORS

Perhaps the best way to amplify the notion of mixing investment alternatives is to consider some generalized investor types.

1. The Retiree. Colonel Robert Richardson is retired from a thirty-two-year career in the United States Army, living in the suburbs of San Antonio near Fort Sam Houston. He and his wife live on his military pension together with what can be derived from an investment equity of roughly $400,000.

Realistically, because they are in their late sixties, neither the colonel nor his wife can expect to begin new careers. The pension is large enough for frugal living, but doesn't enable them to travel or enjoy other indulgences, so the difference in having an enjoyable retired life comes from returns on investment. They can expect to live another ten to fifteen years, so for them it makes sense to use about 70 percent of their estate to obtain maximum safety of principal and high liquidity. Even with low to moderate inflation, this proportion of the estate will be depleted by the time they are no longer mobile, so part of their equity should be working to overcome the damage from currency devaluation and taxes. About 20 percent can be devoted to a higher current yield, probably Federal Agency notes or their equivalent, and the last 10 percent can be dedicated to the growth of principal.

2. The Affluent Surgeon. Dr. William Malone, a middle-aged neurosurgeon living in Chicago, is married, has three children, and lives in a silk-stocking neighborhood. His wife runs his clinic; she has as good a head for business as he does for surgical artistry. Since they bring in an income that more than satisfies basic needs and wants, and the clinic's traffic is steadily increasing, they have no need to protect their investment equity much, nor to use it to generate income. A far more pressing matter is relief from taxation, and their investment adviser recommends a portfolio emphasizing about half their total equity in municipal bonds and half in securities producing a growth of principal. A bit in between is used to create trusts for their children, within gift tax permissible limits, so as to lighten their current tax burden while creating the children's equity foundations.

3. The Young Engineer. Edward Elkins, an aeronautical engineer in Seattle, is recently married. His wife of six years has borne

two children, who she will stay home to rear at least until they begin school. Edward has a salary of $48,000 per year, out of which
he has lately saved an estate valued at $20,000. Since job security
in Edward's field is tenuous, and taxation is not onerous, they
would be best advised to keep around 10 percent of their equity
liquid and 20 percent working to earn them a higher current yield.
The balance of their equity should go into solid, nonspeculative
long-term growth investments, preferably healthy common stock
shares, with a little thought about speculation now and again.

4. The Single Nurse. Nancy McAshan is a registered nurse
working for a hospital in Winston-Salem, North Carolina. It was
her decision not to marry until past thirty, the age she is now ap-
proaching. She earns $28,000 per year and recently inherited
$15,000 in cash, with which she consults a professional about set-
ting up a brand-new portfolio. The adviser notes that since nurses
rarely need worry about becoming unemployed, Nancy should
keep only about 10 percent of her equity liquid. Her salary from
the hospital is enough to pay basic living costs; probably 30 percent
of her equity should go toward generating higher current income,
either to reinvest or to pay for the special one-time purchases that
make life so much more fun. About 50 percent should be put into
growth of principal, building her estate and already lining her up
for a retirement income; 10 percent can go into speculation.

AN INVESTMENT STRATEGY

John Tracy is a plumbing contractor who brings in more than
$45,000 per year plus company benefits that cover health and life
insurance for him and his wife, Janice. She works part-time in a
picture frame shop, arranging her hours to coincide with the
schedules of the couple's two grade-school children. The extra
$10,000 per year she earns helps the family budget, including
building investment equity. This equity has reached encouraging

proportions as each is reaching age forty, no less than some $68,000.

They feel, correctly, that the growth of principal is their best orientation, since taxes aren't a problem and they don't have extravagant tastes. The Tracys decide to put together an investment distribution analysis worksheet (see Table 1-1 on page 13) to help their thinking about what they will do.

At the bottom of the worksheet they note their current investment proportions, wherein long-term growth at the moment is at 35 percent, income is at 57 percent, and speculation is at 8 percent. They set a goal of shifting emphases to a 60-30-10 mixture. At the moment, their $68,000 equity is earning $3,444 annually, a yield of 5.0 percent. These returns come from long-term growth stocks in Colgate and Winn-Dixie, a tiny total of $544, and from the current income-oriented securities of United States Treasury notes and Ohio Edison, a utility, totaling $2,900. Their stab at a speculation stock, XYZ Intergalactic, recommended by Uncle Charlie, brought in nothing at all.

Place your desired distribution by objective in the blank spaces to the left of the percent signs before the rest of the table is completed. It's a good idea to fold under the part about desired objectives so that they do not prejudice your actual allocations. When you have completed the rest of the chart, unfold it and put in the actual distribution. It may be similar to your desired distribution or disturbingly different.

The Tracys decide to begin adding equity each month to either Colgate, Winn-Dixie, or another growth stock. They could sell some of their Treasury notes to pull things into the new investment proportions they want, but they are used to the little bit of income being derived from that quarter and leave matters there as they are.

In a few years, as personal circumstances alter, they will sit down again with their figures and alter proportions. Once Janet goes back to full-time work, easing the cash flow each month, they will probably further emphasize long-term growth and even make greater efforts in speculation, this time definitely not on a tip from Uncle Charlie.

CONCLUSION

Most investors spread their risks around by using two or more of the investment routes. It is necessary to watch over what is happening to your portfolio, as an investment array is called. Given an unexpected inheritance or the passing of years, and of course success or failure in your career, the best courses for you may alter with time, and usually do.

Once again, the main thing is to overcome inertia so that you do a little investment thinking each month. Procrastination is the only thing you have to fear. Look investment opportunity in the eye, put yourself on a mild regimen, and one day you will suddenly realize that your estate has become significant. The sense of fulfillment and security derived in that moment will more than make up for the effort used to make it come about.

TABLE 1-1:
INVESTMENT DISTRIBUTION ANALYSIS WORKSHEET

For Long Term Growth			For Current Income			For Speculation		
ITEM	PRESENT VALUE ($)	ANNUAL YIELD ($)	ITEM	PRESENT VALUE ($)	ANNUAL YIELD ($)	ITEM	PRESENT VALUE ($)	ANNUAL YIELD ($)
Colgate	20,000	424	US Tsy Notes	20,000	1,400	XYZ	5,000	0
Winn-Dixie	4,400	120	Ohio Ed	19,500	1,500			
Ⓐ TOTAL 24,400		Ⓑ 544	Ⓒ TOTAL 39,500		Ⓓ 2,900	Ⓔ TOTAL 5,000		Ⓕ 0
Annual % Yield 2.22%			Annual % Yield 7.5%			Annual % Yield 0%		

Total Value (Ⓐ + Ⓒ + Ⓔ)   Ⓖ $68,900

Total Yield $ (Ⓑ + Ⓓ + Ⓕ)   Ⓗ $ 3,444

Total Annual Yield (Ⓗ ÷ Ⓖ × 100)   5.0%

- - - - - - - - - - - - fold

Distribution By Objective		Actual	Desired
Long-term Growth	(Ⓐ ÷ Ⓖ × 100)	35 %	60 %
Income	(Ⓒ ÷ Ⓖ × 100)	57 %	30 %
Speculation	(Ⓔ ÷ Ⓖ × 100)	8 %	10 %

fold - - - - -

2

UNDERSTANDING KEY INDICATORS

JAMES GALBRAITH

INTRODUCTION

Determining the health of a business is easy once you know what to look for.

Companies that trade on the main public stock exchanges in the United States are required by the Securities & Exchange Commission (SEC) to provide basic, truthful data for their stockholders in quarterly and annual reports. A company's annual report is usually available without charge from its corporate secretary, and the larger brokerages hand them out as a service. Value Line, Standard & Poor's, Market Base, and other data collection businesses gather and summarize a considerable amount of financial information on thousands of companies, and make it available for a fee. The new investor is probably best off asking for annual reports.

There are seven basic parts in an annual report: (1) management's message to the stockholders; (2) the annual income statement; (3) a five-year (or more) summary of operations; (4) a breakdown of sales and earnings; (5) the annual balance sheet; (6) the auditor's opinion of what all this means; and (7) notes to the financial statements. After a little practice it becomes second nature to use these resources to determine some fifteen key indicators of the health of a company.

The best way to introduce the indicators is to explore a real annual report of an actual company. SYSCO is a Houston-based company engaged in marketing and distributing a wide range of food and related products to the food service, or "away-from-home-eating" industry, from outlets in the United States and Canada. Our example is SYSCO's annual report, presented at the end of the second quarter of 1991, the end of its fiscal year. As we proceed, please refer to Tables 2-1 through 2-4 on pages 32–34. These summarize the basic financial data used in this chapter, present the formulas of the various indicators, and show the values calculated for them in the SYSCO example.

THE BUSINESS STRUCTURES

We start by acknowledging the forms of today's modern businesses. With rare exceptions, business is carried out under one of three legal structures. These are the proprietorship, the partnership, and the corporation.

The simplest and probably the oldest form is the proprietorship, left over from those times when all businesses were one-man (or one-family) affairs. The proprietorship continues to be used for smaller businesses such as retail shops and dentists' practices. If you own an investment as a single proprietor, the total assets working for the business belong to you. You share them with no one. If the investment does well, the gains belong solely to you. Of course, you also carry the entire burden of failure. When you lose, you lose alone. You get sued alone, too, since the business is you.

Setting up a business in the basement or a corner of the dining room is a common way in which individuals without much experience or funding start up a way in which they hope to make an income from some product or service. Others may set up shop in rented quarters, using savings or inherited money. The search for buyers or clients is particularly rough for tiny, untried enterprises, and their casualty rate is high—according to some sources, in the neighborhood of 90 percent within four years. Yet the attraction of working for oneself, without a boss, is strong enough to keep newcomers trying to beat the salary treadmill.

If an enterprise is complex enough, two or more individuals can become united as a partnership. This is also an ancient idea, traceable back to mankind's earliest communal hunting expeditions. By their very nature, some sorts of business efforts are too much for one person and his family to handle. They may be highly complicated or demand a great deal of starting capital. Whatever the case, the private individual may wish to share the benefits and risks with someone, or several someones. Two individuals usually agree to an equal investment and an even split in the profits, but different ratios of contribution and return are not uncommon. The same thing goes for greater numbers of partners.

Since partnerships are only as comfortable as the relationship between the partners, and because partnerships—like proprietorships—are subject to direct risks, corporations are the most popular way to configure businesses. The corporation dates back to the late sixteenth and early seventeenth centuries in Europe, when private enterprise began to become involved on a large scale in trafficking with the rest of the world, first through trade but shortly thereafter through overt conquest. Investors bought pieces of the action in a "company of their fellows" and were able to vote on what would be done commensurate with how large a stake they had in the "incorporated" venture.

The substance of the corporation is the same today. The individuals who own shares generally elect a supervisory board to keep track of what is going on, the members of which may be stockholders themselves and direct participants in the day-to-day operations of the business. If the corporation issues 2,000 shares and you own a 10 percent segment, you have 200 shares. That's the proportion of net profits you will receive if the company prospers, and usually the proportionate voting weight you wield on matters put to the stockholders. A particularly attractive characteristic of corporations is that, other than losing their capital, the investors are not liable for the consequences of failure. Only those directly involved in the business are responsible for lapses in judgment or ethics.

All businesses keep track of operations in one way or another, be it a one-man operation's receipts tossed into a cigar box to be tallied along with the monthly reconciling of the checkbook, or a megacorporation using computer files to follow hundreds of thousands of daily transactions. The conventional approach to record-keeping, and the one insisted upon by Internal Revenue auditors, involves the keeping of a "consolidated financial position" (commonly called the balance sheet), a "consolidated income statement" (also known as the profit and loss statement, or the P & L), and other assemblages of data.

The double-entry approach to bookkeeping uses the concepts of assets and liabilities as its central premise. Assets are elements owned; liabilities are elements owed. Businesses always have a mix of both to show on the balance sheet, starting with current assets and current liabilities.

CURRENT ASSETS (CA) AND CURRENT LIABILITIES (CL)

Balance sheets represent an instant in financial time, a frozen frame of a company's situation at that particular moment. Current assets (CA) refer to those assets that either are or can be converted into cash within a period of one year: cash, marketable securities, accounts receivable (short-term debts owed to SYSCO), inventories, and prepaid expenses.

Cash refers to actual specie (dollar bills, coins) and "cash equivalents" such as checking account deposits and highly liquid instruments with maturity typically impending in three months or less. On June 29, 1991, SYSCO had $70.2 million in cash. That was up from $56.0 million on June 30, 1990.

Marketable securities include United States Treasury securities and what is called "short-term commercial paper," the unsecured promissory notes corporations sometimes use to obtain quick financing. These assets must be measurable tangibly and are expected to be used up within the fiscal year. If a company owns bonds issued in a foreign country, these are not considered marketable securities. They must be listed as "other assets." SYSCO did not report marketable securities in the last two years, so in this case the category is not even noted on the balance sheet.

Accounts receivable are debts owed but not yet paid off by regular customers or clients. It is common practice for bills to be paid on a monthly, that is, a "thirty day" basis. Since the expense of taking legal action against remitting dawdlers is high, some debtors frequently take their own sweet time in sending in payments. If a customer fails, for whatever reason, to make payment for over ninety days, the accounting practice is literally to write off the debt from accounts receivable. In its footnotes to its annual report, SYSCO reported about $13.6 million of dubious, deducted accounts. That left a net accounts receivable for SYSCO of $600.6 million.

Inventories are the fourth defined type of current asset. Inventories may be raw materials that will soon be made into the product line, partially processed material, or finished products available for shipment. SYSCO's inventories consist primarily of food and related products held for resale. SYSCO reported inventories of $460.3 million for 1991.

The last item usually included in current assets is prepaid expenses. These represent items or services paid for in advance, like discounted insurance, supplies, rents, and commissions. SYSCO had made prepayments of $12.8 million by the end of fiscal year 1990–91.

The total current assets for SYSCO increased in 1991 to $1.1 billion from about $1.0 billion in 1990, a healthy 10 percent advance. That's intriguing enough to warrant further investigation.

Current liabilities (CL) are the reverse face of current assets, debts which must be paid off within the impending fiscal year. These are: notes payable, accounts payable, accrued expenses, accrued income taxes, and the current portion of long-term debt.

Notes payable represent written promises by a company to pay back short-term loans from banks or other lending institutions. All are due during the coming fiscal year. In SYSCO's case, these represent short-term bank borrowing of $7.88 million. Accounts payable represents the total amount owed in the course of normal business operations from those who provided goods or services, raw materials, utilities, and the like on credit. Accounts payable for SYSCO for 1991 were $445.9 million.

Accrued expenses are business expense items obligated but not yet paid, such as interest on borrowed money, attorneys' fees, insurance premiums, pensions, and payrolls. Accrued expenses for 1991 amount to $139.8 million. Accrued income taxes of $12.5 million is a separate item because of its distinctive importance. The final item under current liabilities is the "current" part of long-term debt (LTD), in other words, payments coming up quickly on debts that are being repaid over more than a single year. SYSCO was required to pay $5.68 million on these debts during fiscal year 1991.

Altogether, the total current liabilities of SYSCO came to $611.8 million for 1991. This represented about a 6.6 percent increase over the previous year.

CURRENT RATIO (CR)

The first key indicator is called the current ratio (CR), defined as the ratio of current assets to current liabilities of an enterprise. What is considered an acceptable value for current ratio varies from industry to industry, but conventional wisdom holds that in most cases the number ought to be around 2.0. Working from SYSCO's balance sheet, simple arithmetic yields a current ratio of 1.87 for fiscal year 1991. This is close to 2.0, and most analysts would agree that there is a comfortable margin for the company to meet this year's obligations, expand volumes, avoid minor crises, take advantage of opportunities, and generally operate effectively. Companies with low inventories and accounts that are easy to collect, like utilities, can operate safely with a lower current ratio, one as low as 1.5.

Executives, and investors, keep a close eye on the current ratio. A current ratio very much greater than 2.0 could mean that the company is building up the assets needed to take over another enterprise, or that the company itself is expecting to be bought and is "primping" for a higher price. A more mundane alternative is that inventories are too high, meaning that their product is not moving fast enough.

A related ratio to mention in passing is the quick assets ratio. Quick assets are current assets less inventory; the quick assets ratio is found by dividing quick assets by current liabilities. A quick asset ratio of less than 1:1 implies a precarious financial situation, with funds ready to meet emergencies comparatively low in relation to funds tied up in inventory. SYSCO had quick assets of $683.6 million for 1991, and a quick asset ratio of 1.12:1.

TURNOVER RATIO (TR)

Turnover ratio (TR) provides an idea of how quickly the product is being moved. It is calculated by dividing the past year's sales, found on the profit and loss statement, by average inventory, inferred as being the average of the last two inventories shown on the balance sheet.

How much inventory a company ought to have on hand varies according to the industry. Bookstores turn over their inventories between three and four times a year, while newspapers turn over their inventories daily. Food distribution companies have high inventories, as do convenience stores and even supermarket companies. In general, the company within an industry that turns over inventories the fastest is considered the best managed.

In the SYSCO example, sales were $8.1 billion, while inventories were $460.3 million for 1991 and $431.9 million for 1990, giving an average of $446.1 million. SYSCO's turnover ratio for the 1991 fiscal year was 18.3, meaning that goods were purchased and resold close to eighteen times per year. This implies a successful, quick movement of well-selected items in inventory and very competent management.

FIXED ASSETS (FA) AND OTHER ASSETS

Fixed assets (FA), sometimes called plant assets or property, plant, and equipment, have an expected useful life beyond the current fiscal year. They are usually not sold, but provide the physical armature within which a company manufactures, warehouses, and transports its product. Land is a fixed asset. Fixed assets are always reported at their original purchase cost, not their current replacement cost. Actual loss of value over time is recorded separately as "depreciation," as fixed assets like machinery wear out. The useful life span of different assets is defined by the federal government, with depreciation whittling away at them at a government-specified rate.

Other assets include intangibles, assets that cannot easily be measured or sometimes even touched. They include the values of patents, trademarks, copyrights, and franchise rights. Goodwill, the mystique or reputation of a business, is another intangible, and any excess over the fair market value of tangible net assets that were added on in a corporate merger. SYSCO also records miscellaneous other assets under a category termed simply "other."

Current assets, fixed assets, and other assets combined add up to the total assets for the year. For SYSCO in 1991 this was about $2.16 billion.

LONG-TERM LIABILITIES (LTL)

Long-term liabilities (LTL) are financial obligations that will not be paid off in the current fiscal year. They may include bond debts or money owed to companies, mortgagors, or bondholders. Those that are debts held with property as collateral are mortgage obligations; any debts backed by a company's good name and credit are referred to as debentures.

A bond is a formal promissory note by the company to repay a debt at a specific time in the future—the maturity date—and also a pledge to pay interest at a specified rate. Theoretically, mortgage bonds give greater security to the bondholder because they are backed by actual company assets. If a company is unable to meet its obligations and goes into receivership, the holders of the mortgage bonds have first claim on the specified company assets. Obviously, companies prefer to issue debentures rather than mortgage bonds. SYSCO discusses their bond positions in their notes, and shows a bonded indebtedness of $543.2 million for 1991.

Another form of long-term liability is deferred taxes. Deferral of income taxes involves accepting tax penalties that, in the opinion of corporate management, are acceptable losses. Putting off the day of reckoning means leaving usable money in hand for use right

now, a good ploy if interest rates impose a bigger hit than the penalty attached to late tax payments. SYSCO reported accumulated
deferred taxes of $86.5 million for 1991. Their total long-term
liabilities of debts and taxes came to $629.7 million for fiscal
year 1991.

STOCKHOLDERS' EQUITY

Stockholders' equity can be divided into four distinct parts: the par
value (an arbitrary money value) of preferred stock; the par value
of common stock, also arbitrary and stipulated when this corporation was first organized; paid-in capital; and accumulated retained
earnings.

Corporations issue preferred stock, whose holders get a set dividend from annual profits, and common stock, whose holders get
what, if anything, is left after preferred stock and debt payments
are made. SYSCO has no preferred stock issued despite having
been authorized for 1.5 million shares with a par value of $1 per
share. The common stock shareholders only need worry about the
company's bond interest payments and loan interest payments separating them from a disbursement of the profits.

Common stock shareholders receive increasing or decreasing
amounts each year depending upon the earnings of the company.
When earnings are high, the dividends paid to common stock
shareholders could also be high, unless the decision is voted to use
the profits for some company purpose. SYSCO has 500 million
shares of common stock authorized at a par value of $1 each. In
1991 there were about 92.6 million shares outstanding, thus the
total par value for these stocks was $92.6 million.

This doesn't mean that SYSCO common stock sells at $1 per
share on the stock exchanges. There they sell at over $40 per share.
Any stock shares that have been bid up to prices over the par value
are called capital (stock) surplus or paid-in capital; for SYSCO, in
fiscal year 1991, this amounted to around $49.6 million. If we add
par value of preferred, the common stock's par value, the additional
paid-in capital, and the retained earnings, we get a total stockhold-

ers' equity of $918.6 million. It turns out that this was a 19 percent increase over the previous year's equity of $770.8 million, good progress by any measure.

BOOK VALUE OF COMMON STOCK

Book value is the theoretical value of a share of common stock. It is calculated by subtracting the value of intangibles from total assets, further subtracting total liabilities and the par value of preferred stock, and dividing the remaining sum by the number of outstanding common stock shares.

To find SYSCO common stock's book value for fiscal 1991, start with total assets of $2.16 billion, subtract intangibles of $274.7 million and total liabilities of $1,241.5 million, and the value of the preferred stock (zero, since no preferred stock is actually out). This leaves $643.9 million net assets to be divided by the 92.6 million shares of common stock, and yields a book value of $6.95 per share.

Book value often isn't anywhere near actual market value, so some analysts urge that it be calculated without subtracting intangibles so as to get a larger final value notation. If we do not subtract intangibles, as SYSCO prefers, we derive a book value of $9.92 per share.

When a stock's market price is at or below book value, the stock could be a fantastic bargain. A more likely possibility is that the company is undergoing some difficulties, thereby nudging down the price as word of this circulates through the investment world. Usually such difficulties will be well publicized in the business news outlets.

CAPITALIZATION RATIOS: BOND RATIO (BR), PREFERRED STOCK RATIO (PSR), AND COMMON STOCK RATIO (CSR)

Companies are commonly described in terms of their total capitalization, meaning the amount of money raised through the sale of all long-term bonds, stocks (common and preferred), additional paid-in capital called "capital surplus," and accumulated retained earnings. The slippery category of intangibles is usually not included. Sometimes the total capitalization of a corporation is referred to as "stockholders' equity plus long-term debt."

Three measures, taken either as ratios proper or as percentages, have been devised to help understand capitalization. The bond ratio (BR) is the total value of all its bonds maturing in more than one year divided by total capitalization. The preferred stock ratio (PSR) is the par value of all actually issued preferred stock shares divided by total capitalization. The common stock ratio (CSR), also known as the equity capitalization ratio, is the par value of all actually issued common stock shares, capital surplus, and retained earnings divided by total capitalization. Capital surplus and retained earnings are included in the ratio as a convention because they support the value of the common stock.

What do these ratios tell us? In general, a high ratio for debt in bonds suggests that fewer profits after debt payments will be available for the common stockholder during years when earnings are low. How much is available will depend on the industry, management, the business's ability to generate profits in the face of debt, the size of the company, and a host of other considerations. By the same token, a high value for the preferred stock ratio and a low one for the common stock ratio might suggest that investing in common stock would not be particularly advantageous. Because the averages for different industries are so different, these ratios should be considered as only a general comparative measure.

Here is an example. SYSCO's long-term debt amounted to about $543 million in 1991, with intangibles of $274.7 million. Total capitalization for fiscal year 1991 came to about $1.19 billion. These numbers yield a bond ratio for SYSCO of 45.8 percent in fiscal year 1991. Because total capitalization consists of only common stock equity plus long-term debt, the equity capitalization ratio becomes 100 percent minus the bond ratio. Here we find that 100 percent minus 45.8 percent leaves 54.2 percent. This would be considered a healthy equity position by most analysts, especially for a rapidly growing corporation.

LEVERAGE

In physics, "leverage" means increasing the effect of force through the use of some device, such as a fulcrum or a pulley. This notion has been borrowed by investment specialists. In the present context, it means the use of money obtained at one rate to achieve a return at a higher rate. Financial analysts express leverage as the ratio of long-term debt plus outstanding preferred stock divided by stockholders' equity.

Building up capital through saving it is time-consuming and expensive, since currencies always gradually devalue. Lending institutions are in the business of making collected money available now, for which they are repaid the amount of the loan plus an interest fee. Leverage, adroitly applied, means making a profit on that borrowed money over and above the amount of the loan and its interest cost. Businesses borrow money so that they can take rapid advantage of new opportunities. This produces expansion, which in turn attracts investors.

Leveraging is not restricted to companies. One can exert leverage in a personal investment portfolio in a number of ways, such as in margin accounts and real estate investment. For example, suppose you have $200,000 in a brokerage margin account that allows you to borrow $100,000 at 10 percent interest. If you do so it costs you $10,000 a year, but if you have invested this borrowed money in investment instruments that reliably yield 15 percent, your gross profit will erase the loan interest and leave you with a net profit of $5,000 before taxes. That's a return on money you did not even own in the first place, always a surprisingly pleasant experience.

How much borrowing makes sense is one of the continuing questions with which management deals. A lot has to do with pure optimism, based on estimating what opportunities the future seems to hold. The danger here is to wind up in a position where the profits derived from borrowed money do not measure up and the company or individual cannot meet interest payments. Investors are therefore well advised to stay clear of highly leveraged companies, particularly if the international economy is in the part of its cycle when it slows or declines.

One final remark about leverage. Interest paid on debt created by a corporation or an individual is tax deductible. The higher your tax bracket, the more you save. This tax provision was devised to encourage use of the "saved" money in further investment.

SYSCO would not be defined as an overly leveraged company. In the previous section it was noted that SYSCO's total equity amounted to about $918.6 million in 1991, and bond and preferred stock obligations came to about $543 million. This means that the company's 1991 leverage position amounted to 0.6, or 1:1.7 when expressed as a ratio. A company with a leverage of about 1:1 is probably not using margin to its fullest extent but is in good financial health. If leverage gets as high as 4:1, the situation could be precarious for a company manufacturing goods, particularly those with volatile sales. Companies like utilities, with relatively assured markets, can work with high leverages because of their secure cash flow situations.

NET EARNINGS (NE)

The sales figure on a company's income statement is the revenue received by the company from sales of a product or service. This revenue will eventually have an effect on the owner's equity in the form of earnings.

SYSCO's consolidated income statement shows how much the assets of the company changed during the most recent accounting period. SYSCO's remarks on sales in their annual report proudly point out that sales in fiscal year 1991 increased by 7 percent over the previous year. Total sales for 1991 were about $8.15 billion.

In the course of generating sales, costs are incurred for materials, payroll, overhead, interest on borrowed money, and income taxes. The largest item under SYSCO's cost and expenses was the cost of sales. For 1991 this was about $6.69 billion, and it ate up 82 percent of its sales income. Operating expenses for 1991 were about 1.16 billion, or about 14 percent of the sales figure. By subtracting the cost of sales and operating expenses from sales, it turns out that for 1991 SYSCO had an operating profit of about $292 million, or about 3.6 percent of sales.

The next two items shown in the income statement are interest expense and other income. The interest expense is the interest paid to bondholders for borrowed money. Because this is considered a fact of life in doing business, interest is subtracted from revenue before taxes are calculated.

Further taxable revenue could be derived from other sources such as dividends and interest received from the company's investments in external stocks and bonds. For SYSCO, other income was derived from storage, drayage (the cost of hauling), rental income, and miscellaneous other activities. This income is placed in parentheses in income statements to indicate that it must be added to total revenues.

If you subtract the interest expense from the net sales profits and add in other income, you are left with profit before income tax (PBT). A comparison of SYSCO's 1991 PBT with the 1990 PBT shows an approximate 16 percent increase. The 1990 PBT had represented a 22 percent increase over the previous year. A ten-year synopsis in the annual report showed that these increases were derived both from enlarging sales and from improved operating efficiency.

Each company falls into a tax bracket that derives from income, credits, depreciation, and capital gains. SYSCO had an effective tax rate of about 39 percent in 1991 and paid about $97 million in taxes. This gave them net after-tax earnings of about $153.8 million, referred to as either net earnings (NE), net profit, or net income.

EARNINGS PER SHARE (EPS)

Companies are now required to present earnings per share (EPS). There are two accepted ways to derive this. One is to divide net earnings by the number of outstanding shares at the end of the fiscal year. An alternative is to divide net earnings by the *average* number of shares outstanding for the year. SYSCO reported 92,599,733 shares outstanding at the end of fiscal year 1991 and used the average approach, deriving earnings per share of 1.67.

If a company experiences either highly unusual earnings or losses, it reports this as a line item at the base of the income statement. These are benchmarks expected to occur only once in the lifetime of the company. Examples of extraordinary items might be the sale of some significant fixed asset, or the dropping of a product that had produced a lawsuit, or the nationalization of a foreign branch of a company by its host government. The practice of reporting extraordinary items separately allows you to compare recurring regular earnings from year to year in spite of unique glitches.

When a company issues one or more of the so-called "common stock equivalents" (which include such vehicles as convertible bonds, which can be converted into stock at some prespecified price in the future), those equivalents need to be converted into their equivalent number of common stock shares and listed with the already outstanding quantity of common shares. This second presentation on the income statement is referred to as "fully diluted earnings per share," distinguishing it from the normal calculation termed "primary earnings per share." The rationale here is to make investors aware of the potential dilution in earnings should all convertible securities be converted into common stock.

Earnings per share alone should not be used to determine if the price of a stock is reasonable. It is the trend of the earnings that inform, not just the earnings themselves. If a company has earnings that have grown at about 20 percent per year and such growth appears likely to continue, it presents an attractive investment opportunity. This is obviously better than investing in a volatile company with high earnings one year and low earnings the next.

INTEREST COVERAGE (IC)

A highly relevant question for potential investors is whether a company can comfortably meet all interest obligations for the year and still have enough earnings to show a profit, pay dividends, and show growth. Interest obligations are usually fulfilled by using funds in operating profits, as well as income from other investments if available. Interest coverage (IC) is calculated by dividing operating profit plus other income by the interest expense. Operating profit is derived by subtracting the cost of sales and operating expenses from the sales. This lets us know the number of times the interest sum could be covered by profits. As a rule of thumb, interest coverage should be three times the interest or greater.

Operating profit for SYSCO in 1991 was $292.4 million, with other income of $7.5 million. The interest expense was $49.1 million. This gives us an interest coverage of close to 6, a very safe situation indeed for SYSCO.

PRICE/EARNINGS RATIO (PE)

The price/earnings ratio (PE) is the figure derived by dividing the current price of a common stock share by its primary earnings per share. SYSCO reported earnings of $1.67 per share in fiscal year 1991. The price of their stock varied from a low of $28 to a high of $44 per share, so at its low the ratio was about 17, meaning that the stock was selling at 17 times its earnings.

The price, and therefore the PE that a company has, depends on a number of factors, including recent earnings, the company's earning trend, the position of the company in its industry, and the recognition of the company and its industry by investors. High expectations result in investors bidding prices upward, producing high PE ratios, because they expect earnings to continue to increase. In the United States, growth companies have PEs of as high as 20 or greater; the highest PE levels ever recorded were over 50 in Japan in 1989.

RETURN ON EQUITY (ROE)

Another way to consider how well common stock is doing comes from examining return on equity (ROE). This is calculated by dividing net common stock earnings by last year's reported stockholders' equity and multiplying by 100 to convert to a percentage. Last year's equity is used because this year's performance is based on the equity that was available last year.

If SYSCO had been obliged to pay dividends to preferred stock-holders, this amount would have been subtracted from net earnings prior to calculation. As it stands, SYSCO's net earnings in 1991 were about $153.8 million, and common stockholders' equity for 1990 was $918.6 million. Return on equity was 16.7 percent, well ahead of most returns generated at present by United States companies.

RETURN ON INVESTMENT (ROI)

Another way to measure how well a company is doing comes from return on investment (ROI). This is calculated by dividing net income *before* interest charges by last year's long-term debt plus the equity of all common plus preferred stock shares. SYSCO's earnings before interest expenses came to about $299.9 million in 1991, and total equity and long-term debt came to about $1,354 million for 1990, the prior year. This gives a high ROI of 22 percent. A high ROI is an excellent indicator of efficient management.

OPERATING PROFIT MARGIN (OPM)

Yet another way to measure profitability is with the operating profit margin (OPM), calculated by dividing operating profit by total sales and multiplying by 100. The trend of the operating margin, especially over the last five years, is a good indicator of the health of a company. A drop even when sales increase could mean that costs are not being managed properly, or that product prices have not been increased sufficiently to meet increased costs. An excessively high OPM for industry averages could mean that a peak has been reached and that a drop will soon come along, pulling stock prices down with it.

SYSCO has an operating profit of about $292.4 million on $8.15 billion in sales in 1991, meaning an operating profit margin of 3.6 percent in a highly competitive industry. SYSCO's ten-year summary of performance shows that its OPM has hovered around 3 percent over that time span, indicating consistency of performance.

DIVIDEND YIELD

The profit a company makes can be reinvested in company growth, paid out to the shareholders, or both. The dividend, that portion of the earnings or profits that are paid to common shareholders, is tangible evidence that a company is profitable. As an analogy, dividends could be compared to the interest you receive on money deposited in a bank savings account. In the stock market you deposit a certain amount of money for each share you purchase, and you receive a certain dividend for each of those shares. Thus the dividend yield (also called the "current yield") is the percentage of the price per share that the dividend represents. This is calculated by dividing the dividend per share by the recent price per share and multiplying by 100.

Growth companies like SYSCO usually plow a large part of their profits back into the company as retained earnings. More staid companies, with limited growth opportunities, are more income oriented and tend to pay higher dividends to stockholders.

In SYSCO's case, a dividend that increased steadily each year from 6 cents per share to 24 cents per share has been paid since 1982. The 24 cents per share on a price of $28 dollars per share gives a dividend yield of about 0.9 percent. This is typical for a fast-moving growth company, and good if an investor is primarily interested in increasing net portfolio worth. It is hardly the type of investment wanted by an investor seeking living expenses from an estate.

CONCLUSION

Working with key indicators is a practical way for anyone to size up how things are going. With nothing more than a calculator and a pencil, the health and prospects of the enterprise become perfectly clear. After working up the indicators for a few dozen companies in a given industry, the normal patterns emerge and the best alternatives start showing a profile.

TABLE 2-1:
CONSOLIDATED FINANCIAL POSITION, SYSCO CORPORATION

(IN THOUSANDS)			(IN THOUSANDS)		
Assets	**6/29/91**	**6/30/90**	**Liabilities**	**6/29/91**	**6/30/90**
CURRENT ASSETS			CURRENT LIABILITIES		
Cash	70,201	56,031	Notes Payable	7,884	10,028
Accounts Receivable	600,596	548,289	Accounts Payable	445,941	418,664
Inventories	460,286	431,865	Accrued Expenses	139,783	125,366
			Accrued Income		
Prepaid Expenses	12,830	11,130	Taxes	12,498	14,509
			Current Part of LTD	5,678	5,088
TOTAL CA	1,143,913	1,047,315	TOTAL CL	611,784	573,655
FIXED ASSETS			LONG-TERM LIABILITIES		
Land	63,903	56,153			
Buildings	498,386	432,443	Long-term Debt	543,176	583,496
Equipment	495,699	450,808	Deferred Taxes	86,545	64,090
Depreciation	(358,887)	(303,507)			
TOTAL FA	699,101	635,897	TOTAL LTL	629,721	647,586
OTHER ASSETS			STOCKHOLDERS' EQUITY		
Goodwill and Intangibles	274,700	269,786			
Other	42,417	39,072	Preferred Stock, par value $1 per share Authorized 1,500,000 shares, issued none	—	—
			Common Stock, par value $1 per share Authorized 500,000,000 Issued 92,599,733 & 91,753,955	92,600	91,754
			Add'l Paid-in Capital	49,616	34,345
			Retained Earnings	776,410	644,730
TOTAL OTHER ASSETS	317,117	308,858	TOTAL EQUITY	918,626	770,829
TOTAL ASSETS	2,160,131	1,992,070	TOTAL LIABILITY + STOCKHOLDERS' EQUITY	2,160,131	1,992,070

TABLE 2-2:
CONSOLIDATED INCOME STATEMENT,
SYSCO CORPORATION

(IN THOUSANDS)	6/29/91	6/30/90
Sales	8,149,700	7,590,568
Cost and Expenses		
Cost of Sales	6,693,822	6,246,372
Operating Expenses	1,163,450	1,078,804
Interest Expense	49,082	56,548
Other Income, Net	(7,518)	(7,242)
Total Cost and Expenses	7,898,836	7,374,482
Earnings Before Income Tax	250,864	216,086
Income tax	97,034	83,625
Net Earnings	153,830	132,461
Common Shares Outstanding	92,600	91,754
Earnings per Share	1.66	1.44

TABLE 2-3:
SUMMARY OF KEY INDICATORS OF HEALTH FOR SYSCO

Key Indicator	Value	Comments
Current Ratio	1.87	Close to 2, quite healthy
Turnover Ratio	18	High, rapid turnover of inventories
Book Value	$6.95	Price is about 6 times book value
Bond Capitalization Ratio	45.8%	Slightly low, but financially sound
Preferred Stock Cap Ratio	0%	No Preferred Stock outstanding
Common Stock Cap Ratio	54.2%	Conservative
Leverage	0.6	Low debt, conservatively operated
Earnings per Share (EPS)	$1.67	Positive increase each year for 10 yrs.
Interest Coverage	6.1	Very healthy
Price/Earnings Ratio (PE)	26	Premium PE due to performance
Return on Equity (ROE)	16.7%	Excellent
Return on Investment (ROI)	22.0%	Excellent
Operating Profit Margin	3.6%	Sound for its industry
Net Profit Margin	3.1%	Sound for its industry
Dividend Yield	0.5%	Positive increase each year for 10 yrs.

TABLE 2-4:
FORMULAS TO CALCULATE KEY INDICATORS

1. Current Ratio $= \dfrac{\text{Current Assets}}{\text{Current Liabilities}}$

2. Quick Assets Ratio $= \dfrac{\text{Current Assets} - \text{Inventories}}{\text{Current Liabilities}}$

3. Turnover Ratio $= \dfrac{\text{Sales}}{\text{Average Inventory}}$

4. Book Value $= \dfrac{\text{Stockholders' Equity} - \text{Intangibles} - \text{Preferred}}{\text{Shares Outstanding}}$

5. Stockholders' Equity $=$ Total Assets $-$ Total Liabilities

6. Bond Ratio $= \dfrac{\text{Long-term Debt}}{\text{Total Capitalization}}$

7. Pref. Stock Ratio $= \dfrac{\text{Pref. Stock}}{\text{Total Capitalization}}$

8. Common Stock Ratio $= \dfrac{\text{Com. Stock} + \text{Pd.-in Capital} + \text{Ret. Earn.}}{\text{Total Capitalization}}$

9. Leverage $= \dfrac{\text{Long-term Debt} + \text{Pref. Stock}}{\text{Stockholders' Equity}}$

10. Earnings per Share $= \dfrac{\text{Net Earnings}}{\text{Shares Outstanding}}$

11. Interest Coverage $= \dfrac{\text{Operating Profit} + \text{Other Income}}{\text{Interest Expense}}$

12. Price/Earnings Ratio $= \dfrac{\text{Market Price per Share}}{\text{Earnings per Share}}$

13. Return on Equity $= \dfrac{\text{Net Earnings}}{\text{Last Year's Stockholders' Equity}} \times 100$

14. Return on Investment $= \dfrac{\text{Net Earnings}}{\text{Last Year's Debt} + \text{Equity}} \times 100$

15. Operating Profit Margin $= \dfrac{\text{Operating Profit}}{\text{Sales}} \times 100$

16. Net Profit Margin $= \dfrac{\text{Net Earnings}}{\text{Sales}}$

17. Dividend Yield $= \dfrac{\text{Dividend per Share}}{\text{Market Price per Share}}$

3

THE BIRTH PROCESS OF
STOCKS AND BONDS

LAWRENCE LYNN

INVESTMENT BANKING

In the securities community, investment bankers are critically important players. These are the broker/dealers in the large houses who make it possible to gather money together so that businesses can carry out projects without borrowing from conventional banks.

Investment bankers have markedly different duties than their savings and loan, institutional, and commercial cousins. They do not handle deposits for the public and do not make small loans, nor do they handle any of the functions of the commercial or institutional bankers. They are concerned solely with raising money to finance business or government projects, usually on a large scale.

Their challenge is to see that this is done in the most efficient manner possible. It requires constant study of conditions in the world economy, particularly within the equity and debt markets. Which are the most appropriate securities for a corporation to issue depends on many variables, including the market for the securities of competing firms, the possible debt issues of governmental bodies, and the time frame during which an offering is presented to public or private investors.

In addition to advisory functions, investment bankers shoulder more direct involvement in the release of securities. As underwriters, they may buy an entire issue and broker the securities to the investing public. This is a tremendous responsibility, because a typical bond or stock issue amounts to tens of millions or billions of dollars in value. If they buy an issue that turns out to be seriously flawed, they will be unable to move the issue quickly enough to profit, a major calamity.

Investment bankers may also retain a portion of an offering. They either keep these "retention" securities in the hope that they will increase in equity rapidly, or release them after the offering if their movement in the "after market" indicates that pulling in cash for them makes sense. By setting up "retention" levels of securities, bankers can help maintain stable pricing by their own buying and selling.

The scale of investment banking today is so immense that the biggest events are usually joint efforts linking two or more banks. In these instances, there is a "managing" or "lead investment bank" that guides the "syndicate," normally a group of investment firms with which the banker's firm has previously cooperated and in which it has confidence. A syndicate is a short-lived form of business structure whose life is intact only until a specific objective has been reached.

HOW SECURITIES ARE ISSUED

Start-up funds for a business obtained through an "initial public offering" (IPO) of stocks and bonds are followed later, as needed, by offering "subsequent distributions." No matter how long a company has been in existence, if it offers new securities, these are called "primary distributions." It is only after the original purchasers begin selling them that securities enter the phase known as a "secondary distribution."

Not all distributions become public offerings. A very small offering, or one of only local interest, may be sold to the public without the involvement of an investment banker or a review by the Securities & Exchange Commission (SEC). The determining factors are the number of shares being offered and how many people will be asked to buy. This offers relief because it permits investment with-

out having to put down overhead money on formulations by consultants or print an expensive prospectus, required for major
public offerings.

This sort of offering—to a private individual, a small group, or
a financial institution—is the way in which many small companies
get started. Some specialist insurance firms, or "venture capital-
ists," invest in small growth companies, later taking their stock
shares to the public market after the companies have demonstrated
what they can do, thereby increasing the offering value of the
shares.

Although it is usually done through brokers, on occasion a corporation may organize a "rights" offering directly, without an investment banker's help. A rights offering gives the current
stockholder the option to buy new stock share issues at a predetermined value within a specified period of time. The rights can either
be exercised by the shareholder or sold to other investors who want
to get in low before the conditions of the marketplace bid prices
up. For example, a corporation selling at $40 per share might offer
a right for each share held and permit the purchase of its new
shares on the surrender of 10 of these rights plus $36 per share
in cash.

For a public distribution of stock shares, there are a series of
steps the investment banker addresses when preparing the offering. The first is an intensive period of investigation and analysis.
Government agencies are reviewed for internal competence, and
in the case of a corporation, not only will the efficacy of the firm
itself be studied but also its competition.

Next a "preliminary registration statement"—sometimes called
a "red herring"—must be prepared and filed with the Securities &
Exchange Commission. This paperwork is required under the provisions of the Securities Act of 1933, another legacy of the Crash
of 1929 and the subsequent Great Depression. This protects the
investment world from impulsive investors throwing money at new
issues before careful supervision has been instituted. The slow
wheels of government take several months to turn, by the end of
which time the amended "final registration statement" is worked
out. Only then can stock shares be sold.

As investment bankers start putting together the preliminary statement, usually during the latter phase of the investigation and analysis period, they may also begin assembling a compatible group of associates. These come from other investment banks that frequently have helped by sharing the underwriting. The selections are based on their interests, size, capabilities, and geographic areas of activity, as well as other factors. Associates will be compensated by the underwriting fee, shared in proportion to participation. A contract called "Agreement Among Underwriters" is drawn up to spell out the responsibilities of all members of the syndicate. American issues were once handled exclusively by American investment banks; today, investment bankers from abroad may be invited to join. On the largest issues it is not uncommon to find Deutsche Bank of Germany or Nomura Securities of Japan included in the syndicate. Of course, if the issue is a relatively small, local one—for example, a chain of restaurants in Ohio—it would be logical to invite in regional firms with Ohio headquarters and branch offices.

After the underwriting group has been formed, and near the end of the waiting, or cooling-off, period, the lead underwriters will meet with representatives from the company's financial and legal staffs to review recent history and current situations. This is to ensure that the statement is as accurate and up-to-date as possible. Once this is done, information about the issue is registered with the securities regulatory bodies wherever it will be offered. In the United States, securities laws differ from state to state, usually in minor ways. These regulations are sometimes still called "blue sky laws," because before federal and state regulatory agencies established controls, and stock offerings came "out of the blue sky" with no information, the value of shares in a public stock offering were impossible to define.

Just a few days prior to the effective date of the offering, the underwriters and corporate representatives finalize the revised prospectus and determine the public purchase price of stock shares. The members of the syndicate are allowed an "underwriting spread" of a slightly lower purchase price.

When serving as a broker, a brokerage firm acts as the client's agent and charges a commission for its trading services. If the firm acts as a dealer, it buys or sells securities for itself as well as for its clients. Some brokers obtain new issues at their reduced "spread" price and later pass them on to clients at a slightly higher price. Reputable brokers keep the difference conservative, profiting by about the same amount as if they were simply earning a straight commission. A normal underwriting spread turns into a profit of about 8 percent on public offerings and 5 to 6 percent on private placements, since the latter requires less effort.

The underwriters may have contracted with the corporation to act as their dealer, in which case they must sign a "fixed commitment" agreement to buy the whole issue, thus taking on the total risk. Alternatively, they may sign a "best efforts" agreement, in which case they act only as agents for the issuer and make no firm commitment to buy any of the securities to be distributed.

MARKETING OF THE NEW ISSUE

As soon as registration of the new security becomes effective, the selling group swings into action. Some of the brokers will have already informed clients about the new issue, but without knowing the price.

Price may have been determined through a negotiated underwriting, in which the company's officers get together with the investment bankers and find a price that is acceptable to all. In some cases, particularly for public utilities and transportation enterprises, investment bankers are notified about a coming issue and are invited to prepare competitive bids for the underwriting. The highest bidder is awarded the underwriting, and the presented price is adjusted accordingly.

Some underwriters, such as Salomon Brothers, are purely underwriters and do no public brokerage. Others, like Merrill Lynch, Oppenheimer, or A. G. Edwards have extensive retail brokerage departments that deal with a host of clients. Generally, the selling group will include many or all of the same firms that participated in the underwriting, but sometimes a firm that was not involved is invited in. This might be done, for example, if the firm is relatively small but has brokerage distribution precisely where the corporation intends to market its products.

The various member firms of the selling group generally receive volumes of the new issue proportionate to their size. A major firm such as Merrill Lynch will get a much larger proportion of the distribution than will a small firm. Allotments also tend to favor the country of origin of the issue. The selling group firms parcel out their issue among the branch offices, which in turn split up the shares for their brokers. This is done based on whomever has shown interest in the issue or whom the branch manager thinks has the clientele to whom the issue will appeal.

A "hot issue" is one whose price, immediately following its release, is expected to trade upward as it moves into secondary distribution. In this case the highest-producing brokers will be awarded the lion's share of the security. If the issue is considered mediocre or a dud, each of the office's brokers gets some of it and tries to move it as best he or she can.

For very attractive growth issues, most brokers have clients in mind to whom they will first turn to suggest a purchase, and the most attentive brokers also see to it that clients overall receive at least one invitation a year to a high-yielding public utility offering. These are good producers for the client, and sales are made without a broker's commission being involved.

There may be a clause built into the original underwriting agreement in which the bankers are obligated to step into the market and buy in order to support a security if the secondary distribution falters and pricing does not bid upward, or upward fast enough. The bankers may also have to sell off parts of their retention if the security goes up too much.

All attempts are made to prevent fraudulent handling of security issues. Brokers in the underwriting firms are generally forbidden to buy or sell the new stock for their own or family accounts lest they corner a hot new issue. "Stock parking," setting up phantom companies and accounts in which to hold the best public distributions in secret for knowledgeable insiders, is also anathematized. These rules are generally adhered to, and instances of firms bilking the public have become rare.

THE OVER-THE-COUNTER MARKET

Most new issues are traded, at least for a while, on the over-the-counter market (OTC). Although it does not receive the same press as the major exchanges, it is actually the largest market of all. The total of all government and corporate issues of stocks and bonds traded in the United States probably exceeds 60,000 in a year, and over half of these are OTC trades. The total value of all securities traded on the OTC market is greater than that traded on all the major registered exchanges combined.

The OTC market is a market of thousands of dealers all across the country, many of whom trade only in OTC issues. Some deal only with specific types of securities like municipal bonds or United States Treasury issues or Federal Agency notes. This is not an auction market like the major listed stock exchanges. Prices here are set through negotiations between dealers.

What types of securities are traded on the OTC market? Mainly primary distributions just emerging from investment banking activities, initial public offerings that have never been listed or traded. Sometimes subsequent distributions of unlisted stocks and bonds are kept on the OTC market too. Other issues trading on the OTC market include mutual fund shares, United States Treasury and Federal Agency bonds and notes, municipal bond issues, and most foreign issues.

The National Association of Securities Dealers (NASD) oversees the OTC market, including price formulation. Some OTC securities are on a restricted list called the NASDAQ (NASD Automated Quotation System). To be included here, the security must have either a minimum of 1,500 stockholders throughout the country, with at least 300 in each of 2 of the 4 regions established by NASD, or have 2,000 stockholders in the United States and a current value of at least $5 per share.

Securities too small or local to satisfy the requirements for NASDAQ may qualify to meet the minimum standards of the local quotation committees that furnish quotations in more limited areas. The prices quoted in the newspapers for these do not reflect the last price on actual trades as do those for the New York Stock Exchange; they reflect the last bid and offer prices between dealers.

The host of OTC stocks that are not quoted in NASDAQ or by regional NASDAQ committees are recorded publicly by the National Quotation Bureau. These are also dealer bid and offer prices, not last trades. They are reported on daily "pink sheets," named for the color of the paper on which they are circulated. These are frequently "penny stocks" that are less than $5 per share, and sometimes even less than 50 cents per share. Most brokerage offices receive the pink sheets and circulate them daily to interested brokers.

On the OTC market, completed trades must be settled in one of three ways. "Regular way" trades refer to transactions that must be settled within three business days following the transaction. "Cash way" delivery, mainly involving small sales, means that the securities are paid for in cash on the same date as the transaction. "Seller's option" means that settlement will be at some time from five to sixty days following the transaction date, as specified in a contract between the buyer and the seller. Most traders use regular way.

SECURITIES EXCHANGES

After initial sales, securities of successful companies inevitably move into the secondary markets. Much of the trading is handled through the stock exchanges. The largest is the New York Stock Exchange, accounting for nearly three-quarters of the dollar value in world secondary securities trading. Other prominent domestic exchanges include the American Stock Exchange, also located in New York City; the Pacific Stock Exchange; the Midwest Stock Exchange, in Chicago; and the Philadelphia Stock Exchange. Those exchanges outside New York are referred to as the regional exchanges. Issues may be listed both on the New York and the regional exchanges.

For option trading, the largest exchange is the Chicago Board Options Exchange (CBOE), followed in size by the American

Stock Exchange, the Philadelphia Stock Exchange, and the Pacific Stock Exchange. The New York Stock Exchange is the smallest of the organized options exchanges in the United States.

The exchanges provide a venue and a facility wherein securities may be bought and sold in a well-regulated environment. They also provide some internal regulation, monitoring facilities to try to ensure fair trading within their rules, public educational aids explaining securities trading, and a continuing stream of information on what is happening during trades. Furthermore, when asked, the exchanges provide representatives to mediate broker/client disputes.

Trading on the floor of each exchange is done by members only, most of whom today are corporate entities. Membership, or the "seats," are bought and sold from time to time with the price fluctuating as in any other free-market context. When the exchange is experiencing a high-volume market with a roaring uptrend, seats are bid up in price; if the exchange is in the doldrums, experiencing down volume or lack of interest by the investing public, seats carry reduced prices.

When all the exchanges were set up in the first place, the memberships were primarily held by family-owned enterprises. The registered traders who trade for accounts in which they or their family group have an interest are a remnant of that beginning. These wealthy individuals trading for themselves have decreased in number as the cost of exchange seats has increased in the past century and the most affluent families turned over the mundane matters of security trading to hired brokers.

The most familiar type of membership is the commission brokerage that acts for clients. Local offices transmit orders to the New York office, which forwards them to its representatives, known as the commission brokers, on the floor of the exchange. The floor men go to the correct "post" where trading in that security is done. When the trade is completed, the floor broker informs both the main and branch offices, and confirmation is relayed to the client. Telephone and computer facilities make communication rapid and accurate.

"Two dollar" brokers handle orders for other brokers if the immediate load of the other brokers' orders gets too large to handle easily. The expense of retaining them is covered by the commission broker, not the client.

The last type of member is registered with the exchange as a "specialist" in one or a small group of stock issues. It is his function to generate a profit by maintaining order in rapidly changing markets through buying and selling based upon his own equity inventory. The specialist steps in when a temporary impasse is reached between supply and demand for an issue.

The main difference between trading on the organized exchanges or on the OTC is usually scale. The very largest capitalization firms trade on the New York Stock Exchange, which has the most stringent listing requirements. To list a company's security, there must be at least 2,000 stockholders who own at least 1 round lot (100 shares is a round lot for most issues). At least 1 million shares must be publicly held, valued at no less than $16 million. Annual earnings of the company before taxes must have been at least $2.5 million during its most recent year of business, and more than $2 million must have been earned during each of the two years prior to that. The company must meet certain requirements for assets held and earnings capability, publish quarterly and annual reports, and maintain a registrar and transfer agent for its stock in the Wall Street district in New York City. The bulk of the listed common shares must have voting rights in the company's annual elections of directors and on other key corporate matters (these are the Class A stocks; other stocks do not assure voting rights). Last, financial data on the company must be audited by an accepted public auditor that publishes its findings in the annual reports. The key benefits of the listing requirements are to protect the prospective stockholder and ensure that there will be an adequately large market for the continual trading of shares.

Different types of orders can be transacted on the exchanges. The most common order is a plain buy order, given to the broker to execute "at market," which means at the best price that can be obtained at the time the order is placed on the floor of the exchange. With this type of order, no further information is needed other than the amount and the identity of the security desired.

Sell orders are a little more complicated, since orders may be designated as "short," meaning that the seller does not yet actually own the shares in question. In the case of a short sale, the investor must buy shares in time to fulfill the commitment. If actual stock is owned, orders to sell are referred to as "selling long."

In addition to plain buying or selling of orders, orders can be made that designate conditions. A price for buying or selling, called a "limit order," is a common requirement. An order might also have a time of purchase definition. For example, a "day order" is an order that expires if not executed by the end of the trading day. The New York Stock Exchange also accepts some "week" and "month" limit orders, but these are rare. A "good until canceled order" is one that remains on the books until the security is bought or sold, or until the client cancels the order. Brokers must confirm such long-term orders with clients if they remain unexecuted on the last trading days of April or October. A "stop order" is activated as soon as the price of the security touches or passes through a price. Stop orders are used to protect profits gained in a stock when that stock starts to decline, or to protect against a further loss in an unsuccessful situation.

For new investors it is risky to sell or buy with anything other than plain market orders. The main reason is that new investors are not habituated to keeping close track of what is going on, and may find themselves committed to securities transfers they didn't anticipate. For example, a client enters an order to buy 400 shares of IBM at $93 a share when the stock is currently trading at 93 1/8 a share. A few days later, forgetting by then that he already ordered, when the stock dips to $92 he orders a buy of 400 shares. Due to the mix-up, he finds himself committed to buying twice as many shares as he actually wanted—or probably could afford.

The money rules for the payment of transactions are the same as for OTC orders. "Regular way" settlements are the general practice, in which orders must be paid for in full in a cash account within three business days. In a margin account agreement with a brokerage firm, the purchase is immediately charged to the account; interest starts being charged in three business days. Clients who are selling can either wait for credit for three business days or can get an immediate "cash delivery" for a small fee. Normally one should use regular way settlements whenever possible, since the alternative is putting out "cash way" money immediately.

CONCLUSION

All stocks and bonds are created; not all reach a demise. Some, as with the old original joint stock companies, date back to the beginning of the group investment concept. However, new or ancient, virtually all are sold over the counter, then move into the exchanges.

The investment bankers who supervise all of this are the linchpins holding everything together. Essentially, it is their confidence in a venture that makes its realization possible. This is power entirely outside the realm of politics, if not outside the influence of law. The expediters of investment are therefore arbiters of the world as we know it, and as it will be.

But they are not magicians. Without the securities investor, making his own decisions to buy or sell, nothing actually happens. In this valuable counterweight lies the wonder that is the birth process of stocks and bonds, and the genius that fosters their value.

4

FIXED-INCOME
INVESTMENTS

OTTO GLASER

INTRODUCTION

Bonds, arguably the most popular investment category for cautious investors, are promises to repay loaned money. For the use of the money, the lender will receive back the loan amount plus an agreed-upon fee, usually defined as an interest rate (called "the coupon") on the amount loaned, usually in semiannual intervals until the maturity date of the bond.

Borrowers typically are government bodies or large corporations. Since the fee is set, bonds are referred to as "fixed-income" securities. There are certificates of deposit (CDs), U.S. Government Treasuries (Treasuries) and their agencies, corporate bonds, international bonds, and tax-free municipal bonds (Munis). In the United States most types of "marketable" bonds, those offered and for sale prior to their maturity, are sold and quoted in units of a $1,000 face value, which in turn is referred to as "par." The exception is municipal bonds, usually issued in denominations of $5,000.

The basic rule of thumb to remember about any fixed-income investment is that when interest rates rise, current market value falls. The political control of currency values and interest rates has a direct affect on when to buy bonds and when to sell.

COMMON FEATURES OF BONDS

All bonds are not created equal, but they have some features in common.

The official name of a bond is that under which it is originally sold. Because a borrower can and does issue several types of bonds, it is important to identify the exact "issue" of a particular bond, whether it is a first mortgage, or a debenture for a manufacturer, or a general obligation, or the revenue for a tax-exempt municipality.

In the jargon of securities sales, the "dated date" is the date when a bond is issued. This can be a critical identifying feature because bonds often have similar names, maturity dates, and interest rates. The dated date, unless stated otherwise, is the date from which interest normally starts to accrue on a bond. There are times when the first interest payment will not be for an exact six-month period from the date of issue. The reason borrowers (usually tax-free municipal issuers) use a date other than six months is to align the payment schedule with their cash income.

There are three ways in which a bond can be issued. A "registered bond" is issued with the buyer's name on it. The owner information is maintained by the issuer's paying agent. The owner of the bond can take physical possession of the certificate. Interest payments will be paid directly to the owner by check.

A "book entry bond" is not issued to an individual owner, and the investor cannot take physical delivery of a certificate with his name on it. Instead, a master certificate is deposited with a central depository institution. Brokerage firms and banks maintain accounts with this depository, which keeps their total ownership position on record. The brokerage firm or bank maintains its own composite record of individual investors' positions in that particular bond. Interest payments are routinely credited to the individual investor on the payment date, with the money coming from the central depository institution to the bank or brokerage account, which in turn credits their individual investors' accounts with the proper payment.

A "coupon" or "bearer" bond is issued with coupons physically attached to it, to be redeemed for each interest payment. Most of these types of bonds are issued with no owner's name on the certificate. The owner is presumed to be the individual who is the "bearer" of the certificate. When the interest payment is due, the payment coupon is detached from the bond and redeemed through the banking system. Ownership of coupon/bearer bonds can be transferred by physically delivering the bonds, in the same way that currency changes hands. In the same way that currency can be stolen, security for coupon bonds has always been a drawback. Effective June 1983, these types of bonds were no longer being issued. They are now only available in the resale or secondary market.

The "maturity date" is when the principal amount, the face value of the bond, comes due and is payable in full to the owner of the bond. Most bonds pay interest semiannually, and the dates are noted on the certificates. The payments are usually made on the first or the fifteenth of the month in which the bond matures and again six months from that date. The interest, or coupon rate, is the stated rate of interest, usually expressed as a percentage, and this, too, is on the certificate. The interest rate that a particular bond pays is basically determined by the rates of return prevalent in the economy at the time the bond is issued. This explains why a number of similar bonds of the same issuer can have different interest rates: the bonds were issued at different times in the past when interest rates varied.

If you purchase a five-year bond with a yield of 5 percent and hold that bond until it matures, you will have received a 5 percent yearly return on that bond for the full five years and will then receive your principal back at maturity. On the other hand, a bond's current market price will fluctuate up or down, or will stay the same. If a bond originally purchased at "par" (a $1,000 face value) is held to maturity, the investor will have received the stated yield on that bond and the full principal back regardless of any interest rate gyrations prior to its maturity. The only time a bond investor should be concerned with the fluctuation in current interest rates as they relate to his bonds is if he sells a bond prior to its maturity. Then and only then does he need to concern himself with his bond's current price and effective yield.

When interest rates go up, the current market value of a bond declines to reflect the state of currently available higher-yielding bonds. This applies inversely when current interest rates decline. For example, if two bonds are for sale from the same issuer with the same maturity, but each has a *different* interest rate, the bond with the higher interest rate will command a higher price in the marketplace because it will be paying out more money over its remaining life span.

Bonds can be priced at "par" (their face value), at a "premium" (above face value), or at a "discount" (below face value). When a bond price is quoted, it will be expressed as a percentage of "par" (a $1,000) face value. For example, if expressed as par 100.00, the value is $1,000.00—100 percent of par value. Premium might be 105.25, meaning $1,052.50—105.25 percent of par value; discounted to 82.50, the value is $825.00—82.50 percent of par value.

A bond's yield to maturity (YTM) is the rate of return the owner earns from payments of principal and interest, with the interest compounded semiannually. Yield to maturity presumes that the bond will remain outstanding until its maturity date. When YTM is calculated, any premium or discount is amortized over the remaining life of the bond, thereby taking into consideration the amount of the premium or discount and the time value of the money—the time remaining for the maturation of the bond.

It is important to understand the relationships among YTM, coupon yield, and dollar price because the YTM is the investor's actual "in his pocket" rate of return on his money at maturity. Consider these examples.

If a 9 percent (coupon yield) bond maturing in 15 years is selling at a price of 113.373, the dollar price of one bond at par would be $1,133.73. This premium bond is above the $1,000 "par" value. Because the bond is selling at a "premium" over "par," the actual yield to maturity (YTM) is less than the stated "coupon" rate of 9 percent because that rate remains based on the original par value of $1,000, not on the premium selling price of $1,133.75. In this case, the actual YTM will be only 7.50 percent when you figure in the extra premium you are paying for the bond.

If a 7.25 percent, ten-year maturity bond is selling at 95.00, meaning 95 percent of par, or $950, it is a "discount" bond under par. This bond would have a YTM of 7.99 percent because, if held to its maturity date, this bond will mature at par ($1,000) and you will realize an extra $50 more than the price you paid in the market. The YTM increases to reflect the added return realized on the bond at maturity.

The formula for computing YTM is:

$$\text{YTM} = \frac{\text{Coupon} \pm (\$ \text{ Discount or Premium})}{\text{Purchase Price} + 1,000 \div 2}$$

Many, but not all bonds, are "callable." This means that the issuer has the right to prepay the bond before its stated maturation date. Prepayment dates and prices are always defined when the bonds are first issued. The bond is usually prepaid at the issuer's discretion, and of course only if such a course of action is to the issuer's advantage. One of the more common reasons to call in bonds is an interest rate decline: the issuer wants to stop paying the higher rate and does so. The investor receives his principal back earlier than expected and is faced with the unhappy prospect of reinvesting the monies at rates significantly lower than what he had been receiving on the called bond.

You can see why it is important to know about a bond's call features, if any. The early call date can, in some cases, significantly reduce an investor's yield. For instance, if an investor paid a premium on a bond, he will lose the premium he paid because of the shorter time period during which he received payments. On the other hand, if he purchased the bond at a discount, his yield will have been greater than anticipated because the discount was accreted over a shorter period of time. Yield to maturity, obviously, means different things under different circumstances. Always ask what, if any, callable dates a bond may have and what the prices are on those bonds at their callable dates. In some cases, a bond that is called early can also be called with a "premium" call price. In that case an investor could actually realize a higher rate of return than the stated YTM on the bond.

In addition to yield to maturity and yield to call (YTC), bonds have a "current yield" (CY). The current yield on a bond is determined by the annual interest payment of the bond divided by its current market price. Say a 6 percent bond selling at a "discount" of 96 ($960) has a CY of 6.25 percent. In this case the annual interest on a 6 percent bond (with a par value of $1,000) is $60. To determine CY, you simply take the annual interest payment of $60 and divide it by the current price of the bond $960 ($60 ÷ $960 = .0625). Simply move the decimal over two places to the right and you get your CY, which is 6.25 percent.

Bonds pay their owners interest every six months. Should an investor buy a bond between payment dates, he must pay the seller his fair share of the next interest payment sum. Let's assume that you have just purchased a bond paying 6 percent, or $60, annually. The bond pays its twice yearly interest of $30 on June 1 and December 1. The bond was bought on September 1, so the seller is paid $15—three months' worth of interest, since he owned the bond for three months into the next scheduled interest payment. This is called the "accrued" interest on the bond.

When the bond pays interest on its next scheduled interest date (December 1) you, the new owner, will receive the full $30 interest payment, but since you have already paid the prior owner of the bond his "accrued" interest of $15, you have actually only earned $15 interest ($30 − $15 = $15). You only declare that amount of income on this bond for that year, not the full $30.

One criterion investors and financial professionals use to determine the value and/or relative safety of a particular bond issue is its credit rating. The two best-known independent debt rating services are Standard & Poor's Corporation (S&P) and Moody's Investors Service. They rate both municipal bonds and corporate bonds, as well as long- and short-term "issues." The ratings themselves are based, in varying degrees, on several factors: (1) the estimated ability of the issuer to pay interest and repay principal in a timely manner in accordance with the terms of the obligation; (2) the nature of the issue, and its security provisions; (3) the relative position of the obligation in the event of adverse conditions, such as bankruptcy, or issuer reorganization, or changes in laws affecting creditors' rights (see Tables 4-1 and 4-2 on pages 66–67).

When rating short-term bonds, the primary focus of the rating services is the liquidity of the borrowers or the issuer. Long-term bonds, with maturities in excess of three years, are bonds that are identified as AAA or AA or A, etc. for S & P's ratings, or Aaa, Aa, A, and so on for Moody's. The term "investment grade" is used to describe bonds whose risk level is acceptable for most investors. These bonds are any bonds with a rating of BBB or better for S & P and Baa or better for Moody's. Bonds with lower ratings are considered speculative. The lower the rating on a bond, the higher the risk. "Junk bonds" have typically earned a BB (S & P) and Ba (Moody's) or lower.

Frequently, new issues are sold on a "when issued" basis. That means the bond certificates will be available for delivery to the purchaser as soon as they are printed, authenticated by the issuer, and cleared by bond counsel. "When issued" bonds are not paid for by the investor until they are available for delivery.

Some bonds have a "sinking fund" provision that requires the bond issuer to retire a certain amount of outstanding bonds before maturity. The number of bonds to be retired and their schedule is always detailed in the bond indenture. The bond indenture is the complete description of all the terms of payment, call provisions, and security of the bond being sold. The issuer has the option of retiring the bonds by purchasing them in the open market if they are trading below par, or by instructing the trustee to call in the bonds through a lottery device.

TAXABLE COMMERCIAL BONDS

Certificates of deposit (CDs) have a fixed maturity date. The maturity dates can range from as little as one month to as long as ten years, but most CDs mature in no more than five years. The interest rate on the CD is fixed at the time of issue. Interest can be paid monthly, quarterly, semiannually, or annually.

An agency of the United States government insures CDs for payment of both principal and interest up to $100,000. Larger CD amounts can be insured at a single institution by using the device of multiple ownership of the CDs—you, your spouse, your children, or the like. However, coverage rules can be highly technical and should be reviewed carefully with the institution's representative and understood before more than $100,000 is tied up. Improperly arranged, principal over the insured $100,000 could conceivably be at risk should the institution fail. This used to seem impossible until the vast savings and loan collapses during the 1980s; since then, hard pragmatism means a skeptical attitude about banking institutions.

CDs can be issued by banks, savings and loans, credit unions, and brokerage firms. The interest paid on CDs issued directly by all outlets except brokerage firms can be reinvested, compounded, and bought in any amounts. When an investor buys a CD directly from a bank, savings and loan, or credit union, the purchase, by law, can only be sold back to the issuer. Brokerages are not so limited, and they market CDs in multiples of $1,000. The interest received on "marketable" CDs sold by brokerages cannot be reinvested in the same CD.

Bonds issued by corporations are available in many forms. For this discussion, we'll limit ourselves to publicly traded issues. Maturity periods for most publicly traded corporate bonds range from five to thirty years, although shorter-termed maturities are available. Corporate bonds are further identified by the types of credit or assets that back up the bond. Corporate bonds are rated by Moody's and Standard & Poor's in the same manner as described earlier.

In "debenture bonds," the full faith and credit of the corporation is behind the bond. No specific asset is pledged to back up the bond, just the corporation's good name. "First mortgage bonds" are backed by a specific asset of the corporation, such as land or a generating plant. If the corporation is unable to pay the principal and interest as agreed, the bond owners can take title to the pledged property. "Sinking fund bonds" require the issuer to prepay specific quantities of bonds each year prior to maturity. This provision can be satisfied in two ways: by buying them back on the open market or by the issuer calling in the bonds.

"Zero coupon bonds" present an interesting perspective on accounting conventions. Instead of a defined principal and interest formula, these bonds are purchased at a discount from face value and upon maturity pay out their full face value. The difference between the maturity value and the price paid is the "interest" earned. The value of the bond increases each year by the original accretion rate (OAR), which is the appreciation stated when the bond is originally sold. Upon maturity, the zero bond pays out at par value.

Here's an example. A zero coupon bond was originally sold for $500 with an OAR of 10 percent. At the end of 1 year, the bond's value would be $550 (10 percent on $500 for 1 year is $50). At the end of the second year, the bond's 10 percent OAR would have added another $55 for a total of $605 (10 percent of $550 = $55) and so on until it matures at par. Even though the owner does not receive this annual income in cash, the income is taxable. This "phantom" income is taxed each year the same as if you were receiving the interest income every six months like most bonds pay out. Should the owner of the bond ever sell the zero bond, he would need to know the accredited value of the bond. The original purchase price plus the annual accretion is the cost basis for income tax calculations. "Convertible zero coupon bonds" are zero coupon bonds that automatically convert to interest-paying bonds on a specified future date.

"Convertible bonds" contain a conditional option that allows them to be converted into common stock. The intention at the time of the bond's issuance is that they will eventually be transformed. It is typical that at the time the convertible bond is issued, the conversion value is set at higher than the current price of the company's common stock. The stock must appreciate to a level higher than the conversion price before conversion is allowed or considered. Usually, the interest rate on a convertible bond is lower than for a comparable nonconvertible bond, due to the added conversion feature. Some convertible bonds have been issued as zero coupon bonds, but the majority pay interest semiannually.

United States Treasury bonds—"Treasuries"—are the safest bonds issued anywhere and will continue to be so unless the dollar collapses or an insurrection brings down the White House, both fairly unlikely events. The full faith and credit of the United States federal government backs these securities 100 percent. When held to maturity, you are absolutely guaranteed the return of your principal and the payment of interest. The United States federal government is the largest single borrower in the domestic market, and new bond issues are sold on a regular basis. An attraction of the

Treasuries is that the interest paid on government bonds is exempt from taxation in individual states. Treasures are not, however, exempt from federal income taxes.

Treasuries are identified according to their length of maturity (see Table 4-3 on page 68). "Bills," or "T-bills," have the shortest term of maturity—one year or less. They require a minimum investment of $10,000 and are sold in additional increments of $5,000. T-bills are different from other government securities in that they are purchased at a "discount" to their maturity value. When you purchase a minimum $10,000 T-bill, you pay less than the $10,000 par you'll receive at maturity. The difference between the discounted price you paid for the T-bill and the par of $10,000 at maturity is the interest you receive on it.

Then there are the other federal government bonds, each with its own nickname (see Tables 4-4, 4-5, 4-6, and 4-7 on pages 69–72). Treasury "notes" have a maturity of from one to ten years and are sold in $1,000 increments. Interest (coupon) payments are made semiannually. "Bonds" are the treasuries with the longest maturity periods, from ten to thirty years. They are sold in minimum increments of $1,000. Coupon payments are also made semiannually.

United States government agency securities, as a group, are the second largest borrowers in the domestic market. The complement of agencies is quite large; among them you may recognize Government National Mortgage Association (GNMA, or "Ginnie Mae") bonds and Federal National Mortgage Association (FNMA, or "Fannie Mae") bonds, two of the better-known agencies. Table 4-4 lists the various agencies.

With a few exceptions, federal agency bonds do not constitute a direct obligation of the United States federal government. Because of this, to make up for the slight risk, agency interest yields are a little higher than direct obligation Treasuries. Agencies that pay interest and principal monthly are backed by mortgages purchased by the agencies and grouped together into a "pool" of mortgages. The agencies then sell parts of the pool to individual investors so that each holder owns a part of many mortgages, not just an individual mortgage. These mortgage-backed securities pay monthly interest and principal because payments of interest and principal are made monthly by the home owners making up the pool of mortgages.

If you have ever owned a home, you know you have the option of prepaying all or part of your mortgage at any time. The same rule applies with agency mortgage-backed securities. Because a homeowner can elect to pay off his mortgage early, the investor cannot be guaranteed that he will collect his full interest for the stated maturity of the security. To allow for early prepayment, there is an assumed "average life" indicated in the tables that is an estimate of prepayment rates, based on past experience. How quickly or how slowly your mortgage-backed security pays your interest and principal back is directly related to current interest rates. In times of declining interest rates, borrowers will prepay their mortgage loans faster. In times of rising interest rates, borrowers prepay more slowly. Mortgage-backed pools generally pay a higher interest rate than bonds of a similar quality because of this flexible maturity factor.

Each agency backs the mortgage pools it issues for both full and timely payment of interest and principal. In addition, mortgages in GNMA pools are backed by the full faith and credit of the United States government. None of the mortgage-backed agency securities is exempt from state income taxes, and most agency securities are in "book entry" form only, which means that certificates cannot be physically delivered to you. Only GNMA pools can be registered and a certificate delivered to the investor.

Collateralized mortgage obligations (CMOs) are a more sophisticated (and hence more complicated) form of mortgage-backed security. These are also pools of mortgages, but with the peculiarity of multiple maturities and different yields in the same pool. The pool is further split into classes, with all principal payments going to one class until it is completely paid, after which the principal payments are shifted to the next class. Each class will have a much narrower maturity range than a regular mortgage pool in which all participants receive equal principal payments. All classes receive interest income on a monthly basis. Yields are quoted on the estimated average mortgage life.

Investors should exercise caution in selecting CMOs because of the different characteristics of each class. Yields are generally higher on CMOs than similar bonds because of the unknown maturity dates. CMOs also tend to be a more aggressive investment, as they can consist of mortgages backed by the United States government, its agencies, private backers, or backed only by the borrower on the mortgage. It all adds up to a higher degree of risk, consequently the various classes are ranked by volatility: below average, average, or above average.

Most countries issue bonds similar to the federal government bonds issued in the United States. Foreign banks and companies issue bonds as well. Some of the bonds are denominated in United States dollars but most are issued in the currency of the country of origin. International bonds, in addition to the usual credit and maturity risks associated with all bonds, possess the added risk of currency fluctuation in relation to the United States dollar. The World Bank and Inter-American Development Bank issue bonds denominated in United States dollars, and trade in them is similar to that of federal agency issues.

TAX-FREE MUNICIPAL BONDS

The thinking behind buying a Muni is simple. If the price and rate of return are attractive, what is its rating? For how long are you willing to tie up your principal? Do you intend to keep the bond until maturity, or do you think it likely that you will trade out beforehand? Develop a strategy, then get moving on the tactics to make it happen.

Under current law, municipal bonds (Munis) are the "last of the Mohicans," the only investment available in which interest income is still free of federal income tax obligations. With one exception, naturally, federal tax law being what it is. If you happen to be subject to the alternative minimum tax (AMT), which few of us need to be concerned with, there is some tax liability. Municipal bonds can also be state and locally tax-free if you purchase a municipal bond issued by the state in which you reside. If you happen to live in one of the few states with no income tax, it hardly needs to be pointed out that this particular benefit obviously has no effective meaning.

Because of the tax advantages inherent in Munis, the higher your tax bracket, the more attractive they become. Investing in tax-free bonds can get complicated when you delve into all the special little nooks and crannies of definition in this very diverse category. But all that the novice investor needs is an overview of the basics.

General obligation/public purpose bonds are among the safest of the municipal bond categories. Just as the name implies, general obligation bonds (GOs) are direct obligations of the issuing municipality backed by the full faith and credit (including taxing and further borrowing power) of the municipality. These bonds repay their lenders directly through tax revenues. They are issued by state and local governments or their agencies to finance essential government projects such as schools and highways.

Revenue bonds can involve more risk to the investor. The income to pay the interest to bondholders is derived directly from revenue generated by the project the bonds were originally sold to finance. These bonds are not backed by the taxing authority of the issuer. Common projects financed by revenue bonds are toll roads, toll bridges, airports, and hospitals. If they do well, investors will have no problems; if they don't, then all bets are off. There is no obligation that the sponsoring municipality bail anyone out, so naturally they don't. When purchasing a revenue bond, pay attention to the institution's credit rating and consider how essential the project is to the municipality. The better the rating, and the more essential the project, the more secure the revenue bond.

Limited tax and special tax bonds are the next step down in safety from a GO bond. The issuer of the bond backs the bond's principal and interest with proceeds from a specific tax. These taxes might be derived, for example, from a gasoline tax, an ad valorem tax levied at a fixed rate, or a special assessment. Since people don't like to pay for government or agency mistakes, the bond buyer should attempt some understanding of how likely such a tax backup actually is before investing. If a vote is required from the public to levy a tax, the odds of it coming off are a lot smaller than from the closed-door decision of a city council.

Double-barreled bonds are backed by guarantees from two

sources, typically from a taxing authority and revenue pledged from the funded project, hence the "double-barreled" designation. The risk is spread out some, reducing the risk of default.

Private purpose/nonessential/nongovernmental bonds are best understood if one puts the emphasis on the key word "nonessential." These are bonds issued to finance facilities or functions such as industrial development projects for airports, student loan bonds, multifamily housing projects, or single-family mortgage revenue issues, to name just a few. Before investing in this type of bond, examine the issue carefully. In some cases, private purpose bonds are *not tax-free*, as for sports facilities and convention centers. Another caveat for the investor is that interest income earned on such bonds issued after August 7, 1986, must be treated as a preferential item for purposes of the alternative minimum tax (AMT). This was the date the U.S. government changed the tax law. AMT bonds are now partially taxable to individuals that are subject to the tax.

Certificates of participation/lease-secured bonds (COPs) are becoming popular with municipalities because issuing the bond does not require approval of the dreaded voter. Because the municipality is not backing the issue with unlimited taxing power, and interest payments and the return of principal on the bonds are only backed by annual appropriations of the issuer, and there is a higher degree of risk with COPs than with tax-based bonds.

States and local housing authorities issue revenue bonds that are secured by mortgage payments on single-family or multifamily dwellings. Additional protections for bondholders on these issues are sometimes provided by Federal Housing Authority insurance, Veterans Administration guarantees, or private insurance. These bonds are more likely to be called in than other types of municipal bonds due to the greater potential for prepayments when home owners refinance or pay off mortgages early.

Investors can be afforded an interesting option on "put" bonds. These typically long-term bonds allow the holder to "put" back to the issuer his bond prior to its maturity at a specific price on a specific future date or dates. The bondholder simply sends the bonds to the trustee bank or his/her brokerage with written instructions that he wants to avail himself of the "put option." Put features can be optional or mandatory. If optional, the bondholder makes the decision whether to put the bonds back to the issuer; if mandatory, the bondholder has no choice but to put the bonds back to the issuer on demand. Yields on these bonds can be different than issues of comparable maturities and ratings.

Zero coupon bonds are purchased at a deep discount to their face value and bondholders receive no interest payments. When the bond matures at par, the difference between the discounted purchase price and the maturity value of the bond is considered federally tax-exempt interest. Investors saving for future expenses, who have no need for more current income, find zero coupon bonds an attractive investment. Because you are purchasing the bonds at a deep discount to their eventual maturity, zero coupon bonds are an efficient way to leverage an initially smaller outlay of cash for a much greater amount of tax-free cash later on. Zeros are popular choices for college funding because you know exactly what the bond will be worth when it matures and you can select a specific maturity that will coincide with your child's matriculation to college—and they are tax-free.

Convertible zero coupon bonds begin life as zeros and end it as coupon-paying bonds. Just as zero coupon bonds pay no interest, these bonds pay no interest for a set period (usually several years) during which the interest accrues within the bond. When the bond eventually reaches its conversion date, it begins paying regular semiannual interest at the original offering yield until it reaches maturity.

MUNICIPAL BOND
TAX OBLIGATIONS

The major attraction of Munis is that their income is federally tax-exempt. However, there are still some tax implications that must be considered.

State taxation on municipal bonds varies from state to state. The worst cases are states which, metaphorically devouring their young, tax both domestic and other states' bonds. Other states protect

their own Munis but tax everybody else's. Some helpfully let everyone have a break. Check with a local brokerage to find out how
your state stands on this.

In the case in which a Muni is purchased at a premium, the
premium is amortized. Current value is reduced by a portion of
the bond's total premium each year. By so doing, the bond's basis
(cost) is reduced for tax purposes, but there is no tax deduction
generated from this exercise. Should you sell the bond prior to maturity, you will still have a capital gain or loss of the difference between the sale price and the cost less amortization.

When a bond is purchased at a discount, the tax treatment depends on whether the bond was an original issue discount or simply
was bought at a market discount on the secondary market. The
most extreme version of an original issue discount bond (OID) is a
zero coupon municipal bond, but there are also regular coupon-
paying municipals that are original "issue" discount bonds as well.

An OID is any bond that was originally sold by the issuer at less
than its maturity value. The difference between the purchase price
and the par value of the bond is the original issue discount. The
Internal Revenue Service assumes a certain rate of appreciation on
OID bonds each year until maturity. No capital gain or loss is incurred provided the bond is sold for that estimated amount. Should
the bond be sold at a price higher than the assumed amount, a
capital gains tax or a tax at the bondholder's ordinary income rate
is due.

Some municipal bonds bought on the secondary market are purchased at less than their maturity value, the reason being that current interest rates on similar bonds are higher than what that bond
is paying. The difference between what you paid for the bond and
the bond's par value is your market "discount."

Capital gains on bonds in the secondary market is yet another
intriguing bit of accounting legerdemain. Consider this: If you buy
a $10,000 face amount municipal bond originally issued twenty
years ago at par, you might pick it up for $8,000 and two years later
sell it for $9,000. Here you have a capital gain of $1,000. Perhaps instead you hold the bond until maturity, when your capital
gain equals the difference between the bond's maturity value—
$10,000—and your purchase price—$8,000. With this, your capi-

tal gain is $2,000. On the other hand, you might find yourself a little short of cash at some point and sell out for $7,000, taking a capital gains loss of $1,000 in order to get liquidity without borrowing. What does the Internal Revenue Service think about all this?

Several things. The returns on bonds purchased before April 30, 1993, are treated as capital gains or losses when sold at a profit or loss. Profits or losses on bonds purchased after that date are treated as ordinary income. Now *that* was a change the investment community sat up and stared at, for obvious reasons.

Sounds complicated? It can be. For most of us, it is best to turn things over to a professional tax adviser and get on with our business rather than fight through the tax thickets.

UNDERWRITING MUNICIPAL BONDS

There are a number of private insurance companies that specialize in guaranteeing municipal bonds in case of default. Should the bonds default, the insurance companies guarantee that they will buy back the bonds at par from the investors or will continue the scheduled payments until their scheduled call date or maturity. The trade-off for the investor is increased security in return for a somewhat lower profit rate. Bonds that are insured receive the highest credit rating—AAA. The major companies specializing in bond insurance are Ambac Indemnity Corporation (AMBAC), Financial Guaranty Insurance Company (FGIC), Municipal Bond Insurance Association (MBIA), and Financial Security Assurance, Inc. (FSA).

An added enhancement for certain housing municipal bonds is federal agency backing. The issues are from collateralized government agencies or public companies with the implied support of the federal government. The principal and interest payments may or may not be guaranteed by the underlying agencies, but the mortgage payments covering the debt service on the bonds are guaranteed by the agencies. Two such agencies are Government National Mortgage Association (GNMA), the "Ginnie Mae," and the Federal Housing Administration (FHA). The Federal National Mortgage Association (FNMA), or "Fannie Mae," is now a public company and no longer an agency of the federal government, but it retains the implied backing of the government. Bonds that have been collateralized by GNMA and FNMA receive a AAA rating by Standard & Poor's and Moody's. Bonds with an FHA backing are typically rated AA by the two rating services.

While letters of credit (LOCs) enhance a municipal bond's credit standing, they are not equivalently desirable as municipal bond insurance. In essence, LOCs are issued by commercial banks that promise to make interest and principal payments on a bond should the issuer be unable to do so. The LOCs are backed by the full faith and credit of the bank. LOCs are typically AAA or AA rated.

TAXABLE EQUIVALENT YIELD

As mentioned, the big attraction of municipal bonds is in their income tax-free status. The higher one's tax bracket, the better the taxable equivalent yield on a municipal bond. If you are not in at least the 28 percent federal income tax bracket, tax-free bonds offer a negligible advantage over taxable bonds.

To figure taxable equivalent yields, there is a simple procedure. Subtract your tax bracket from 100 percent, then divide the municipal bond's yield by the resulting number and compare it with the unprotected tax rate for corporate bonds.

Let's walk through a calculation for an investor in the 28 percent tax bracket. Should he buy a 6 percent municipal bond or a 7 percent corporate bond? He compares the taxable equivalent rate of the Muni with the taxable rate of the corporation:

$$(1) 100\% - 28\% = 72\%; 6\% \div 72 = 8.33\%$$
$$(2) 100\% \text{ taxable} = 7.0\%$$

You're now comparing apples with apples. In this case, the Muni gives you a 1.33 percent taxable equivalent yield higher than the corporate bond. If all other considerations are equal—same credit ratings, maturity, and so on—the Muni is clearly a better value for the tax-conscious investor.

UNIT INVESTMENT TRUSTS

Under the Investment Company Act of 1940, unit investment trusts (UITs) can be created in one of two forms. The most popular is the "fixed trust," a mutual fund resembling a portfolio of securities, of which units are sold and holders of the units profit proportionally. In "participating trusts," the holder profits both from the trust and from the underlying mutual fund. Corporate, municipal, or government bonds, mortgage-backed securities, and preferred stock shares are the more popular types of securities in UITs. Unit holders receive both shares of net income and, as underlying securities are sold or mature, a return of principal. Because the trust is composed of a "fixed" portfolio, the investor knows exactly what bonds are in the portfolio, when they will mature, and the income stream the bonds will generate.

Most brokerage firms maintain a secondary market in UITs, so they can easily be resold prior to their stated maturity. Brokerage firms maintain a secondary market in UITs to give investors the option of selling all or a portion of their UITs at any time. Of course, the selling price of their units is determined by current market conditions.

There are compelling attributes of UITs. UITs are available with state-select municipal bond packages such as Texas UITs or Florida UITs to provide unit buyers with the potential for double and, in some cases, triple tax-exempt income. Bonds selected for inclusion in all UITs are carefully selected by bond professionals of the sponsoring company. Most UITs tend to be of investment grade quality—BBB or better by Standard & Poor's, Baa or better by Moody's—because bonds compiled by UIT portfolio managers are usually selected with an eye to providing investors optimum income with the least amount of risk. UITs can also come with insured bonds that provide investors with an even higher rate of security. These assure prompt payment of principal and interest and are rated AAA by both rating services.

Typically, a UIT will have anywhere from ten to thirty different bond issues, diversified as to type and location of issuer. No more than 10 percent of a portfolio is generally invested in one particular issue, with the net result of further spreading out any potential risk. Investors can choose how they want to receive income from the UITs—monthly, quarterly, or semiannually. Additionally, investors can elect to take out no income and use the distributions to reinvest in additional units. A trustee is secured to handle the various administrative details inherent in a portfolio of municipal bonds. Unit holders receive concise details of any activity in the trust along with their regular payments.

CONCLUSION

Bonds are a useful form of securities investment, particularly during periods of slow currency devaluation. They are a highly liquid way to protect equity, and municipal bonds offer the last genuine haven against income taxes. All portfolios should include a section devoted to bonds, whether municipal or not.

TABLE 4-1:
SHORT-TERM RATINGS OF BONDS

Moody's	S & P	
MIG-1°	SP-1	Best quality—very strong protection from established cash flows; superior liquidity support.
MIG-2	SP-2	High quality—protection margins for credit risk are satisfactory.
MIG-3		Favorable quality—while issues carrying this designation have a capacity for timely payment, they are more vulnerable to adverse changes in short-term economic circumstances.
MIG-4	SP-3	Adequate quality—can be affected by changing market conditions or short-term difficulties. There is specific market risk.

°*MIG stands for Moody's Investment Grade.*

TABLE 4-2:
LONG-TERM RATINGS OF BONDS

	Description	Moody's	Standard & Poor's (+ or −)*
Superior	Almost negligible degree of investment risk. Interest payments protected by large or exceptionally stable margin, and secure principal. Economic changes unlikely to impair strong position.	Aaa	AAA
Excellent	Margin protection not quite as great as AAA-rated securities, and economic fluctuations may have slightly greater effect on long-term risk factors.	Aa	AA
Favorable	Security of principal and interest is adequate, but long-term risk of issuer is more susceptible to economic changes.	A**	A
Average	Neither as highly protected nor as well secured as A-graded issues. Interest and principal security appear adequate in the short term but may be unreliable in the long term.	Baa**	BBB
Fair	Protection of principal and interest is moderate and not well safeguarded against economic changes.	Ba	BB
Marginal	Generally lacking desirable investment features. Little assurance of interest and principal payments over any long period of time.	B	B
Poor	May be near default or have circumstances leading to problems with interest and principal payments.	Caa	CCC
Speculative	In default or has severe credit deficiencies. Extremely poor possibility of ever attaining any real investment-grade standing. Income bonds on which no interest is currently being paid. Not yet declared in default but not currently making interest payments.	Ca C	CC C C1
Default	In default, and payment of interest and/or principal is in arrears. Traded flat "f" appears in bond tables.***	D	D
Not Rated	No rating has been assigned, or rating has been suspended or withdrawn. May be too small an issue to get itself rated.	NR	NR

*The ratings from AA to B by Standard & Poor's may be modified by the addition of a plus or minus sign (+ or −) to show relative standing within the category.
**Bonds in the A and Baa categories that Moody's believes carry the strongest investment attributes are designated with the symbols A-1 and Baa-1.
***"Traded flat" means that the buyer does not pay the seller any accrued interest at the time of purchase.

TABLE 4-3: UNITED STATES TREASURY SECURITIES

Type of Issue	Minimum Denominations & Increments	Maturities	Interest Payments	Delivery Form
U.S. Treasury Bills	$10,000 with increments of $5,000 thereafter	• Issued at a discount from par • 1-year bills auctioned every fourth Thursday for settlement on the following Thursday; 3-month and 6-month bills auctioned weekly on Monday	• Issued at a discount from par • Discount is based on the actual number of days to maturity on a 360-day basis • Earned discount is ordinary income	Book Entry Only
U.S. Treasury Notes	2 & 3 year notes: $5,000 min. with increments of $5,000 5 years & longer: $1,000 min. with increments of $1,000	*Maturity* 2 year, 5 year 3 & 10 year 7 year *Auctioned Monthly* Months: 2,5,8, & 11 Months: 1,4,7, & 10	Semiannual, accruing on the basis of actual days in the month and half-year	Book Entry, except notes issued prior to 1/01/83 are available in book entry, registered, and bearer form. Notes issued between 1/01/83 and 8/01/86 are available in only book entry and registered form. Notes issued after 8/01/86 are available in book entry form only.
U.S. Treasury Bonds	$1,000	30-year bond auctioned in months 2, 5, 8, & 11	Semiannual, accruing on the basis of actual days in the month and half-year	
U.S. Treasury Bonds with a "Flower Bond" feature*	$500	Outstanding bonds with coupon rate of 4.25% and below with a max. maturity of 1998	Semiannual, accruing on the basis of actual days in the month and half-year	
STRIPS (Separate Trading of Registered Interest and Principal Securities)	$1,000 face amount	6 months to 30 years	Zero coupon bonds traded at a discount from par, face value paid at maturity	Book Entry Only

*The government will redeem them at full face value plus accrued interest in payment for federal estate taxes if the bonds are purchased by the beneficial owner prior to death.

TABLE 4-4:
FEDERAL AGENCY SECURITIES

Type of Issue	Minimun Denominations & Increments	Maturities	Interest Payments
Federal Farm Credit Bank Bonds (FFCB)	• $5,000 on issues 12 months and shorter with increments of $5,000 • $1,000 on issues 13 months and longer	• 3- and 6-month bonds offered last week of each month for settlement on the first business day of the following month • Term bonds offered periodically	• 3- and 6-month bonds paid at maturity accruing on a 30/360-day basis • Bonds with maturity of 12 months and longer paid semiannually, accruing on a 30/360-day basis
Federal Home Loan Bank Bonds (FHLB)	$10,000 with increments of $5,000 thereafter	Bonds of various maturities offered in the middle of each month for settlement late in the month	Semiannual, accruing on a 30/360-day basis
Federal National Mortgage Association Debentures, "Fannie Mae" (FNMA)	$10,000 with increments of $5,000 thereafter	Debentures of various maturities offered in the beginning of the month for settlement mid-month	Semiannual, accruing on a 30/360-day basis
Financing Corporation Bonds (FICO)	$10,000 with increments of $5,000 thereafter	30-year bonds	Semiannual, accruing on a 30/360-day basis
Student Loan Marketing Association Notes, "Sallie Mae" (SLMA)	$10,000 with increments of $5,000 thereafter	Debentures of various maturities not offered on a regular basis	Semiannual, accruing on a 30/360-day basis
Federal Home Loan Mortgage Corporation Debentures, "Freddie Mac" (FHLMC)	$10,000 with increments of $5,000 thereafter	Debentures of various maturities not offered on a regular basis	Semiannual, accruing on a 30/360-day basis
Resolution Funding Corp. (REFCORP)	$1,000 with increments of $1,000	30 year and 40 year	Semiannual, accruing on the basis of actual days in the month and half-year
Tennessee Valley Authority (TVA)	$1,000 with increments of $1,000	Various maturities up to 40 years	Semiannual, accruing on a 30/360-day basis

TABLE 4-5:

GOVERNMENT NATIONAL MORTGAGE ASSOCIATION, "GINNIE MAE" (GNMA)

Types of Issue	Underlying Mortgages	Final Maturity/ Assumed Average Life	Denomination	Monthly Payment
GNMA Pass Through	FHA/VA mortgages on one- to four-family dwellings	30-year final maturity/12-year assumed average life	$25,000 min., with increments of $5,000 thereafter	Interest and return of principal are paid on the 15th of each month, accruing on a 30/360-day basis, by the mortgage service company
GNMA "Midget"	FHA/VA mortgages on one- to four-family dwellings	15-year final maturity/7-year assumed average life	$25,000 min., with increments of $5,000 thereafter	
GNMA Mobile Home B	FHA/VA mortgages on manufactured housing	15-year final maturity/7-year assumed average life	$25,000 min., with increments of $5,000 thereafter	
GNMA GPM (Graduated Payment Mortgage)	FHA/VA mortgages on one- to four-family dwellings	30-year final maturity/12-year assumed average life	$25,000 min., with increments of $5,000 thereafter	
GNMA II (All of the above mortgage types have GNMA II Programs)	(All of the above mortgage types have GNMA II programs)	(All of the above mortgage types have GNMA II programs)	$25,000 min., with increments of $5,000 thereafter	Interest and return of principal are paid by Chemical Bank on the 20th of each month, accruing on a 30/360-day basis
GNMA 223F Project	FHA-insured apartment project	Generally a 35-year final maturity; some GNMA 223F projects have call protection	$25,000 min., with increments of $5,000 thereafter	Interest and return of principal are paid by the mortgage service company on the 15th of each month, accruing on a 30/360-day basis

TABLE 4-6:

FEDERAL NATIONAL MORTGAGE ASSOCIATION, "FANNIE MAE" (FNMA)

Types of Issue	Underlying Mortgages	Final Maturity/ Assumed Average Life	Denomination	Monthly Payment
FNMA MBS (Mortgage-Backed Security)	Conventional FHA/VA mortgages	30-year final maturity/ 10-year assumed average life	$1,000 min., with increments of $1,000 thereafter	Interest and return of principal are paid on the 25th of each month, accruing on a 30/360-day basis
FNMA "Dwarf"	Conventional or FHA/ VA mortgages	15-year final maturity/ 6- to 7-year assumed average life	$1,000 min.	Interest and return of principal are paid on the 25th of each month, accruing on a 30/360-day basis
FNMA-REMIC (Real Estate Mortgage Investment Conduit)	Collateralized by FNMA MBS and average lives	Various stated maturities and average lives	$1,000 min., with increments of $15,000 thereafter	Interest and/or interest and return of principal are paid on the 25th of each month, accruing on a 30/ 360-day basis

TABLE 4-7:
FEDERAL HOME LOAN MORTGAGE CORPORATION "FREDDIE MAC" (FHLMC)

Types of Issue	Underlying Mortgages	Final Maturity/ Assumed Average Life	Denomination	Monthly Payment
FHLMC PC (Participation Certificate)	Conventional or FHA/VA mortgages	30-year final maturity/10- to 12-year assumed average life	$1,000 min., with increments of $1,000 thereafter	Interest and return of principal are paid on the 15th of each month, accruing on a 30/360-day basis
FHLMC "GNOME" and "NONGNOME"	Conventional or FHA/VA mortgages	15-year final maturity/6- to 7-year assumed average life	$1,000 min.	Interest and return of principal are paid on the 15th of each month, accruing on a 30/360-day basis
FHLMC-REMIC (Real Estate Mortgage Investment Conduit)	Collateralized by FHLMC PCs and FHLMC "GNOMEs"	Various stated maturities and average lives	$1,000 min.	Interest and/or interest and return of principal are paid on the 15th of each month, accruing on a 30/360-day basis

5

TECHNICAL ANALYSIS

JOHN R. MARKLE

INTRODUCTION

You've done your homework. You've examined the basic characteristics of all the stocks you have an interest in buying. It's time
to take the plunge, but which of the stocks on your list do you
buy *now?*

Determining trends in stock values is a critically important part
of investment research. After an examination of the basic indicators
turns up appealing candidates, the next step is to see what their
pattern of share price uptrends and downtrends have been. The
basic idea is to catch stocks just prior to a rise in price due to competitive bidding on the stock exchanges. To find stocks poised for
an upward surge requires careful attention to what is going on during daily bidding in the exchanges. Buying stock shares in this way,
you maximize your equity's impact.

Part of the story has to do with the overall situation of the economy as expressed in stock exchange activity. For some time this has
been summarized each day by commercial analysis companies. The
oldest and most widely quoted stock market average is the Dow
Jones Industrial Average. The Dow is a price-weighted average of
stock activity of thirty blue-chip companies. The companies are
changed from time to time, alterations being made so that the Dow
represents 15 to 20 percent of the market value of all New York

Stock Exchange stocks. The average is calculated from the closing prices of the component stocks.

Then there are the specialized averages. The Dow Jones Transportation Average is a price-weighted average consisting of the stocks of twenty large transportation companies—airlines, railroads, and trucking companies. The Dow Jones Utility Average is derived from the performance of fifteen gas and electric utility companies around the United States.

As computers became available and reliable, the old Dow Jones numbers were joined by averages taken from much wider samples of companies. The Standard & Poor's 500 Stock Index (the S & P 500) is a market-value weighted index amalgamating the trading activity of "the S & P 400 Industrials," "the S & P 20 Transportations," "the S & P 40 Financials," and "the S & P 40 Utilities." The index represents about 80 percent of the market value of all issues traded on the New York Stock Exchange. The S & P is commonly considered the best benchmark against which the performance of individual stocks or stock groups can be measured, but some analysts prefer the Wilshire 5000 Equity Index. It represents the value, in billions of dollars, of all New York Stock Exchange, American Stock Exchange, and over-the-counter share trades for which quotes are available.

Things can happen fast to a share's value, often for little apparent reason. Once a stock gets hot, investors buying simultaneously can kick the price rapidly upward. Eventually, enthusiasm will peak, causing the stock price to stabilize or retreat. Then the cycle starts all over again. It is a rhythmic matter, and charts of share price histories have an uncanny similarity to pulse, brain activity, and other life diagnostic indicators. The analogy is apt, because the health of a stock truly is revealed in the charted patterns of its recent behavior.

Although the most sophisticated investors use complicated computer programs to calculate share trajectories, by far the majority use graphics to estimate what will soon be happening to a stock share's value. This is called "charting." A surprising amount of deduced information can be taken from looking at the displayed fluctuations. Brokerage firms and investment companies often have technical departments whose whole function is to keep up charts of various types describing individual stocks and various market averages.

The data that is used to make charts can be obtained in several different ways. Professional investors keep instantaneously in touch with the markets around the world through computer subscriptions. This is more than novices require. They can make do with the stock information published by daily newspapers, normally the summaries of what happened the previous day on the New York or American Stock Exchange.

For the new investor with comparatively few stocks to worry about, making charts by hand from this resource if fine. Once a portfolio becomes enlarged, the task of keeping up charts becomes too onerous. Luckily, there are now subscription charting services that use computer graphics and are fairly inexpensive. The individual has to decide when the change should be made. Beginning on page 86 you will find the charts referred to throughout this chapter.

BASIC CHART PATTERNS

The most readable graphic used by the investment community is the bar chart (see Figure 5-1). The top portion of a bar chart displays the trading activity of a stock or market average by using vertical lines. The top of the line represents the high of the day and the bottom indicates the low of the day. Some charts record the daily high and low, while others record the weekly high and low. Either way, the bottom portion of the bar chart shows the volume of shares traded during the trading period.

An alternative graphic approach is called point & figure (see Figure 5-2). Point & figure graphs plot significant share price movement, but not all movement. Rising prices are represented by X's and falling prices are represented by O's. It is a good system for the beginner because chart maintenance is less time-consuming than it is with bar charts and the patterns are easier to interpret.

The fundamental pattern of stock share value fluctuation is the sine curve, familiar to any student of trigonometry. Available stock shares of a healthy company are always eventually absorbed by expanding demand, a process called "accumulation." After the accumulation period, the forces of demand gradually build up power in a base-building phase before the price trend turns upward. Breakout is when a stock's price first exceeds its previously recorded high or low points, or some other predetermined criterion.

After you follow stocks for a while, you notice that price bidding acts to alter prices in a jagged, oscillating fashion. Consolidation can occur at any time, a temporary pause in a trend bidding price up or down, but there may be a definable zone of price within which the share price moves up and down. This is called the "trading channel."

If a share climbs higher than expected, it is being overbought by investors bidding simultaneously and without knowing how many others are doing the same. Near the peak, resistance occurs as buyers begin to worry that a drop is on the way. Potential sellers exceed potential buyers. An inevitable climax of a rising trend is for the distribution of large quantities of stock to occur. Investors become convinced that share value has become extended past its anticipated peak, according to trend history, and some start selling to reap a profit before the downturn. The effect of such a big sell-off itself is to trigger a decline in share prices.

Price declines for a while. Then support comes along when a price level is reached that stimulates buyers to become active enough to absorb available supply. This buying results in a slowing, then a reversal of a decline. At the bottom, overselling may cause the share price to go lower than the trend would predict— a great time to buy, and part of the mechanism that fuels a turnaround.

Looking at Figure 5-2, you can see typical key points in the trading cycle. Base building is underway at A, and B is where there is a period of buying, a bullishness. The trading channel is the range between B and C, and D is where there was a period of extension. At E we see a period of consolidation, and at F a period of accumulation, followed by clearly bearish signs at G and H that buyers think the price will fall. I is that interesting phenomenon, the breakout.

KEEPING POINT & FIGURE CHARTS

Eventually you will need and want to subscribe to a computerized service, but for now your portfolio is small and your charting needs are simple. Here is the standard approach to charting by hand, using the point & figure approach.

Incomplete point & figure charts can be obtained from Chartcraft in New Rochelle, New York. After ordering your chart book, save copies of the *Wall Street Journal* or the business section of a major newspaper, so that you can update the charts quickly after they arrive.

There are conventions in charting (see Figure 5-3). The vertical axis, marked along the left side of the graph, represents the trading price of the stock. Each square in the graph, referred to as a box, represents increasing value from bottom to top. Boxes change in value as follows:

under $5 a box is worth ¼ point
under $20 a box is worth ½ point
under $100 a box is worth 1 point
over $100 a box is worth 2 points

The horizontal axis, marked along the bottom of the graph, indicates time. A price history is traced from left to right, and the intersection between value and date is marked on the body of the chart. Rising prices are indicated by X's, falling prices by O's, except when a new month starts. This is shown as a single figure, the numbers 1 through 9 indicating January through September and A through C to finish out the year.

Except for the month indicators, the chart is marked with X's and O's. X's represent upward motion in price, O's represent downward motion. Only actually mark a box when a continuing trend has moved at least another full box, or when a reversal of a trend—indicating a new one—has moved three boxes.

Let's look at a chart of Trinity Industries (see Figure 5-4) and practice updating the pattern from a list of highs and lows we gathered from the paper. The chart ends in a series of O's reaching down to 24. The stock must go down to 23 or lower before we can add another 0. If the stock went up to 27 or higher, then we would start a column of X's.

Try actually adding the following data to the chart.

Day	High	Low	Entry on graph
1	25 ¼	24 ⅞	
·	25 ⅝	25 ⅛	
·	26 ½	26	
·	27	26 ⅝	enter 3 X's up—25, 26, 27
·	27 ¾	27 ⅛	
·	28 ¼	27 ½	enter 1 X up—28
·	29 ⅛	28 ¾	enter 1 X up—29
·	28 ¾	28	
·	27 ⅞	27 ¼	
10	27	26 ⅜	
11	26 ⅝	26	enter 3 O's down—28, 27, 26
12	26 ⅜	25 ¾	
13	28	27 ¼	
14	29 ¼	28 ½	enter 3 X's up—27, 28, 29
15	30 ⅜	29 ¾	enter 1 X up—30
16	32	31 ⅜	enter 2 X's up—31, 32

The updated chart pattern should now appear as shown in Figure 5-5.

A helpful way to keep charts current is to use a parameter sheet. Make a list of the stocks you follow, as in Table 5-1. Look at the charted pattern for each stock to determine what impending high or low of the day would cause a significant change in the chart pattern, either augmenting a trend or reversing it, then note these parameters in pencil next to each stock. Columns on the sheet represent trading days of the week. Comparing the highs and lows of your stocks, using data from the newspaper, you can see each day whether the high or low parameter has been reached. If it has, record it and move on. If both parameters were hit by a very active stock, record the high if the stock was rising in value or the low if the stock was declining. After updating the parameter sheet, record the changes on each stock's charts. The last step is to determine and write on the parameter sheet the revised parameters to be looking for next.

Point & figure charting by hand takes time and effort. Is it worth it? Absolutely, because it helps the investor spot trends in stocks as they begin to emerge. The only excuse most people have had for not charting was the tedium factor. Precise, day in and day out, gathering and tracking of data quickly becomes a tremendous bore to most people, even for a few stocks.

Do it anyway, while your portfolio is small. A hands-on approach right now will only take a few minutes a day, and you will benefit by watching the shares cycle up and down. As computers take over more and more of the dull, repetitive work, leaving the investor the task of merely pondering implications, before long virtually everyone will be a subscription chartist. Those who don't will eat the chartists' dust, since their decision making won't have the swiftness and precision derived from closer analytical touch with their investments.

CHART INTERPRETATION

Charts are fine, but how does one interpret them? That is the true art of the chartist. Knowing whether to buy or to sell, and when, makes all the difference in profitable investing.

Let's look at some of the most common buy and sell signals that occur on point & figure chart patterns.

Chartists are always watching for a duplicated pattern of highs and lows. In example A of Figure 5-6, a hypothetical stock starts with a bottom at 31 and a top at 34. The stock then repeats the bottom at 31, then follows it with a move to 34. This called a "double top," which frequently means that the stock is about to jump upward a point or more. Here the wise investor would give his broker a "double top buy signal," namely, telling him to buy in if the stock reaches 35. It does, indicated by the letter B. The happy chartist watches as the stock continues to rise, soon reaching 41.

The same sort of pattern applies when a stock sinks. In example B of Figure 5-6 a top occurs at 45 followed by a bottom at 42, then a top again at 45 followed by a bottom at 42. This is called a "double bottom." The investor senses a coming plunge and at 41 he gives his broker a "double bottom sell signal," indicated by the letter S. The stock is unloaded, and as expected, it continues to fall, winding up at 35. Yes, the blow fell elsewhere, but this is not the investor's affair. He saved his equity. Moreover, whoever bought the stock will eventually see the stock rise again, unless there is something fundamentally wrong with the stock's corporation. Double tops and double bottoms do not necessarily have to begin after long falls of O's or long rises of X's. However, when they do, they usually appear at market tops and market bottoms.

In Figure 5-7 there are three variations of "triple top" formations. They are all equally potent forecasters of a new upward movement in the stock. In example A, tops occur at 34, 34, and 34, a "straight triple top." The buy signal, indicated by the letter B, is given when 35 is reached. In example B, tops occur at 35, 34, and 35, a "V triple top." The buy signal is given at 36. In example C, tops occur at 34, 35, and 35, an "angle triple top." The buy signal again comes at 36, when the stock climbs above the three tops. The triple top formation is easy to spot and very reliable.

Triple top formations are usually found at the beginning of a new uptrend, but they also occur in the middle of a rising trend before a stock propels itself into a steeper climb. After a long decline in the stock market, watch for triple top formations. When a high percentage of stocks show triple top buy signals, it usually means that a new bull market is starting.

There are, naturally, three types of triple bottom formations. In example A of Figure 5-8, bottoms occur at 42, 42, and 42. Since the three bottoms are in a straight line, this formation is called the "straight triple bottom." The sell signal, indicated by the letter S, is given at 41. In example B, bottoms occur at 41, 42, and 41. Since these bottoms form an upside-down V, this formation is the "V shape triple bottom." The sell signal is given at 40. In example C, bottoms occur at 42, 41, and 41. The bottom at 42 occurs at an angle to the others, so we call this formation the "angle triple bottom." The sell signal is given at 40.

Triple bottom sell signals are quite common at the beginning of a new downtrend of a stock. This signal often forecasts a major stock-exchange correction, the beginning of a bear market when there is a prolonged period of falling stock, bond, and commodity prices. Since stocks usually fall faster than they rise, triple bottom sell signals often precede a rapid decline in a stock. For that reason, they are commonly used in selecting stocks to sell short.

In addition to tops and bottoms, chartists inspect "support lines" to determine trading channels and forecast overall trends. A support line indicates the pricing area in which buyers normally come in to support a stock or market average and drive the price higher. The bullish support line is more reliable an indicator than the bearish support line.

Here are the rules for drawing support lines.

The bullish support line (see Figure 5-9) is drawn at a 45-degree angle. After a stock has given a buy signal, note the lowest X in the formation. Start your line in the box under the X. Most point & figure charts use a plus (+) sign. Insert a plus sign in the box under the X, and just go up one box and over one box as you add each successive plus sign. This is an easy way to draw the 45-degree line. Bullish support lines stay in effect until they are broken by two open boxes. It is profitable to own a stock as long as the bullish support line is in effect. Once the line is broken, you should consider selling.

The bearish support line forms the bottom half of the bearish trading channel (see Figure 5-10). It is a 45-degree line drawn from the open box next to a wall of X's. It can be drawn with dots or slashes and should be next to a wall that is at least 7 to 9 boxes long. The bearish support line is often temporarily broken as a stock trades downward, and should also be drawn to reflect a stock's normal trading pattern. Sometimes there will be several walls of X's. Choose the one to the immediate left of the sell signal formation, unless this would create an uncomfortably tight trading channel.

The other primary line to think about in a trading channel is a resistance line. This is the area in which a stock or market average usually stops rising in value. A bearish resistance line is more powerful than a bullish resistance line, and must be penetrated before a meaningful uptrend can begin.

The bearish resistance line is a 45-degree line drawn from the top X in a sell signal formation (see Figure 5-11). Place a plus sign (+), slash (\), or dot (·) above the top X in the formation and then proceed down one and over one, to continue the line. As long as a stock has this type of resistance line, it will stay in a bearish trend. Even if a stock has given a buy signal, it is best to wait until the bearish resistance line is broken before buying it. Once resistance is gone, a stock has the best likelihood of starting a new uptrend. Bearish resistance lines, along with triple bottom sell signals, are quite common at the start of new bear markets.

The bullish resistance line forms the top half of a bullish trading channel (see Figure 5-12). It is not as powerful as the bullish support line, and is often temporarily broken as a stock trades in an uptrend.

Here are some things to remember about indicators supporting a buy:

1. In the absence of a triple top buy signal, look for a stock that has two or more buy signals in its base. This will often have the same significance for you.

2. Buy stocks that have broken the bearish resistance line by two open boxes. By doing so, you increase the chances that the stock is in a new uptrend, as opposed to merely a short reversal. Notice the encircled area in Figure 5-13.

3. Look at a long-term chart pattern that covers at least eight years of trading. This will give you a broader perspective on how the stock traded in previous bull and bear cycles. It will also help you see whether the stock is in the early or late stages of a bullish trend.

4. Buy stocks in an industry where several companies at once are giving buy signals and starting new uptrends.

5. When a bull market is already underway, it is sometimes difficult to find stocks that are just starting an uptrend; most have already started. In this kind of market, buy a stock that is in a well-defined uptrend, as it pulls back in the trading channel near the bullish support line. In this way, you can avoid chasing a stock, can get a fair price, and can still have a lot of upside potential. An example of this is shown in the encircled area of Figure 5-14.

DECIDING WHEN TO SELL

The hardest decision for an investor to make is not when to buy, it's when to *sell*—foregoing further possible increases in stock value so that known current profits can be made, or selling and taking a known loss rather than waiting for a stock to bottom out and bounce back. There are several reasons why this decision is so difficult.

First, there is plenty of information available from brokerage firms about stocks to buy, but not much on ones that should be sold. Part of this is psychological—successful brokers tend to be positive, optimistic people always looking for an improved world— and part is political—they don't want to slam a shaky stock now because it could easily make a comeback, and for that matter, making statements of a negative kind actually further weakens a stock. So the investor can't count on much help here.

What about the fundamental analyses traditionally used to assess a company? These have their limitations, because they track matters comparatively slowly. They summarize generalized corporate behavior, but not the rapid oscillations of the exchanges.

This brings us back to point & figure again. It provides a disciplined mechanism with which to spot upturns, and the same thing goes for spotting downtrends. Watching for sell signals on the charts can help an investor get out of a dipping stock before too much equity damage occurs.

Here are some basic guidelines for deciding when to sell:

1. Sell a stock that has given a triple bottom sell signal or has given multiple sell signals. This often precedes a top building process. Notice the circled area in Figure 5-15.

2. Sell a stock when it breaks the bullish support line by two open boxes. This usually marks the beginning of a new downtrend. An example of this can be found in the circled area in Figure 5-16.

3. Stocks that have been in a long uptrend, are building a top, and give several sell signals form a "curling-over" pattern. An example of this can be found in Figure 5-16. Sell a stock with this pattern because it usually occurs at the beginning of a significant downtrend.

4. Sell a stock when your predetermined profit objective has been met. When buying a stock for a quick trade, use the following guidelines. Consider selling a double top when the stock has increased by 35 percent or eight months have passed. Consider selling a triple top when the stock has increased by 28 percent or six months have passed. If you purchased a stock that has a well-defined trading channel, consider selling when it hits the bullish resistance line.

5. Sell when a stock drops by 20 percent. Once a stock has fallen this much, you have to find a stock that will rise 25 percent just to break even, not factoring in brokers' fees. If you let a stock fall much more than 20 percent before selling, it may well be best just to grit your teeth and wait out the whole cycle of down and back up. Of course, there is always the risk that the stock may *never* come back!

STICKING WITH IT

When you begin your portfolio, and get into point & figure charting, start with no more stocks than ten of the Dow Jones 30 Industrials, ten other corporations from the S & P 500, and ten corporations in which you have a special interest, probably derived from working up the fundamentals. This way you will follow enough stocks to get a feel for the market, but you won't have so many that you are overwhelmed with the task of charting by hand.

As you begin to add to the stocks you follow, it is important to make sure that there is balance among the industry groups. Besides charting the major manufacturing companies, it is a good idea to follow a few oil stocks, gold and silver stocks, consumer product marketers, transportation stocks, and utility stocks.

Published chart books come in short and long-term formats. The short term is set up to cover two to four years of trading on a stock and is quite helpful in showing immediate trends. The long term covers eight to ten years of trading and shows a stock's primary trends.

A cautionary reminder: Charts show *trends* in the impact of supply and demand, not guarantees of profitability. Unpredictable influences such as wars, political events, buy-out offers, or surprise business decisions can suddenly come out of nowhere and produce violent wobbles in formerly sturdy patterns.

Most novice investors maintain that they understand this, but they really don't. The first year they lose money using charts, they want to scrap the whole system.

But then where do you go? To reading tea leaves or consulting tarot cards? Inspecting chicken entrails, seeking out the aid of second-sighted crones, or doing business with wizards peddling cloaks of invisibility might be valid choices. . . .

Seriously, the fact of the matter is that novices become wearied, and a dip yields the excuse needed to cease doing the daily chore of charting. By stopping they gain blessed free time with which to watch television or pat their dogs. They also pass into the mass of knee-jerk investors without much to guide them except emotion.

There's no longer any reason for this, due to computerization. A couple of years of disciplined charting by hand should produce good results on the basic portfolio, and after that introductory period a turn to subscription charting and the use of a personal computing system at home are well worth the investment. After that, the routine of tracking investments will resolve itself to little more than a few odd minutes each day in front of the computer, and watching for the signals of when to buy or sell.

Figure 5-1: Common Bar Chart of Price Movement with Volume Traded Shown at the Bottom

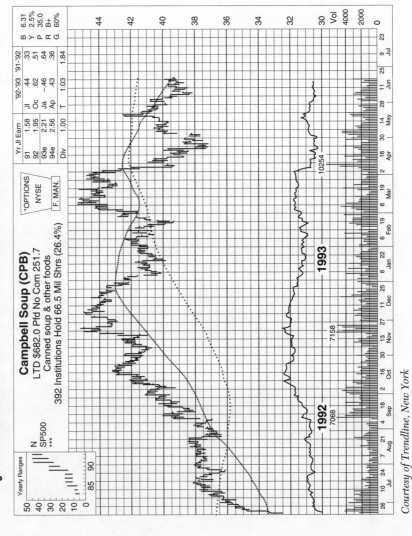

Figure 5-2: Illustration of Technical Terms Such as Accumulation, Uptrend, Trading Channel, etc.

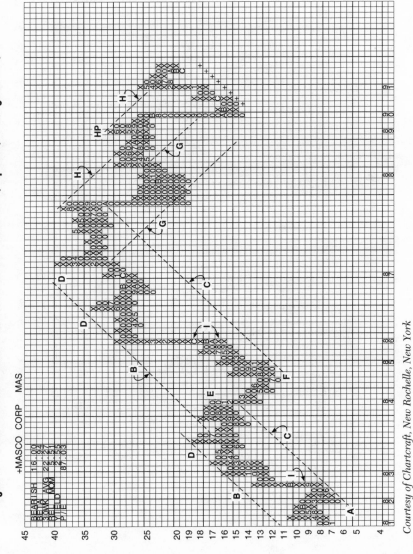

Courtesy of Chartcraft, New Rochelle, New York

Figure 5-3: Common Point & Figure Charts Showing How Point Values Change at Various Price Ranges

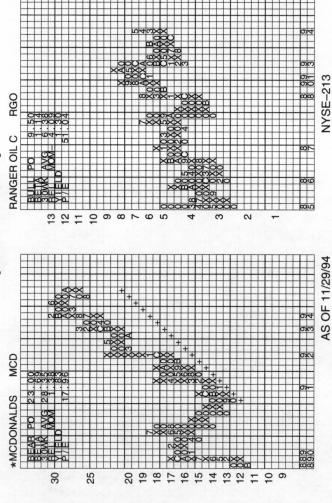

Courtesy of Chartcraft, New Rochelle, New York

Figure 5-4: Chart Pattern of Trinity Industries Before Updating from the Parameter Sheet

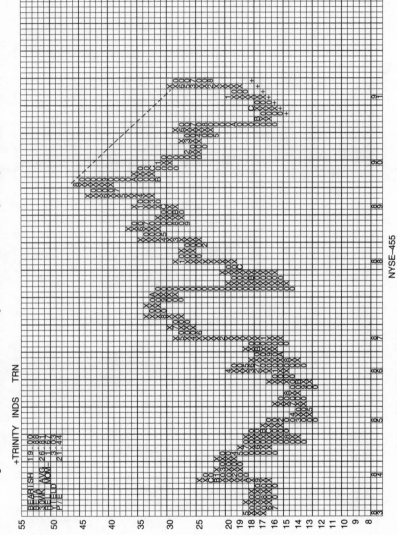

Courtesy of Chartcraft, New Rochelle, New York

Figure 5-5: Trinity Industries Chart Pattern After Updating

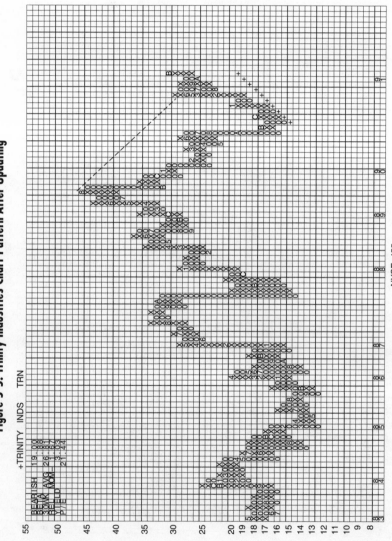

Courtesy of Chartcraft, New Rochelle, New York

Figure 5-6: Classic Double Top and Double Bottom Formations of a Hypothetical Stock

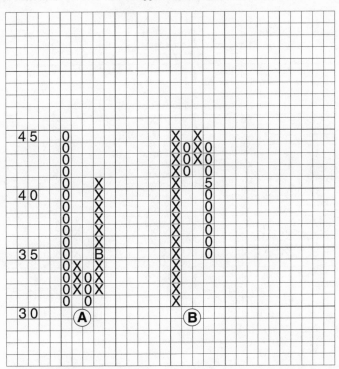

Courtesy of Chartcraft, New Rochelle, New York

Figure 5-7: Different Classic Triple Top Formations of a Hypothetical Stock

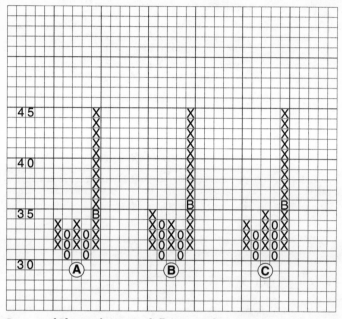

Courtesy of Chartcraft, New Rochelle, New York

Figure 5-8: Various Classic Triple Bottom Formations of a Hypothetical Stock

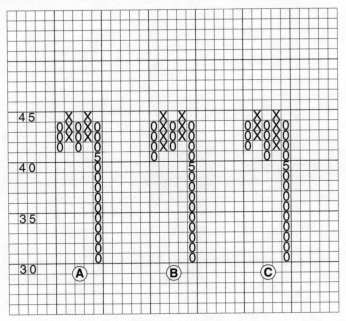

Courtesy of Chartcraft, New Rochelle, New York

Figure 5-9: Example of a Bullish Support Line Represented by Plus Signs

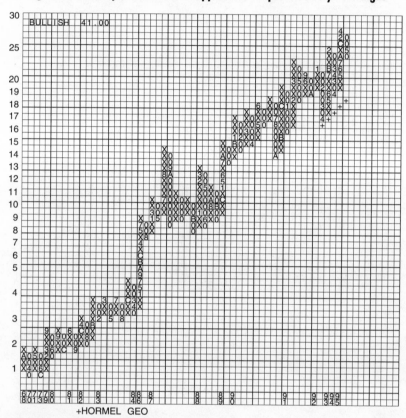

Courtesy of Chartcraft, New Rochelle, New York

Figure 5-10: Bearish Support Lines Illustrated by Lower Sets of Dots

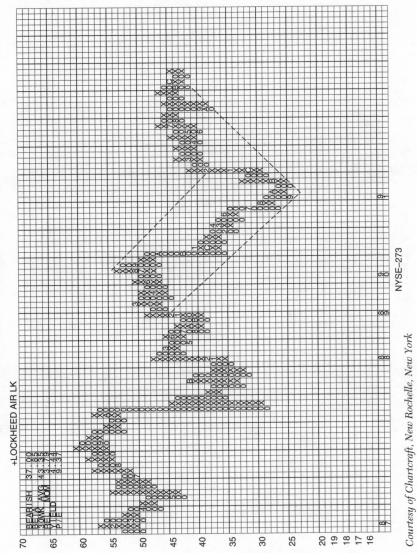

Courtesy of Chartcraft, New Rochelle, New York

NYSE-273

Figure 5-11: Example of a Bearish Resistance Line Represented by Plus Signs

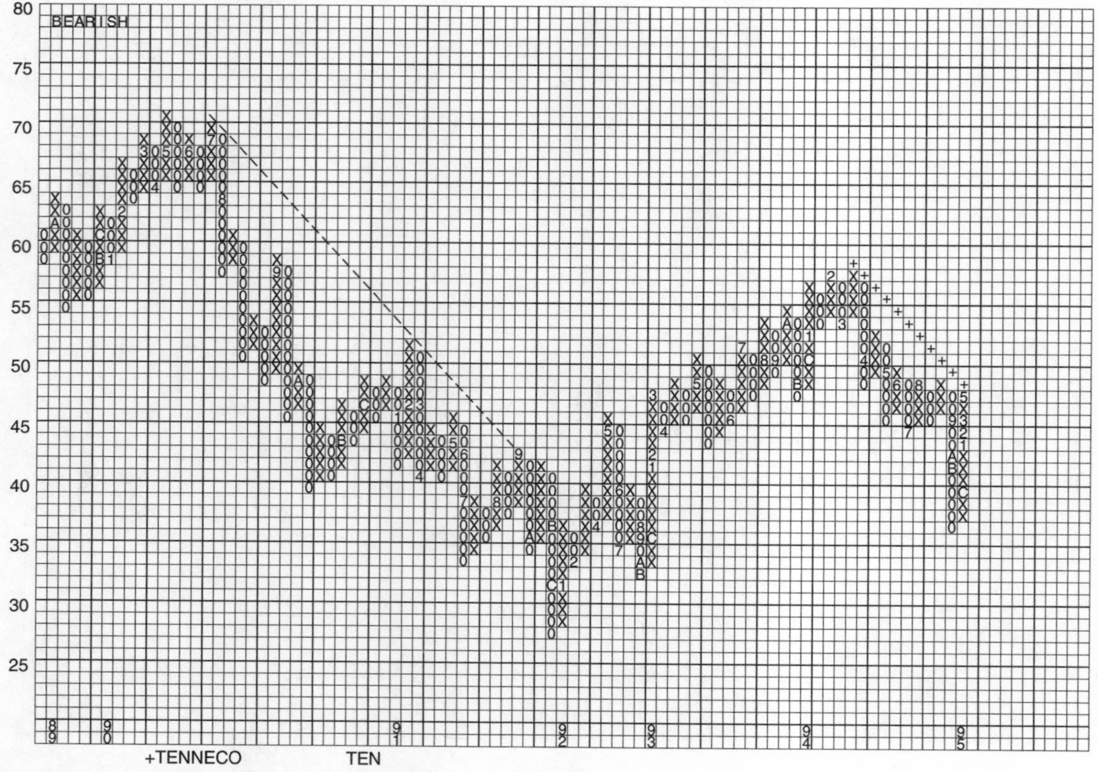

Courtesy of Chartcraft, New Rochelle, New York

Figure 5-12: Bullish Resistance Line Illustrated by a Rising Set of Dots

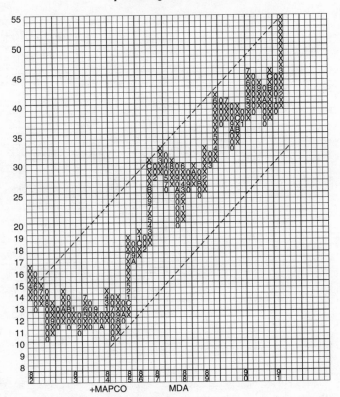

Courtesy of Chartcraft, New Rochelle, New York

Figure 5-13: Monsanto Shows a Typical Reverse Check Mark Pattern as the Price Goes from 62 to 39, Then up to 50

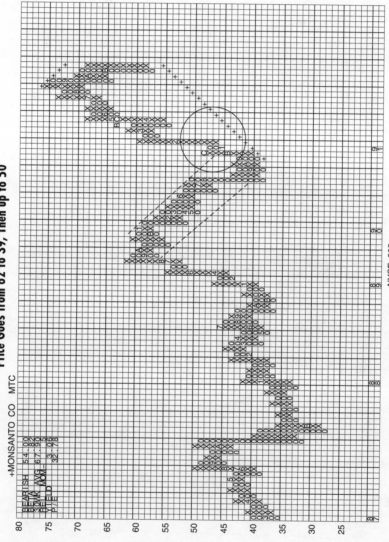

Courtesy of Chartcraft, New Rochelle, New York

Figure 5-14: Example of Buying as a Stock Hits the Bullish Support Line at 16 1/2 and Again at 23

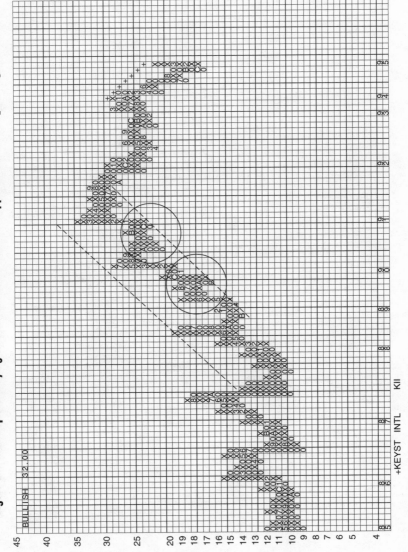

Figure 5-15: Strong Selling Signals Given by Triple Bottom Sell Pattern at 28 and Again at 27

+SAFECARD   SVC   SSI

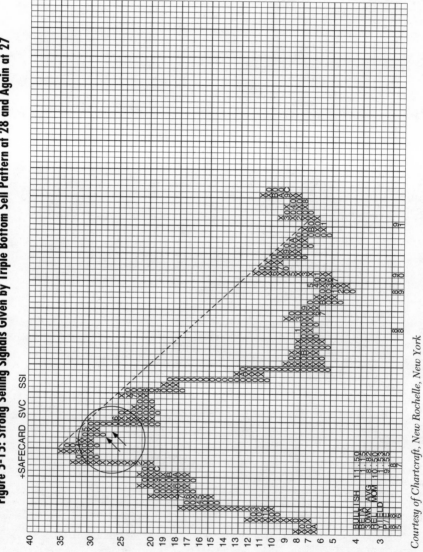

Courtesy of Chartcraft, New Rochelle, New York

Figure 5-16: Examples of Curling-Over Patterns Mean "Head for the Hills"

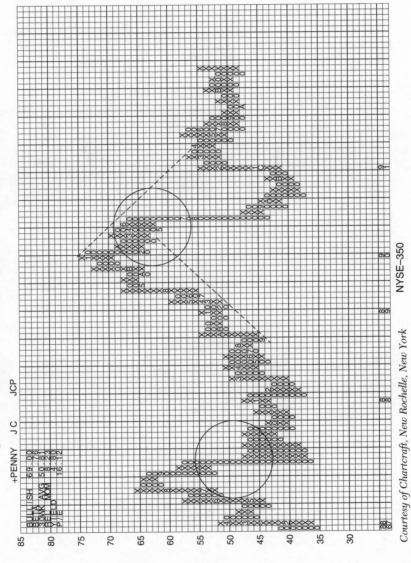

Courtesy of Chartcraft, New Rochelle, New York   NYSE–350

TABLE 5-1:
A PARAMETER SHEET IS USED TO COLLATE DATA
BEFORE POSTING TO POINT & FIGURE CHARTS

	2/12 W	13 T	14 F	2/17 M	18 T	19 W	20 T	21 F	2/24 M	25 T
Alcoa			68		70	73				
71-67								70		68
Boeing										
49-45	46									
Chevron										
64-60		63			62			61		
IBM	92	93								
92-88			90						89	

6

PORTFOLIO CREATION
AND NURTURING

LAWRENCE LYNN

INTRODUCTION

When joint stock companies first began nearly four hundred years ago, printing was still rudimentary and business documents, as a matter of course, were drafted and copied by hand. The scriveners who did this work excelled in calligraphy, priding themselves on creating manuscripts distinctive as much for their beauty as for their clarity. Many were large affairs, written on sheepskin. Investors took to keeping these works of art in the portable, flat cases used by artists for their paintings. Eventually the documents within these "portfolios" became known jointly by that name themselves, and the practice has continued to the present.

Assembling a modern investment portfolio requires thought and caution. If you live in a moderately affluent neighborhood, sooner or later you will begin getting annoying telephone calls from stockbrokers. New brokers just getting started have to find clients, and investors aren't likely to walk in their office doors. Some brokerage houses even have policies about this, with rookie hires providing cannon fodder to build up the house's list of clients.

Making "cold calls" is legitimate. Virtually all salespeople use this tool, and hearing from an earnest young person about investment alternatives may be the way you are inducted into investing.

Be aware, however, that there are both creditable brokers and boiler room "bucket shop" brokers out to sell you absolutely certain winners, like oil property or drilling partnership participation, for a surprisingly modest amount of money. If these folks get your attention, this pitch will be followed by an urgent proposal that you take part in some commodity deal that "simply cannot lose." These propositions almost always start with the word "only" before the dollar amount you must pony up.

Whether from the hard-sell cadre or a tip from your aunt Harriet, who has heard about a wonderful investment from a dear neighbor with a terrific broker friend, kindly but firmly just say no. As ever, if something sounds too good to be true, it usually is. The cold-calling quick-deal salesperson is out to get your money, and Aunt Harriet's neighbor is a bubblehead in the process of being cleaned out. Initiating your investment portfolio ought to start with calm deliberation, not hype.

A BASIC PORTFOLIO

All professions have their cherished traditions and dogma on how to project and proselytize central tenets. In securities investment one of the most hallowed educational analogies is to compare a solid portfolio to a pyramid (see Figure 6-1 on page 115). It is a well-taken comparison because the pyramid is the sturdiest architectural shape known; the famous pyramids of ancient Egypt are weathered now but still there after 5,000 years.

In a securities portfolio, your pyramid has eight levels, progressing upward from level A through level H. The foundation is level A, a footing consisting entirely of investment blocks without a hint of speculation. Here are the structural components that are instantly convertible into cash should the need arise: passbook savings accounts and certificates of deposit, money market securities, and short-term federal securities. An important feature is their interchangeability. With relatively small service commissions, one can easily move from United States Treasury Bonds to Treasury Bills to certificates of deposit and money market funds or the reverse.

Always remember, though: High safety has been traded for growth. Level A is a parking place for money, no more.

What portion of your equity should be put into easily available locations? This depends upon your situation in life. If you are in a secure, well-paying job, you need a lot less of a nest egg than someone whose company is downsizing. Depending upon whom you ask, financial experts suggest that having a six- to twelve-month survival fund makes sense if times are getting rough and you are in middle or higher management. Those who have more modest incomes but higher job security, solid medical insurance, and good health can be comfortable with three to four months' worth of living expenses to draw from. For those who are retired but who do not qualify for federal medical assistance, adequate cash to cover the emergencies of old age could be a good topic to discuss with a doctor. To broadly generalize, the average person should keep no more than eighteen months' worth of living expenses readily at hand, and someone with very secure employment needs no more than four to six months' worth. More than this in the foundation level means giving up too many opportunities for growth investment returns.

Once an investor has estimated how substantial the pyramid's foundation should be, it becomes possible to begin building the growth portion of the portfolio. You want a tier of investments with some risk, but not too much. Level B holds the lesser-known federal agency notes backed by federal taxation, like student loan long-term bonds, the better issues of corporate bonds, and tax-exempt municipal bonds. These investments typically keep slightly ahead of losses due to currency devaluation.

How much should be invested in level B again depends upon one's situation. All other variables in balance, when the economy is in a recession, and currency devaluation is low, bond investment should be enlarged; in more robust economic times, with growth and higher currency devaluation, investment in level B should be reduced in favor of securities that are more dynamic. Of course, for most individuals, age and employment characteristics and security are considerations. If your portfolio is large, and you can absorb possible reverses on the riskier securities, you might well put here as little as a fourth or a third of your net worth. The elderly, with little chance of earnings to offset market losses from stock or real estate investment, and those with shaky job situations, should put more into level B than into the burgeoning but more risky levels.

The idea is to cultivate net equity growth without betting the farm. Common stocks of highly capitalized corporations with a demonstrated pattern of growth in good times or bad are called "blue chip stocks," referring to their solidity through a poker analogy. Big corporations like Procter & Gamble, Colgate-Palmolive, General Electric, Du Pont, and Merck have common stock that doesn't appreciate quickly in value and doesn't pay out large dividends, but is almost impervious to economic fluctuation. The emphasis in such corporations is on major reinvestment in the research and development of new products, technologies, and businesses.

Similarly stable are the shares of top mutual funds such as Investment Company of America, Templeton Growth, World Fund, and Merrill Lynch Capital Fund. Mutual funds indirectly enable you to invest in fifty to one hundred companies at a time, yet pay only a small brokerage commission on transactions. Mutual funds, through sheer enormity and breadth of investment, have an outstanding history of growth, in some cases reaching levels of 14 to 20 percent per year over extended periods. Their very diversity is the hedge against inevitable periodic industrial and regional economic fluctuations.

Investment in public utility stock offers a nice balance of low risk and fairly high returns to investment. Although they are private corporations, they are legal monopolies in protected geographic areas. Most public utilities offer dividend yields at over twice the return of passbook accounts. Some utilities offer regular dividend reinvestment programs wherein the quarterly dividend is reinvested in their own stock at zero commission. This compounding causes actual yields to escalate over time.

Annuities are, on occasion, an investment alternative of interest. Annuities are vehicles set up to guarantee a continuing return of income to the recipient during the life of the annuity. During the 1980s rates were at 8 percent or more for periods of up to ten years, but in the 1990s annuity writers were only willing to guarantee rates of about 2 percent. Annuities are not an investment tool that belongs in most investment programs unless rates outdistance passbook accounts.

For the active, highly involved investor, the practice of covered stock optioning is a possibility. Since this is a fairly complicated alternative, detailed discussion is deferred until this book's chapter on options for a fuller description and explanation.

The neophyte investor typically takes the advice of his most conservative friends already in the investment game. The portfolio is launched, and for a while the newcomer watches it with mixed pride and apprehension. Unless some catastrophic turn in the market occurs, happily a rare event, all is well and equity is being protected. Inevitably the investor decides that this is not enough. Why not start experimenting a little to see if investments can be found that will make the whole package a bit larger? This leads to adding on the pyramid's higher levels of investment, where greater profits, and greater risks, are involved.

Level D is like a capstone layer to consolidate what has been built below. In level D we find two investment forms. The high yield bonds—called "junk bonds" because of their somewhat lower ratings than the blue chips—are bonds issued by companies with a fairly low credit rating and comparatively uncertain futures. The attraction is higher yields than the garden variety bonds offer; the risk is that the companies themselves are quirky. The attraction? A possibility of annual yields of up to 12 percent. Due to the higher risk it is imprudent to have over 10 percent of your total estate in junk bonds.

Level D is also where you find the use of a brokerage firm's "margin account" to borrow investment money, a considered risk in which you obtain money at a lending rate that you anticipate to be lower than what will be returned from the investment for which it is used. It should ordinarily be kept to no greater portion of your total equity than 10 percent. The Cassandras of investment argue that the total ought to be a lot smaller than that.

Most brokerage firms are willing to loan part or all of the money needed for an investment transaction, assuming that the equivalent equity in your securities or liquidity is there to back it. Suppose you have a portfolio account valued at $90,000. If this consists of healthy, listed stocks, your brokerage will permit you to buy further such stocks on credit up to the amount already in your portfolio at a given interest rate. In this case, that means $90,000 in buying power.

Say that, after careful study, you find a healthy company whose common stock shares have been increasing in value by at least 15 percent per year. If you buy 200 shares at the current asking price of $35 per share, the purchase will cost you $7,000, borrowed from your brokerage. If your annual interest rate on this $7,000 loan is 7 percent, you will be obligated to pay the brokerage firm about $490 per year for the use of its money. Since that cost will be more than matched if the stock keeps increasing in value, as it has in the recent past, you can expect a market gain of $1,050 (0.15 × $7,000) per year on your investment, giving you a net gain on the transaction of $560 ($1,050 − $490) or 8 percent.

How confident are you that the stock price will continue to increase at the estimated 15 percent per year? Is the charged interest rate on the borrowed margin money low enough so that a downward fluctuation in the estimated stock price rise will not dip below what you have to pay for the money? These questions form your risk factor.

Why hold down borrowing to invest? You do it voluntarily, out of prudence, and there are federal and brokerage rules to guarantee it. The reason is that from time to time the market goes through huge palpitations that come out of nowhere. On October 19, 1987, for example, the market dropped like a poleaxed mule, 508 points (20 percent) in a single day. An unexpected hit like this could cause all your calculations to go by the board, and if you can't absorb paying up on a loan, you find yourself with problems.

Level E in your pyramid is where you find growth stocks, oriented toward concentration on internal growth to the point of offering low or no current dividends regardless of profitability. Investors attracted to these corporations are comfortable with deferring pocket-money results in return for the enlargement of an estate. Such companies tend to have been in stride for a number of years, most of which were distinguished by sustained increases in earnings and sales. They have favorable capital ratios, underlying debt structures that are quite reasonable, and a solid niche for their activities. Examples of this sort of company are Carnival Cruise Lines, Winn-Dixie Stores, Albertson's, Dollar General Stores, Hospital Corporation of America, and Chiron Corporation.

The reinvestment-oriented companies have stocks whose prices trend upward along with net earnings. Occasionally there will be setbacks, either because of the general market or because of some temporary hiccup in the growth pattern, perhaps caused by bad press concerning a product line. These corporations inevitably weather such setbacks, sometimes actually gathering further momentum by turning problems into answers.

Some growth companies haven't yet had the time to produce an extensive track record, without which proof of stability they must be considered a somewhat higher-risk investment. They need not be avoided by the novice investor. Hot new issues, particularly in an area of exciting new technical discoveries, can turn out to be real winners in a hurry. Careful study of the key indicator numbers even over just a few years can suggest meaningful interpretations, and that you sign on with a laudable company in its early stages of taking off.

Once in a while, a brand-new corporation issues stock that may be attractive to you. Most new issues are sold outside the securities exchange system, or "over the counter." The over-the-counter (OTC) market listings often show fairly modest prices, low enough for an investor simply to have a go and hope for the best. If it doesn't work out, the loss isn't bad; if it zooms, self-praise for insight is in order.

Occasionally you may want to consider a temporarily depressed issue in a region or country that appears to be emerging from hard times and moving into good. Another possibility would be to buy a stock you believe has suffered a depressed price for no particularly good reason. Do these occur in real life? Yes, but they tend not to be easy to find.

A choice of higher risk level E investments demands greater diligence than otherwise because it is easier to make mistakes. There is also no question that at this level of investment the novice should ask for the help of an interested and well-trained broker or investment consultant. How much of an investor's portfolio should be dedicated to these investments? Since these companies are very much future-oriented, part of one's thinking about this should involve a candid estimation of how much the future means. Elderly persons may feel that getting some use now out of their capital is the best idea; a major proportion of the vacation travel industry depends on this feeling. Some of the elderly have more of a family capitalization sense and work to build long-distance returns even though they know these will be enjoyed by someone else. For nearly all investors, the consideration of income needs and wants comes into decision making here. A reasonable middle-of-the-road position is to maintain at least 10 percent of your portfolio in high growth/low dividend investments, but probably no more than about 40 percent even for investors in very comfortable circumstances.

With level F you enter the realm of high-risk investments. This part of the pyramid should not be built until the foundation and lower levels are completed and the new investor has several years' experience behind him. Uncovered stock options are the selling and buying of the right to purchase shares at a predefined price, should fluctuations of the market bid it into place, but without already having the shares purchased. While legal, this practice is controversial and requires very careful attention, as described in chapter 10.

The highest, and headiest, levels of your pyramid are the highly speculative investments. Level G holds speculative stock investment, such as in selected common stocks in foreign currencies or terribly depressed former hot issues that could turn around in a big way—or languish indefinitely. Level H, investment in raw land or the most volatile commodities (orange juice, for example, or pork bellies), is in the ozone layer and not for the beginner. Even the more experienced investor should never expose more than 10 percent of his equity to efforts in these levels, for here is where extreme caution is the rule.

Whatever speculation is done, it should be small enough so that possible losses will not badly damage overall equity. If a loss would mean having to sell off less risky long-term growth stocks, don't take the plunge. You don't need wild growth, and you don't need to endanger your hard-won progress.

USING A MARGIN ACCOUNT

Cautious or aggressive, once you are under way with your investment portfolio you will quickly recognize the advantages of using a margin account. Essentially, your brokerage firm provides lender services to you so that you can operate outside the avenues of conventional banking. Your margin account is underwritten by either a cash deposit or by equity in securities already on hand in the account.

A margin account can earn money when the margin interest rates are low. Margin interest rates are directly influenced by the prime lending rate established by the Federal Reserve Bank. When the rates dip, if investments backed by loaned brokerage firm money generate returns greater than the margin rate—the "call rate"—you make a profit commensurate with that difference. For example, if sound corporate bonds are returning a reliable 9.9 percent per year, and the margin rate is down to 7 percent, an investment would hand you an easy profit of 2.9 percent.

Margin accounts can also be used to sell securities "short." If you detect that a security is significantly overpriced, you can legally borrow shares and sell them before the price adjusts itself downward. Your cost is the interest for the loan and a handling fee. Later, when you have to return the shares, you cover yourself by buying back shares after the stock has adjusted down to the lower price. Your profit is the difference between the price for which you sold the borrowed stock and the later reduced price you paid so that the borrowed stock could be returned. Such borrowing cannot be done through a cash account.

Margin accounts are also used for personal or business loans. Since brokerage firms have cleared clients for borrowing to buy stocks, most provide the same service for outright cash. Again, one avoids the ponderous, slow decision making of the conventional bank lenders.

The more experienced investor uses his margin account to trade, buy, or write options—market action on a defined quantity of securities at a set price within a set time period. The settlement time for regular stock trades is three business days; for option trades it is twenty-four hours from the time of the trade. With a margin account, the brokerage covers option deals automatically. This disposes of logistical problems if the investor trades often and the broker's office is inconveniently located for frequent visits.

The rules on using margin accounts are set by the Federal Reserve Board (see Table 6-1 on page 116). The Board's Regulation T (Reg T) was set in 1934, after wild speculation based on little cash led to the Crash of 1929 and the initiation of the Great Depression. Prior to then it was possible to buy stock with very small down payments. During stock rises buyers were able to pyramid holdings tremendously, starting from almost nothing. All was well so long as the stocks gained in value. Big problems came about when stocks declined and investors were unable to meet their payments. This started a spiral of desperate security sales whose value was rapidly bid downward as cash-weak investors clamored for aid. It took fifteen years and the punch of the government war industry to turn the market around.

The Federal Reserve Board uses "Reg T" as one of its tools to define just how much actual equity an investor must have to back margins. This percentage has varied since 1934, depending on the estimated stability and strength of the economy. The lowest required rate has been 40 percent, the highest occurred for a short period following the start of United States involvement in World War II, when no margin at all was permitted because the Federal Reserve Board was concerned about blocking runaway enthusiasm in certain wartime industries at the war's end. The rate has stabilized for years now at 50 percent.

Not all securities can be bought on margin. Marginable securities conform to certain guidelines stipulated by the Federal Reserve Board. All New York Stock Exchange listed securities over $5 per share are usually marginable, the fundamental exception being most stocks being traded through over-the-counter sales. New stocks have no track record, are therefore considered a higher-risk investment, and are not marginable. Foreign stocks and municipal bonds are also outside the scope of permitted margin buying. The "penny stocks" are also considered excessively volatile and hence too risky for margin.

Reg T works this way. Suppose you buy $10,000 worth of stock, 200 shares at $50 each. Because of the 50 percent rule, you must pay in a minimum of $5,000 to hold the stock in your account. If the stock then advances to $60 before you sell it, you have a gain of $2,000 (10 × 200). Without the margin you would have been able to buy only 100 shares for a profit of $1,000 on your $5,000 investment. Because of margin, your money is able to earn you twice as much, yet the rule prevents extremism that might endanger the process of borrowing to invest.

If you put $2,000 more into the account than the minimum required to satisfy Reg T when you bought the stock, your account is said to have "Reg T excess" of $2,000. You have what amounts to a line of credit for the purchase of an additional $4,000 worth of marginable securities.

What happens if someone makes a margin commitment and does not swiftly cover the Reg T percent with cash or marginable securities? The regulators supervising security trading notice the lapse at once and the errant trader receives an admonishing telephone call warning that Reg T must be followed. This warning is known as a Reg T Call. The investor has five business days of grace to come up with the equity, failing which his broker can sell enough of the investor's securities to match the obligation and hold the funds. The red-faced investor may also be hit with making good on market price damages that may have occurred after the unfulfilled transaction was underway.

The various stock exchanges have rules about margins that go beyond Reg T controls and into the domain of "maintenance." The New York Stock Exchange, for example, requires that all margin accounts must maintain an equity position of at least 30 percent of the current market value of funds and securities in the account, a safety cushion of 5 percent over the federal maintenance requirement of 25 percent. Federal regulators make warning calls immediately about maintenance of equity if it dips into the danger zone below 30 percent.

Let's take an example to pursue this idea, using parameters from the guidelines in Table 6-1.

Consider the purchase of 200 shares of Dagmar Production Co. (DP) at $50 per share, for a total of $10,000. Since you have current equity in investments of $5,000, your brokerage provides a margin of $5,000. If the price of shares then goes up to $70 per share there is no problem with the regulators. The "long market value" (LMV) of your investment becomes $14,000, the equity is now $9,000 ($14,000 − $5,000), the maintenance requirement is $4,200 (0.3 × $14,000), and the "firm maintenance excess" (FME) is $4,800 ($9,000 − $4,200). Your maintenance requirements are satisfied and everyone is happy.

But suppose the market becomes bearish and the price of Dagmar drops to $40. The LMV now becomes $8,000 ($40 × 200 shares), the equity changes to $3,000 ($8,000 − $5,000), the maintenance requirement is $2,400 (0.3 × $8,000), and the FME is $600 ($3,000 − $2,400). This is getting close to the maintenance limit, but no problem has yet arrived.

Now the market deteriorates further and the price of Dagmar sags all the way to $30. Now the LMV is $6,000 ($30 × 200 shares), equity is only $1,000 ($6,000 − $5,000), the maintenance requirement is $1,800 (0.3 × $6,000), and the FME is −$800 ($1,000 − $1,800)! You will quickly be getting a regulator call requiring you to pony up $800, thereby boosting equity back to 30 percent.

Supervising accounts—particularly complex accounts with many securities, all of which constantly fluctuate in value—is a formidable task. Luckily computers have come to the aid of all involved. Brokerage firms provide brokers with desk terminals that allow them to monitor accounts and head off problems before they become severe.

Once an investor becomes familiar with the routines and requirements of security trading, it becomes second nature to remain aware of his "primary margin indicators." The firm maintenance excess (FME) is the key indicator that refers to equity excess over maintenance requirements; the special memorandum account (SMA) defines the line of credit in the account available for withdrawal or for use to satisfy additional Reg T calls. Both must show a positive balance at all times to avoid maintenance calls from regulators. If for some reason the balance drops too low, your broker will let you know at once so that the correct equity can be restored. Most of the time the grace period is three working days, but should a big plunge in the market occur, the cushion of the brokerage's equity situation may decline so quickly that it will cut back on what it can do for you. In the crash of 1987, some brokers demanded action within twenty-four hours to forestall liquidation.

CONCLUSION

Intelligent portfolio management is simply another aspect of intelligent money management. The new investor has realized that developing personal security should be a personal responsibility, and that this is best achieved through the system of corporate borrowing and sales. Once the jargon and rules of the exchanges' and firms' procedures become familiar, safeguarding equity and seeing about helping it to grow turn out to be no more taxing than the time it takes to do a little research. The constant surveillance is well worth the effort.

FIGURE 6-1:
INVESTMENT PYRAMID FOR PORTFOLIO CONSTRUCTION

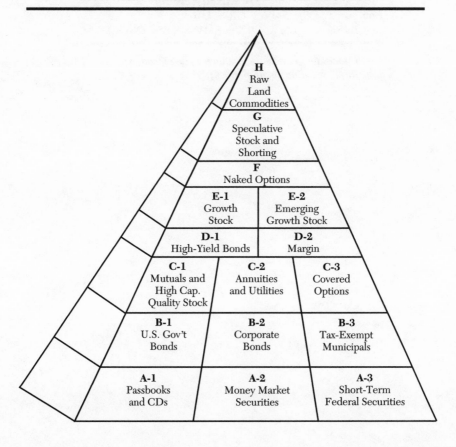

TABLE 6-1:
MARGIN EQUATIONS

CR = Credit Balance   DR = Debit Balance

Long Market Value (LMV) = Price/Share × # of Shares

For Equities Loan Value = LMV × 0.5 + CR°

For Bonds   Loan Value = LMV × 0.7 + CR°

Equity (E) = LMV + CR − DR

SMA = LMV × 0.5 + CR − DR

Maintenance Requirement (MR) = 0.3 × E

Firm Maintenance Excess (FME) = E − MR

Maintenance Call = MR − E

Buying Power (BP) = Lower of SMA × 2 or FME × 3⅓

For Shorting Accounts

Short Market Value (SMV) = Price/Share × # of Short Shares

Reg T Excess = CR − 1.5 × SMV

For Mixed Accounts

Equity = LMV − SMV + CR − DR

Reg T Excess = LMV × 0.5 − SMV × 1.5 + CR − DR

°Both stocks and bonds are assumed to be marginable securities, excluding "penny" stocks.

7

REAL ESTATE

ROBERT FRATER AND CHARLES SMITH

INTRODUCTION

Real estate in its most fundamental sense is land, but often the structures, minerals, waters, and crops found on or under it are included in the term. Interestingly, the concept of owning real estate has varied throughout human history. In some cultures even today land and resources claimed by a group can only be used by the group's individuals, never owned outright. It is the transition from a hunting-and-gathering economy to one based on fixed settlement and farming that marks the divide after which increased population density almost inevitably produces the tendency to assign and parcel out limited land resources.

In the industrialized economies, land is uniformly valued and titled. How much is retained by the state depends upon many variables. Half the area of the United States, for example, is made up of public lands with restricted access. Some of the land is in preserves, some simply offers so little potential return that no individuals have sought to buy it. The other half consists of areas owned by corporations or private individuals. About three-fourths of these have no recognized use and therefore no investment value to be considered in this chapter.

The most distinctive feature of real estate is its individuality.

When you buy a share of stock in a company, the share is just like all the rest. When you own real estate, you own the only property on earth exactly like it. Since no two pieces of real estate are identical, no two real estate transactions are exactly alike.

BUYING REAL ESTATE

In most states private individuals can buy and sell real estate without professional assistance. They are usually helped by a broker because finding property with specific characteristics takes a knowledge of real estate inventory; also, the procedures for transferring the title from one owner to the next can be convoluted.

The broker's job is usually to help people sell their real estate. Unless informed in writing to the contrary, all brokers and agents in a transaction are technically working for the seller, the party usually paying their commission. Conscientious real estate agents actually work as an honest and reliable liaison between buyer and seller with the objective of making a deal that is good for everybody.

Once the broker has gotten seller and purchaser together, next comes the process of clarifying a precise definition of the property and its financial characteristics. Attorneys may be hired jointly or separately to prepare the documents or to find and solve problems. Title companies, in some states called "abstract companies," determine the ownership history of the property and search out any attachments or debts against it. If all is well, a "title policy" is written by this company, ensuring that there are no legal or financial problems with the real estate. In states where abstractors prepare abstracts, attorneys prepare "title opinions" that can serve the same purpose as the title policy. This policy is good for as long as the buyer owns the property with no additional premiums. Title companies also normally coordinate the "closing" of the deal, the meeting where all the paperwork is signed and the title is transferred.

In this country it is customary to negotiate the final sale price of real estate. The first step is for the owners to list their "asking price." This is typically somewhat higher than what they expect to get, unless more than one potential buyer comes in to start a bidding war. Singly or in competition, offers are made in writing to the owners. Making an offer is simply a matter of filling in the blanks on a standardized form, normally prepared by the state real estate commission.

The form is called an "earnest money contract" or a "buy/sell agreement." When the blanks are filled in and the bottom signed, the aspiring buyer has "written a contract." Standard practice is to include a check for up to 1 percent of the purchase price—the "earnest money"—to indicate to the seller that the buyer is serious. The check is normally written to an escrow account to be applied to the purchase price. This earnest money check is usually not cashed until the buyer and seller both agree on all the conditions and both sign the contract.

If the contract, as it is initially written, is not acceptable to the seller, he responds with a "counteroffer" by crossing out the parts of the contract he finds unacceptable and writing in alternatives. The buyer, in turn, responds in a similar fashion. This goes on until an agreement is eventually reached.

Actually, the majority of contracts written do not result in an agreement between buyer and seller, so the potential transaction ends during negotiation. And a surprisingly high percentage of contracts are never consummated because of any number of unexpected glitches that come up prior to or at the closing meeting. The most common surprises have to do with finance, the physical condition of the property, or some legal problem.

If all goes well, and a purchase is worked out successfully, most of the time money is borrowed to pay for a portion of the purchase. If this is the case, the lender files a legal document at the county courthouse that gives the lender the right to repossess the property and sell it if the buyer does not make timely payments. That legal document is called a "lien," or a mortgage.

This brings us to our real estate rule number one: *The time to ask questions is before you close.* The only stupid question is one that is not asked. If you feel uncomfortable about a real estate transaction before you close, don't go through with it.

BENEFITS OF OWNING
INVESTMENT REAL ESTATE

There is a lot to be said in favor of owning real estate. Here are the main points.

Home ownership represents the single largest investment many people ever make. There are many psychological and financial benefits of owning your own home, such as the day-to-day enjoyment it provides, the potential benefit of price appreciation, and tax benefits from deducting interest and taxes. In many states personal residences are an asset legally protected in most litigation. In other words, if your home is paid for and you live in it, no one can force you to leave it even if you are bankrupt.

Investment real estate is generally considered to be property bought for an economic purpose. The buyer purchases it in order to generate income either through personal use or through the rental of space to tenants.

Making money from rental property is no different from any other business. To earn a profit, expenses must be controlled and income collected. One of the most positive aspects of direct ownership of investment real estate is that, with careful attention, the profits generated can sometimes be substantial.

To start with, there are few other investments in which a loan can be secured for over 90 percent of the purchase price, and where the debt can be paid off with income provided by the investment itself. Add to this that as the loan balance is reduced over time, the equity or net worth of the owner increases on a tax-deferred basis even if the property does not appreciate in value, and you have one heck of an investment.

The Tax Reform Act of 1986 and subsequent tax changes notwithstanding, an investor in residential real estate can still derive a significant tax shelter under certain forms of ownership. Assuming active participation in the management of the property, most individuals can benefit from up to $25,000 of real estate tax losses if the individual owns at least 10 percent of the rental property.

Another benefit of owning real estate is the potential for value appreciation. Real estate does not always increase in value, but as

Will Rogers once said: "They ain't makin' any more of it." Except when a regional economy encounters bad times, the usual long-term trend is for property value to increase by at least the rate of inflation.

Let's reiterate these benefits through the use of an example.

Assume a single-family rental house is bought for $80,000 using a conventional loan with a 10 percent down payment. The interest charge on the thirty-year note is 8.5 percent, and there were $2,000 in closing costs. If the market rent, after allowing for vacancy loss, for the house nets $850 per month, and taxes, insurance, and maintenance eat up about $250 per month, then the cash flow would be:

Monthly Rent	$850
Less Expenses	(250)
Net Operating Income (NOI)	$600
Less Mortgage Payment	(554)
Before Tax Cash Flow/Mo.	$46

While the $46 per month provides only a first-year 5.52 percent rate of return on the out-of-pocket $10,000 investment (the $8,000 down payment plus the $2,000 closing costs), this is only the beginning. A second benefit comes from the tax sheltering of income, assuming the activity qualifies for the $25,000 loss provision of the tax code:

Annual Taxable Profits (NOI)	$7,200
First Year's Interest Expense	−6,099
First Year's Depreciation Expense*	−2,618
Equals Taxable Income-Negative	(1,517)
Multiplied by a 31% tax rate	$ 470

$$*\frac{\$80,000 - \$8,000}{27.5 \text{ Years}} = \$2,618 = \text{Annual Depreciation}$$

The $470 represents taxes saved in the first year of ownership in the 31 percent tax bracket because the negative taxable income of $1,517 translates into $1,517 on which taxes are not paid.

Adding the $470 of taxes saved to the $552 received from cash

($46/mo. × 12) provides an actual after-tax rate of return of the $10,000 investment of 10.22 percent in the first year. The rate of return in the first year would be greater than 10.22 percent if any portion of the $2,000 in closing costs consisted of first-year finance charges.

There's more. In thirty years the rental house will be debt-free, essentially purchased by the tenants but titled to you. And again, while local property values do fluctuate with the normal real estate cycle, residential real estate has historically risen in value above each previous peak, following intermediate declines. The odds are good that by the time the mortgage is paid off, assuming competent upkeep, the house will be worth more, even after adjusting for inflation, than when you started.

TAX BENEFITS

One of the particularly attractive things about real estate investment is the special tax treatment involved. The seemingly inevitable tax reform acts may fine-tune and remodel the tax rules on real estate virtually every year, but some basic rules and concepts in place today have been so for some time.

The annual loan interest and property taxes you pay each year on your residence are deductible against your regular income. These expenses, along with charitable contributions and a few other miscellaneous expenses subject to limitations dictated by your adjusted gross income, are listed on Schedule A of the Internal Revenue's tax return. If your expenses exceed the standard deduction, you can deduct these itemized expenses; if not, then you still qualify for the standard deduction. Either way, you win.

Death and taxes may be the only two certainties in life, but how much tax is paid on your home when you die can be adjusted. One way to reduce your estate taxes is to set up a Residential Grantor Retaining Income Trust, or "Residential GRIT." With a GRIT, you give your house to your heirs effective at a specific time in the future, usually ten to twenty years hence. This effectively transfers the home at its current value for tax calculations. Since inflation and natural appreciation will likely raise the value by the time of your death, the net result can be a substantial estate tax savings. A good certified financial planner (CFP) or estate attorney will be needed to look at the merits of this alternative for your particular situation.

With investment real estate, interest and taxes are deductible, but not on Schedule A of your tax return. If your taxable income from all sources is less than $100,000 per year, you deduct it all now. If your income is greater than $100,000, some of these deductions may be saved for use when you sell the property. All expenses such as utilities, repairs, and professional services associated with investment real estate are deductible, off-the-top business expenses.

One of the most important tax benefits associated with real estate is depreciation, what accountants refer to as "noncash expense." If you buy a new refrigerator for your rental house, the refrigerator will have value for more than one year, so the Internal Revenue Service does not let you deduct the whole cost of it at once as a business expense. Instead, you deduct a portion of the cost each year over its useful life. That's depreciation. Since the true useful life of anything is impossible to know in advance, the government provides depreciation tables, charts, and acceptable formulas for determining how much you can deduct each year.

This applies to structures too. Suppose you bought a rental house for $80,000, and on the annual tax statement the county said the value of the land itself was $8,000. Obviously the "improvements" to the land therefore have a value of $72,000. The law permits you to depreciate $72,000 over the useful life of the house, currently (by law) defined as 27.5 years, or 3.64 percent per year. That comes out to $2,618 each time you do your taxes until the whole value is erased. It, of course, is a pleasant fiction that the house automatically loses value. Unless you foolishly let it deteriorate, the place could well increase in value. This is the key tax component that allows investors to build up real estate holdings without being hit by massive income taxes along the way.

People in the United States move around a lot, typically exchanging one house for a larger one when space requirements dictate or increased income permits. When someone sells their home, it will usually be listed for and get more than its original cost. As long as the seller buys another home at an equal or greater value within the next twenty-four months, taxes do not have to be paid on the gain. After age fifty-five, each person is eligible for a one-time-only sale profit of up to $125,000 without it being subject to income tax. The notion here is to provide retirees with a boost if they need it.

This tax saving is not applied to real estate held for investment purposes. Sell it and you pay taxes on the gain. Because of the depreciation we discussed earlier, the taxable gain is often very different than the cash you actually receive from selling your investment. To calculate your taxable gain, you must determine your "basis." Your basis is equal to what you paid for the property, plus the cost of any major improvements, minus the total of all depreciation you have deducted. The taxable gain is equal to the net sales price minus your basis. The amount of any debt on the property, unless you are loaning a portion of the purchase price, is not included in a taxable gain calculation.

POST-MORTEM (AFTER DEATH)

The final tax benefit of real estate passes directly to your heirs. If you die while owning real estate that has appreciated, your heirs will pay no income tax on this gain. The tax savings from this benefit alone could save over 20 percent of your estate from going to Washington, D.C.

MONEY MATTERS

Real estate has the precise characteristics that make it ideal as collateral for debt: it maintains or increases its value over long periods of time, and no one can steal it or move it. As an individual's net worth in property increases, it becomes possible to use this value to negotiate loans so that even more property can be purchased.

Outright buying of real estate with cold cash sounds positive to those who worry about being in debt, but actually a fair amount of the time it is smarter to obtain money from lending institutions. Not to mention the fact that most of us don't keep a few hundred thousand dollars lying around in a checking account waiting until we discover a great deal. The right financing on a land deal can turn out to be the most lucrative way to put your money to work for you.

"Leverage," as a physical term, means the use of a device so that effort is intensified. In finance, it means applying money in a loan context so that its power to generate income is enhanced. It is worth the effort to sit down with a pencil and see how the purchase of property outright or with different leveraged purchase levels will work out (see Table 7-1 on page 140).

If rental income from a property costing $100,000 will yield 10 percent or $10,000 worth of net operating income a year, one has to consider the impact of financing a portion of the investment. If financed with $10,000 down and a loan of $90,000 at 8 percent, then $7,200 of your net operating income goes to the bank, leaving you with only a profit of $2,800. However, the return on your investment of $10,000 is now no less than *28 percent!* That's obviously good leverage.

On the other hand, if the best lending rate the bank can give you is 12 percent for the deal, all is changed. In this case, although the property can still yield $10,000 per year, the bank's interest rate will cost you $10,800, meaning that for your investment you lose $800 a year. At first blush that seems to be a fool's leverage, and in terms of up-front income it is. However, it could well be that expected appreciation of the property and/or the depreciation of improvements tax benefits might factor in to change your mind.

Unless you work at home, buying a family dwelling means acquiring shelter, which will not produce cash income for you. That's not the point: you need somewhere to live. The size and amenities of your home will depend on what you want and what the bank or mortgage company says you can afford. Each lender has its own particular oddities and quirks but most follow the same general procedures to see whether you qualify for a loan and how large the loan can be.

Lenders will not typically loan more than 95 percent of what they think the property is worth, and the standard is to loan between 80 and 90 percent. It is wisest to make 80 percent your personal "Loan-to-Value Ratio" (LTV) limit, because otherwise you will be required to pay for expensive private mortgage insurance (PMI). Paying for PMI increases your monthly outflow of cash but provides no benefit except the dubious one of borrowing more money for your home. All PMI does is provide additional assurance to the lender or mortgage company that they will be repaid. You or your heirs are still obligated for the full note's balance whether you live or die, even if you die and the lender collects on the insurance. So if you can afford it, put the 20 percent down.

An additional benefit of having an 80 percent mortgage or less is that you can sometimes eliminate paying into the escrow account. Lenders normally escrow (charge you in advance) for your annual real estate taxes and casualty insurance. They do this by adding $\frac{1}{12}$ of these costs to your monthly payment and holding this money in a noninterest-bearing account, to be used to pay your taxes at the end of the year and your insurance when it renews. By eliminating this escrow account, you can earn interest on the money until it is due instead of handing it over to the bank to use.

The lender will naturally be interested in your ability to repay the mortgage. Most mortgage companies don't like to see that it will take more than 28 percent of your gross income to cover the mortgage payments, real estate taxes, and insurance on your home. If you have outstanding credit card debt, automobile loans, student loans, et cetera, these payments will be added to your mortgage payment and counted against a 36 percent ceiling. To calculate this yourself, take your gross monthly income and multiply it by 28 percent. This is the maximum amount of the monthly note plus escrow payment for which you would qualify. A look at the current interest rates available on fifteen- or thirty-year mortgages will tell you the amount of the loan for which you would qualify.

Another part of the mortgage company's decision to loan money has to do with how reliable you are. If you have had problems in the past with debt where you have been delinquent or have been in default, it will be revealed on your credit report. This will have a major impact on whether you qualify for the loan. No one wants to be bothered with a potential deadbeat. If you have been a straight-up cash-and-carry type who never bought anything with borrowed money, it would be advisable to take out a loan for your next major purchase even if you have the cash. Then make the payments exactly to the agreed-upon terms. If you are anxious to get a house before the loan is paid off, go ahead and clear it completely. Either way, paying it through term or paying it off, you will garner an impeccable credit record.

Lenders also normally like to see a stable work history and will want to see at least the last two years' tax returns. If you are self-employed, brace yourself. Lenders frequently question the income estimates of such people. Be prepared to justify your estimates of income with financial statements or a letter from someone who can verify your business activity.

Although it frequently is done the other way about, now you are ready to look for a house. You know how much you can pay, and how far your lender will support you.

YOUR HOME IS YOUR CASTLE

Purchasing a home is much more than an investment decision. Your social status, the schools your children attend, your friends and neighbors, your personal safety, your commute time, and your general quality of life are all directly affected by residence. One of the worst mistakes you can make is to fall in love with a house because of its architectural features alone, rather than considering these other factors. Make sure that you spend at least as much time evaluating the neighborhood as you do the house.

The difference between the purchase price of a house and what it is sold for seems pretty impressive, particularly if in the interim a decade or two has passed. Remember, though, that in reality this looks better than it is. Inflation will have devalued the currency either some or a lot, and if you add on all the interest paid on the mortgage, utilities, maintenance, and taxes, the sale price may not produce the profit you thought it would.

Of course, what you wanted was a degree of comfort and you enjoyed what you were paying for. That's the overhead cost of being alive. But it is valid to consider just what you want to do with your money before you spend it. The grasshopper who enjoys himself and devotes a high proportion of his income to immediate pleasures may find himself in trouble later in life, while the diligent ant next door who never threw money around could have a nice nest egg by retirement time.

However you balance today's gratification with tomorrow's security, it doesn't hurt to at least consider the perspective of the cool-minded real estate investor when shopping for a house. The costs of maintaining a large four-bedroom house with a swimming pool are significantly greater than those for a more modest house without a swimming pool. Unless you are actually going to use all that space, and jump in the pool every day, an investment specialist would argue that it would be a better idea to buy the smaller house and invest the balance of the saved money in rental real estate.

Talking pure money, rather than amenities, it is best to buy the smallest instead of the largest house in a given neighborhood. You will also find that as your needs change, you will have more options open to you. All neighborhoods have fairly concise valuation brackets for the houses within them. Starting with a smaller house, if you choose to add on to it someday instead of moving, the house value might increase by as much as you spend on the improvements. If you already have one of the largest houses in a neighborhood, it is unlikely that adding anything on will increase its value in proportion to the money spent on further enhancements.

Another aspect here is value in itself. A part of the planning value of a house is its liquidity—how quickly you can sell the house if you want to. In most areas of the country, a smaller, lower-priced house is usually easier to sell and has the most stable price appreciation. Also, a lower-priced house tends to be pulled up in value by the medium and larger homes nearby. The opposite is true for the most expensive homes. The reason? There simply are not as many people out there with the money to buy them. Any bidding is going to be downward, not upward.

SWEAT EQUITY

Conventional "equity" is the difference between what something is worth if sold and how much is still owed to a lender. In real estate, "sweat equity" means valuation added to a property through your personal work. Instead of paying for repairs and services, you do them yourself. The increased value resulting from that work was derived from your own labor.

There are two different types of sweat equity. The first type consists of "saved" labor: painting, Sheetrock work, trash hauling, carpentry, plumbing, and electrical repairs. For those who know how to do this sort of work, have the time, and want to, the savings can amount to thousands of dollars on a small residential rental property.

The second type of sweat equity is entrepreneurship. It consists of research into estimating when to buy and how much to pay for a property, negotiating contracts for repairs, and shopping for the best prices on materials. Some investors combine a smart use of leverage with this form of sweat equity.

The entrepreneur seeks out either a needful or a poorly informed seller with a property that needs repairs to turn it around. The classic turnaround is a run-down house in an acceptable neighborhood, or one of many in a neighborhood being rehabilitated. The key is to find a potential project and make a "low-ball" offer, low enough so that the cost plus sweat equity will leave a profit when the turnaround is remarketed months later in its new, revived incarnation. In real estate, you make your money when you buy the property, not when you sell it, because a low purchase price at the front end creates a future profit when the property is sold.

A sweat-equity offer to purchase is made subject to arranging suitable financing, usually within a week or two. The entrepreneur may need two loans: one to purchase the property, and one to finance the repairs. Some entrepreneurs get started by using credit-card cash advances to pay for the repairs and try to pay off the debt before losing too much ground to the high interest rates charged. Time is of the essence; the whole point is to buy the property, get it repaired, and sell it or refinance it and rent it. The less time your equity is tied up, the better.

Once established, with a track record, it is possible to visit lenders and scale up your endeavors. It helps to interview several of them prior to making the offer so that you can explain to the loan officer in advance what you intend to do. This convinces the banker that the entrepreneur is a person who plans ahead. Once an amiable, supportive lender is lined up, the entrepreneur will be able to make his earnest money contract and know that the project will fly if the seller goes for it and if the appraiser estimates the value of the property favorably "if and after" all the repairs are made. The appraiser and lender will want to see a detailed list of repairs to be performed and the costs to perform them, including the value of your labor for repairs you intend to perform yourself.

Sometimes a connection is made between an entrepreneur and a bank that already owns a turnaround property, probably through a repossession. Being in the money business, not real estate, it is attractive to the bank to unload the property for equitable terms as quickly as possible.

Some smaller banks will even provide what might be called a "two-stage loan." The first stage is the loan that provides the purchase price money and fix-up money. The entrepreneur has to put up additional collateral, such as trucks, savings accounts, or other valuables, until the house is repaired. Stage two is when the bank releases the additional collateral to back the actual purchase of the house. The added value to the house resulting from the sweat equity means that no additional collateral is required except making monthly payments to the bank with the real estate as the sole collateral. Banks will usually peg the interest rate on the loan for three to five years and provide a loan payment period, called the "amortization period," of between ten and fifteen years.

After the first successful turnaround, the equity in the first property can be pledged for collateral to secure financing for the next turnaround project. The successful use of second mortgages is itself an art. Gradually, profits will increase as the most effective sources of lower-cost products and labor are located. Presently the entrepreneur finds that "sweat equity" has become "sweet equity" as his net worth grows, tax free.

Here are some numbers taken from two real-world "fixer up-per" examples.

Stage 1 Loan

Purchase Price	$20,000
Cost of Materials	+5,000
Cost of Hired Labor	+3,000
Financing and Other Costs	+2,000
Total Borrowed	$30,000
Repaired Property Value	$40,000

Stage 2 Loan

Amount of Stage Two Loan	$30,000
Sweat/Sweet Equity Earned	$10,000

The $30,000 stage-one loan was obtained by pledging a car and a $5,000 certificate of deposit. The distinction is that a stage-two loan requires only the purchased real estate as collateral, while a stage one requires added collateral.

There are times when it is possible to borrow more money on a stage-two loan than you have invested in the property.

Stage 1 Loan

Purchase Price	$8,000
Cost of Material/Labor, etc.	+5,000
Total Invested	$13,000
Sweat/Sweet Equity Earned	$9,000

Stage 2 Loan

Stage Two Loan	$16,000
Repaired Property Value	$25,000

The $3,000 more borrowed money in the stage-two loan over that of the stage-one loan is sometimes referred to as "walking money."

If you buy the right rental house at the right time and at the right price, you will be amazed by how inexpensive some of your purchases will be. Smaller towns and cities offer especially great opportunities to purchase turnaround properties at low prices.

If it takes three to six months to find and buy a house, and another three to six months to repair the house, some entrepreneurs can and do purchase a house a year. This just makes the point that if you start with modest means and are willing to work, you can still attain wealth in a reasonable amount of time. Give up your television watching now and you can get comfortable in ten to fifteen years.

Here's an entrepreneur's true story. We have a friend who recently purchased a house for $95,000 in an inner-city area of Houston. He spent $15,000 to fix it up by using 98 percent hired labor. His only tools were a ballpoint pen and a Hewlett Packard 12C calculator. After the fix-up he had a property worth about $140,000. He then borrowed $110,000 against his equity in the property and rented the house for $1,200 per month, meaning that he now had a small positive cash flow for *no* hard money invested.

APPRAISAL

Anyone buying real estate needs to know what a piece of real estate is probably worth. An appraisal is an estimate of what a house will probably sell for if exposed to the market for a reasonable length of time and bought by a typical person. While professional appraisers have complicated forms and computer programs to use, with some time and practice you can learn to appraise houses the old way: with a piece of paper, a pencil, and a calculator.

There are three commonly used approaches to estimating value: (1) the cost approach; (2) the sales comparison approach; and (3) the income approach. Professional appraisers apply each separately to a house, then synthesize the three values into a single final value estimate. If that sounds a little "by guess and by God," there's a reason: the appraisal process is more art than science.

The "cost approach" to estimating value assumes that the typical buyer will pay no more for a house than an amount equal to the cost of buying a vacant lot and building a similar house there within a reasonable time. It accepts the idea that older houses can decline and that people will pay less for a house if its carpet, paint, and so on need replacing. In other words, age and condition are the driving components of this approach to making an estimate.

Taking an example, assume that you are looking over a house which is 10 years old, has 1,700 square feet of living area, and lies on a 60-by-125-foot lot. You consult with local realtors and a builder or two and find that you could buy a new house similar to it for about $110,000. The existing house, however, needs or could use new carpet, interior painting, and external painting; moreover, the roof is half worn out. So you talk to carpet salesmen, painters, and roofers. You find that new carpet would cost $2,250, a new interior paint job would cost $2,000, new exterior painting would run approximately $3,000, and a new roof would be $2,500. To find a cost approach estimate of value, you simply subtract the cost of repairs from the cost of an equivalent new house:

Cost of New House	$110,000
Less: New Carpet	−2,250
New Exterior Paint	−2,000
New Interior Paint	−3,000
Half New Roof	1,250
Value Estimate	$101,500

Since what repairs would cost has devalued the structure, the estimate of the house's value is $101,500. If fencing, central air, or anything else has worn out, their value would be subtracted as well.

The "sales comparison approach" is similar to costing, except that the appraised house is compared to similar houses that have sold recently. The idea here is that a typical buyer will pay no more for a house than what the equivalent has gone for.

Taking the same 1,700-square-foot house analyzed by costing, the estimator compares it to a similar house in the same (or a similar) neighborhood. The similar house, slightly smaller at 1,600 square feet, recently sold for $105,000. It had newer carpet, adequate exterior and interior paint, a larger garage, and a larger patio/deck area. The sales comparison adjusts value accordingly:

Sale Price of Similar House	$105,000
Adjustment for Extra 100 Square Feet	+3,000
Carpet adjustment	−2,250
Garage size adjustment	−1,500
Deck adjustment	−2,000
Value Estimate by Sales Comparison	$102,250

The adjustments of +$3,000, −$2,250, −$1,500, and −$2,000, respectively, whittled at the base sales price. It is standard for the estimator to evaluate at least three houses in this fashion to get a mean notion of how the price should stand.

The "income approach" is the simplest of the three ways to make an estimate, for it is derived from the income that could be produced if the house was rented. If houses in the area are selling for 95 times the monthly rent, and a similar property is renting for $1,000 per month, then the house you are looking at is worth 95 × $1,000 = $95,000. The multiplier is called the "gross monthly rent multiplier (GMRM)."

Sizing up the results of the three approaches, you can see that the house is probably worth about $100,000. If you pay more than this, you could lose money.

TYPES OF REAL ESTATE OWNERSHIP

Homes are usually titled in the names of one or both spouses. Titles, in litigious states, sometimes further distinguish "joint with rights of survivorship" so that the property transfers title automatically when one partner dies. In some states, the elderly are wise to move all assets including real estate into trusts so that legal squabbling will be reduced to a minimum when their inheritors take possession.

For investment real estate there are even more ownership options available, with dramatic variations between states. Before venturing into any of them you should seek appropriate professional advice.

If a property is large or very expensive, some buyers like to spread the burden and risk through a partnership. There are two broad types of partnerships. In a "general partnership" everyone involved is treated as the same. Decisions, profits, and losses are all determined and divided proportionately to how much each partner has invested. In such partnerships everyone is ultimately responsible for all obligations, a feature that in some instances limits their practicality.

A "limited partnership," on the other hand, has two classes of partners: limited and general. The limited partners' liability is normally restricted to whatever specific liability the partners agreed upon at the beginning. At least one of the partners is ultimately responsible for management decisions and bears the burden of ultimate liability. That person is called the "general partner."

The third form of property ownership is the "corporation," in which investors buy shares and whose operations are run by officers. The primary advantage of corporations is that all liability stops with the corporation. It can be sued, but shareholders cannot, nor are they liable for any corporate debt. Unlike a partnership that only exists as long as do its partners, a corporation lasts as long as it continues to function, or even afterward.

A corporation in most states is relatively easy to set up. There are two types of corporations, a "C corporation" and an "S Corporation." A C corporation is taxed based on an escalating schedule similar to the tax schedule for an individual. When the C corporation distributes income to shareholders, the income is taxed again at the individual level. Because double taxation is considered onerous by most investors, the S corporation concept was invented. The S corporation is not a taxable entity. It passes all of its income, expenses, and deductions on through to the S corporation shareholders. In the United States, S corporations are limited to thirty-five owners and all of the owners must be actual citizens, not partnerships or corporations.

Recently some states have now adopted what is called a "limited liability company" (LLC). This provides some of the best advantages of an S corporation along with some of the best advantages of a partnership. These LLCs, however, are very new and regulations have not been tested or finalized in many states, so a full discussion of the form is not needed here.

The last real estate ownership device is the "syndication." A syndication is normally a limited partnership in which there are many investors with only a financial interest in transactions. They invest their money but will have no involvement in management. Some of the largest syndications now traded on the stock exchanges are real estate investment trusts (REIT). Each year, the REIT is required to distribute at least 90 percent of its net profits to its unit holders. According to the regulations, by doing so the trusts are not subject to taxation.

REAL ESTATE CYCLES

As with all other economic phenomena, real estate values pass through cycles. These can last for ten years or longer.

For quite a long time conventional wisdom in real estate circles held that interest rates had the overwhelmingly greatest effect on real estate values. There's more to it than that, as it turns out. Local employment cycles, in combination with local building cycles, have a considerable regional impact and at times can be more important than interest rates. Pockets of prosperity or recession depend upon local economic conditions.

As new industry gravitates to an area for whatever reason, new jobs are created. This translates into an enlarging population, new stores, and new houses and apartments. Initial shortages develop, causing prices and rents of real estate to increase rapidly in an accelerator effect. It is at this stage in the real estate cycle when the difference between the cost to build a structure and the price at which it sells is very high. For example, if you purchase a lot for $10,000 and build a structure costing $40,000, you have $50,000 invested; but the actual market value is $60,000. The wise real estate investor sells or holds.

All booms slow and then reverse. The value of real estate will then spiral downward for a while, possibly several years, depending on how much the real estate market was overbuilt at the peak. As the cycle reaches its trough, those who are not historically minded speak gloomily of how prices will never get back to their old levels again. Houses can be bought for about half to two thirds the cost of building a new one. Banks, at this point, have large portfolios of real estate that they want to sell and will finance at below market interest rates with little money down. The best time to buy real estate is during the latter part of a trough, just before the next upturn occurs.

How can this be predicted? The key is to watch employment statistics, building permit data, and occupancy rates in rental property, particularly apartments. Be attentive when employment, especially construction employment, has been rising faster each month than the long-term average. Check building permits; are enough granted to satisfy the most optimistic construction needs of an area for years to come? And are occupancy rates in apartments and rental houses running over 95 percent and rising? When these three conditions all occur together, it's a warning that the downturn potential for the real estate cycle is quite high.

It is also important to understand that the biggest changes in value happen when the use changes. In other words, if you buy agricultural land just before it changes to single-family residential property, you will find that it could double or triple in value within a relatively short period of time. Likewise, when property goes from single-family residential to multifamily residential, there will usually be a major increase in the value of the real estate. These factors are true regardless of how the real estate cycle stands.

By the same token, it is possible to unwarily throw money into developing a property that due to geography is never going to pay you back. For example, if you own a single-family rental house surrounded by multifamily properties, making improvements in the house to attract higher-paying tenants doesn't make sense. That sort of tenant doesn't want to be next door to an apartment, no matter what amenities a house may have. Like it or not, the economic realities of location dictate that the best use of your property is to tear the house down and put up yet another apartment building. If that happens, all the improvements put into the house will vanish.

Comprehensive and other planning, and zoning, are considerations independent of cycles too. Maps and other documentation of municipal and regional designs help the investor determine where and what sorts of growth will be coming up, and help avoid painful misdirection. Always remember that the person who recognizes the highest and best use of a piece of real estate, and owns it at the time conversion is made, will be in the position to reap a substantial profit. Location is of critical importance, always.

SHOULD YOU PAY OFF YOUR HOUSE?

There are several considerations when you think about paying off a mortgage earlier than at term.

First, think about taxes. The federal tax laws by 1994 provided a married couple filing a joint tax return a standard deduction of $6,350. This $6,350 is subtracted from adjusted gross income if you do not itemize deductions on Schedule A of your tax return. The point here is that you will have $6,350 of deductions whether your house is paid off or not. Putting current money into it instead of devalued money down the road will make no difference in the deduction.

There is, however, a sense of personal security that goes with outright ownership of a home. No lender can repossess your home, and as long as you pay your taxes the state and federal governments will leave you alone. In fact, some states such as Texas and Florida protect "homesteads" from civil lawsuits. In our suit-happy times, protected assets are comforting, particularly the roofs over our heads.

From an investments viewpoint, though, your home mortgage is likely to hold the lowest interest rate of all your obligations. The payments are also the only ones that you can deduct at tax time. That is good. If you are able to generate enough income to invest, and aren't concerned too much about having the house mortgage paid in full, putting the money to work for you makes the best sense.

SHOULD YOU CARRY A MORTGAGE?

When it comes time to sell property, the new buyer may ask if you would be willing to make a personal loan of some or all of the purchase price. If there is no debt on the property when you sell it, and you were the only one holding a loan against the property, your loan would be referred to as a "first mortgage." Holding the first mortgage means that you would be paid off first should the property subsequently be resold.

If there is financing already on your property, and you are just loaning the buyer a portion of the down payment, then you would have a "second mortgage." If you own a second mortgage, this means that if the property were sold, the person with the first mortgage would be paid off entirely before you. Because this is a less secure position, normally the interest charged is adjusted upward.

The main question is whether it is prudent to get into the lending business. Usually, it isn't. The individual ought to be able to obtain financing through conventional means. Doing him a favor may be setting yourself up for headaches. If he defaults, taking a property back due to nonpayment can be a long and expensive legal undertaking. Moreover, becoming a banker will reduce your cash in hand right now, thereby limiting your investment alternatives. The general rule here is to carry a mortgage only if the buyer has a flawless credit record, if the mortgage does not significantly interfere with your investment plans, and if the payout is for a fairly short period of time.

Make certain that the note is a "contract for deed" in which defaulted payments clearly end all the buyer's rights to the property and improvements. Most lake lots and recreational properties are sold on a contract for deed basis, and many times these properties are sold several times before a buyer actually fulfills the contract. You must always make sure that your rights and interests are properly protected, especially when there is a small down payment or you are in a second or third mortgage position.

RISK IN REAL ESTATE INVESTMENT

There are tremendous potential rewards to be derived through real estate investment, but there are also perils. We would be remiss not to conclude by mentioning them.

"Business risk" is the risk that you will wrongly estimate the cash flow an investment will produce. The "financial risk" of real estate investment is that you will not be able to make your loan payments. "Liquidity risk" is that if you have to sell fast to raise cash, you may be forced to take a hit below current market value. "Interest rate risk" is that if interest rates increase, the market value of your investment will decline. "Management risk" is that you will suffer unexpected losses due to dishonest or incompetent management of your asset. "Inflation risk" is that the value or cash flow from your asset will not keep pace with inflation. Finally, "legislative risk" is that you will suffer unexpected losses due to changes in laws, government planning, or zoning alterations. One of the greatest recent legislative risks of real estate often overlooked by real estate investors is the potential *unlimited* liability associated with real estate that has been contaminated by underground storage tanks, asbestos, or any of a growing list of contaminants. Under current law, the only way to protect yourself is to commission a Phase I environmental study *before you buy* the property. If you have any concerns, or if the property has ever been used for commercial purposes, you should have this study done before you buy. All investments have some amount of legislative risks, with bank savings accounts probably having the least.

But then, there is risk in all investment. There is risk in driving to the supermarket. There is risk when you mow the lawn. Risk is a part of life. The trick is to manipulate risk so that it works for you. Real estate investment is an excellent way to do this.

TABLE 7-1:
LEVERAGED PURCHASING COMPARISON, ONE YEAR

	Cash Purchase	Leveraged Purchase (8% Rate)	Leveraged Purchase (12% Rate)
Cash	100,000	10,000	10,000
Borrowed $	0	90,000	90,000
Total Investment	100,000	100,000	100,000
Net Op. Income (10%)	10,000	10,000	10,000
Interest Exp. (8%)	0	7,200	10,800
Net Return	10,000	2,800	−800
% Return on Cash Invested	10%	28%	−8%

8

ANNUITIES, ESTATE PLANNING, AND INSURANCE

GEORGE S. ECKHARDT JR.

INTRODUCTION

Estate conservation need not be a confusing matter. While taxation laws today border on the confiscatory, opposing legislation has produced ways of paring back their effect. Tax-deferred annuities, estate planning, and selected types of insurance are effective modern financial devices with which to nurture assets while protecting them from the worst impacts of taxation.

ANNUITIES

The tax-deferred annuity is simply a contract between an individual and an insurance company where, for a specific dollar amount up front, the company promises to pay the "annuitant" a benefit over a defined period of time. In many cases the period is five or ten years, but lifetime benefits are not unknown. Annuity sums are *not* protected by the safety net of the Federal Deposit Insurance Corporation, so only buy from a dealer who can promise strong annuity underwriting.

Before the payout begins, during an "accumulation period," the annuity's size grows at a contract-defined rate. A happy financial convention, protected by law, is that during the accumulation period the swelling profit cannot be taxed. A further cheerfully contrived tax logic is that when a contract starts to be "annuitized," meaning that payment starts, the income stream is only taxed in part. The reason? Because some of the payment amount is defined as being part of the original principal spent to activate the contract in the first place.

In most cases the owner of the annuity contract is permitted to withdraw up to 10 percent of the annuity's value each year without a penalty being levied by the insurance company. The withdrawal amount is counted as taxable income, however, and in addition is subject to a 10 percent IRS surcharge if the annuitant is under the age of 59½. This provision was set by lawmakers as a means of ensuring that the elderly would be the predominant beneficiaries of annuity plans.

All annuities have a penalty for early redemption, ranging from as much as 12 percent of the total value to as little as six months' interest. If an annuity is cashed in early, the gained value naturally becomes subject to income taxes. The single exception is when one policy is exchanged for another. This is called a "Section 1035" exchange and refers to a specific section of the tax code.

If an annuitant dies during the life of the contract, all proceeds will be paid to a beneficiary named in the contract. These pass to the heir free of probate costs, but they are subject to income taxes and will be considered part of the gross estate of the owner when the estate tax is determined.

There are two types of annuities: "fixed" and "variable." A fixed annuity has a set rate of return guaranteed for a specified period of time. The variable annuity is nothing more than money derived from mutual funds that has been wrapped within the tax protection cloak of an annuity, where investment in any number of funds is possible without paying any current taxes on the growth.

Fixed annuities last over a defined period, usually one, three, or five years. Afterward a new rate will be offered depending upon current interest rates and the profitability of the insurance company. There is usually a defined floor past which the rate paid cannot descend. The insurance company uses the net funds from sales of policies plus a certain reserve requirement set by its home state and invests the sum in corporate bonds. In general, the company will credit to the annuity the difference between earnings from investments less its operating expenses. Normally that spread is about 2 percent.

Some insurance companies offer enticing annuity "teaser rates" several percentage points higher than current interest rates. Watch the small print, here: the guarantee is normally for only a year or six months, after which the rate suddenly drops to as low as 3 percent. These contracts are also often accompanied by a ten-year, 12 percent penalty for early withdrawal.

During the 1980s fixed annuities were extremely popular because they offered rates equal to or better than certificates of deposit, and held the additional attraction of their tax-deferral characteristic. Once inflation cooled and interest rates fell, people searching for yields on their money past what could be earned from certificates of deposit began finding that the variable annuity was more attractive.

Variable annuities derive income from mutual funds based on United States government bonds, several stock funds, money market funds, and corporate bond funds. The investor can be diversified into several funds at the same time, and some contracts offer international groups of funds. The annuity contract owner can make changes in his investment structure at any time through a telephone switching system.

Because the annuity's underlying funds fluctuate in earning power, so does the potential earning of the annuity. From 9 to 13 percent growth annually should be attainable over a five- to seven-year period, barring unpredictable financial and currency upheavals. Growth can be withdrawn without charge in some instances, and if the investor dies, his beneficiary will receive no less than the full initial deposit at death. Early redemption charges vary from 7 to 10 percent. Figure 8-1 on page 148 illustrates the attractive annuity accumulation over twenty-five years, compared to a taxed investment.

The economics of variable annuities in highly taxed times have pushed this investment product to the forefront of investment choices. Look for the investment community to continue introducing new and innovative variable annuity products through the end of the twentieth century.

ESTATE PLANNING

All estates with a net value of more than $600,000 are subject to federal estate taxes, and most states have inheritance taxes as well. Because state tax laws are so varied, they will not be discussed here, other than to recommend that readers investigate local conditions carefully. A conference with a tax attorney can be one of the best investments you ever made.

Many people who never thought they would have to concern themselves with estate planning have been surprised recently as their assets soared past anything they imagined possible. The rocketing escalation of real estate values in some areas such as California, Florida, and New York has in part been behind this. For instance, a $50,000 home bought in 1980 in any of those states could easily be worth $500,000 to $600,000 today, depending upon conditions of local economic geography. In addition, corporate retirement and thrift plans have appreciated considerably, at least on paper. If funding holds out, the fortunate retiree participants can expect quite a comfortable return.

But what happens upon dying? Without protection, the government will take between a third and a half of estates worth over $600,000 (see Table 8-1 on page 149). The estate tax is an unabashed vehicle of social engineering by politicians intent upon redistributing wealth. Under estate tax provisions, taxable assets are converted to cash, confiscated by the federal government, and used in any fashion Congress sees fit—like buying the Pentagon $500 screwdrivers. It makes sense to develop a well-designed plan to provide not only for your needs but for passing assets on with the least amount of legal thievery.

Even if you do not have a taxable estate, it is important that you have a will so that your assets can be distributed as you wish. It must be properly worked up so that its veracity can be proven before a probate judge. When someone dies without a legal will, called an "intestate" condition, the court can do about anything it wants to with assets. Usually an attorney is appointed to act as the trustee and is charged with the task of settling the estate under the intestate laws of the state, after which point resolving matters can become enormously costly. In essence, the state writes your will for you.

Such court-appointed attorneys are inevitably motivated to boil down their charge into cash and to drag matters out as long as possible. This is because their "reasonable and customary" fees are deducted from the estate's net worth, as are all other expenses that occur during the process of dealing with parceling things out. Just how much value is siphoned off depends on the size and complexity of the estate, the avarice of the attorney, and the attitude of the judge. All too often Solomonic wisdom dictates that nearest kin be assigned proportions of the estate, but huge tax and court costs are imposed that can gut it of over half its value. Minor children will receive a court-appointed trustee to look after their newfound wealth, which worthy is paid fees for the work until the children reach the age of eighteen.

A will is therefore the most important part of estate planning. It is the road map for the estate and directs the executors on how to care for and ultimately dispose of its assets. It should be reviewed at least once every five years to ensure not only that its terms still reflect the wishes of the writer but also that changes in the law have not adversely affected it.

Level-headed elders can, if they want, begin giving away their assets while still in good health. Under the law, each person can give away up to $600,000 without tax penalties, if done in accepted form. Any individual can give up to $10,000 per year to as many people as he or she wants without gift tax consequences and without affecting the $600,000 lifetime exclusion, and one spouse can pass on to the other unlimited property up to a total value of $600,000.

Joint estates of up to $1,200,000 can be passed on to heirs without estate tax if wills are used to create a marital or bypass trust. A "trust" is a bank instrument into which formerly liquid assets are placed for extended periods of time, with terms allocating payments and eventual liquidation. Beneficiaries of the trust can receive their portions over spans of even several generations, avoiding estate taxes each time a disbursement is made. When the first spouse dies, $600,000 worth of the marriage's joint assets pass immediately into the trust. Income from it, along with the remaining assets not placed in trust, supports the surviving spouse during his or her remaining years of life. The trust then passes the protected assets on to beneficiaries after both spouses have died, and of course up to $600,000 of the second spouse's assets are handed on without taxation either (see Figure 8-2 on page 149).

For estates larger than $1.2 million, estate taxes will probably be unavoidable upon the death of the second spouse. Estate taxes can be paid from cash on hand, borrowing, selling assets, or using funds obtained from life insurance. When assets such as a business or real estate are involved, liquidation to raise the tax is a bad idea both because it can mean the end of the business and because sales in a distress situation frequently produce results below assessed valuation. The life insurance option is much better. A "life insurance trust" funds a policy specifically so that the estate tax can be covered, and is not part of the estate.

LIFE INSURANCE

Conventional life insurance provides protection for beneficiaries who have lost the value of the insured's presence and earning power. Although discussing life insurance confronts one with personal mortality, an unsettling notion, the benefits to be derived are important enough to warrant this discomfort.

The proceeds from life insurance are always income-tax free; they are not estate-tax free, therefore it should never be purchased inside a *taxable* estate, increasing asset size. There has never been a life insurance policy in the United States that has failed to pay off as promised, thanks to state regulation and a very protective industry extremely concerned about public relations.

There are several types of life insurance, each involving periodic payments. Term life insurance was designed to cover short-term needs, such as family protection or to guarantee that education funds are available even if the insured parent dies. Whole life insurance is paid over a defined long term, at the end of which— should the insured person have beaten the odds and not died— dividends are repaid, usually at quite a low rate. Universal life insurance is insurance in which the participant pays for insurance plus expenses but also shares in the profits of the insurance company. In a well-managed company the profit dividend should be stable and may enlarge over time. Survivorship, or "second-to-die insurance," is universal life insurance that insures both spouses and pays off when the second spouse dies. It was designed specifically for estate purposes, and because it insures two lives, the costs are considerably less than single life policies.

Variable life insurance is a mutual fund family wrapped within the superficial legal construct of life insurance. Returns inside of the policy grow tax free and stay that way as long as the policy remains intact. Up to 90 percent of its cash value can be borrowed from the policy at low or no charge. The investor has bought a product that provides tax-free growth and a substantial death benefit. Variable life insurance is the one instance in which an insurance product is a true investment vehicle.

Because you are buying something now that pays off years later it is essential that your insurance carrier be large and stable. Your financial consultant or agent should be able to provide both A. M. Best's and S & P ratings on any carrier you are considering.

CONCLUSION

Because estate planning is so important and so complex, take advantage of the expertise of consulting professionals in the fields of investment, estate planning, and insurance to create a coordinated plan that fits your specific situation. The best idea is to set up the framework well before retirement, then to adjust it as needed every few years. A well-protected estate is both a relief for you and a means whereby your financial legacy can be passed on to those you wish, as opposed to being subject to the terms the legal bureaucracy might impose.

FIGURE 8-1:
Comparison of the value of a tax-deferred annuity with a taxed investment where, in each case, the rate of return is 8%. (The tax-deferred annuity produced significantly more retirement dollars. That means more income later—the longer the tax-deferred accumulation, the greater your return.)

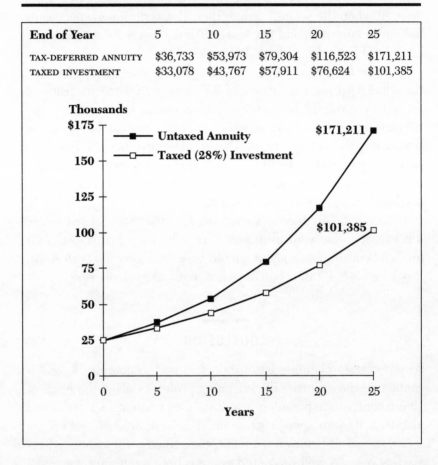

End of Year	5	10	15	20	25
TAX-DEFERRED ANNUITY	$36,733	$53,973	$79,304	$116,523	$171,211
TAXED INVESTMENT	$33,078	$43,767	$57,911	$76,624	$101,385

FIGURE 8-2:

Flow of a decedent's assets of $600,000 into a bypass trust. The income goes to the surviving spouse until death. The assets at the second death flow to the children. This eliminates all estate taxes on a joint estate of $1.2 million or less.

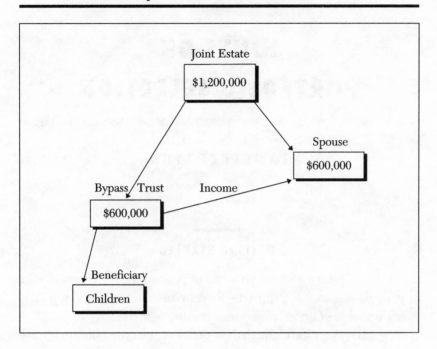

TABLE 8-1:
FEDERAL ESTATE AND GIFT UNIFIED TAX RATES

Taxable Amount	Amount of Tax +	Rate on Excess
Up to $500,000	$155,800	37%
$1,000,000	$345,800	41%
$1,500,000	$555,800	45%
$2,000,000	$780,800	49%
$3,000,000	$1,290,800	55%

9

HINTS ON
PORTFOLIO SELECTION

LAWRENCE LYNN

GETTING STARTED

After developing a general investment philosophy for yourself, with a general strategy appropriate to your needs, the next step is to work up a list of good investment candidates.

A good way to start is with a Saturday visit to your public library. Ask the reference librarian to help you locate their section of reference books on investments. Among the best publications on stocks are the quarterly editions of *Moody's Handbook,* the current compilation of *Value Line,* and the *Standard & Poor's Stock Pages* and their monthly *Stock Guide.* For bonds, find *Standard & Poor's Monthly Bond Guide.* For mutual funds, good sources of information are *Morningstar, Lipper Analytical Services,* and *Weissenberger.* All of these last publish an annual yearbook with the present statistics for all key mutual funds, as well as their historical backgrounds.

Full-service brokerage firms have archival and research departments that publish an abundance of basic data on public companies. You naturally have access to that if you are working with one of the firm's brokers. Keep in mind that brokerage firms also have corporate clients and are not likely to have much that is negative to say about them.

When organizing your potential investments, always remember the reasons for making them. To ward off currency devaluation, the most fundamental investment purpose is to assure enough growth of principal so that your equity at least stays even. Investment is also about creating a reliable, preferably large source of income. Canny investment means watching for "fallen angels" having rough times right now but with the strength to overcome obstacles and spring back better (and bigger) than ever. Wise investing means diversifying outside one currency and one economy, but in the more stable parts of the world, such as the United Kingdom, Canada, Germany, Switzerland, Singapore, or Australia.

Let's consider a few examples to illustrate each of the four categories of investment.

GROWTH COMPANIES

There are some 10,000 investment candidates including equities on the listed exchanges and NASDAQ, a mass of alternatives that at first seems overwhelming. Novice investors should screen out most newcomer companies with little or no track record. Oddball companies seated in a peculiar niche are a bad idea, too, because the first thing that happens during recessions, wars, and political storms is for people to conserve, meaning less spending on curious but not essential products.

After knocking away the young and the infirm, the choice of firms in which to invest is considerably smaller. All the surviving companies are not created equal, however, and this shows up quickly in their sales records and the earnings per share derived from these sales. Have earnings been continuously increasing over many years? Have share prices, both annual highs and lows, been on an upward growth trend? Have the operating profit margins been consistent from year to year, or is there a pattern of periodic drops? Mainly, is the percent return on investment consistently high? These are the critical clues from which to judge whether or not to get involved. They are all right out in the open in annual reports and the financial reference books and data bases, as you saw back in chapter 2.

To underline how one thinks about these things, let's take another look at SYSCO, our food and restaurant service company. We have already seen that SYSCO has honors as a growth company with an excellent track record and fine prospects for the future. SYSCO's leading competitors are: Fleming Companies, Inc.; Super Valu Stores, Inc.; and Wetterau, Inc. SYSCO focuses on providing goods and services for the away-from-home food market—hotels and motels, airports, cafeterias, hospitals, nursing homes, company cafeterias, and other restaurants in over 150 metropolitan areas through 74 distribution centers in the United States and Canada. Its long corporate history is a record of excellence. Moreover, since the business amounts to distributing everything from cups of coffee to toilet paper, it is safe from foreign competition or rapid technological obsolescence (see Figure 9-1 on page 161).

A recent Value Line report for SYSCO shows that it generated an annual average sales growth of about 20 percent over the past ten years, an average price growth of 22 percent per year, an EPS growth of 18 percent per year, and increases in dividend payments of 16 percent per year. These are excellent figures. The price/earnings ratio (PE) of SYSCO has recently been about 24, slightly above the average for all stocks on the New York Stock Exchange but not a high-wire act in the way many Japanese stocks were in the late 1980s. The operating profit margin has varied only slightly from 4.3 to 4.8 percent per year during this period, as seen in Table 9-1 on page 160. The average profit margin was 4.58 percent for the period from 1983 to 1993, which is satisfactory relative to its competitors. SYSCO's management generated a return on total investment dollars (ROI) of from 14.89 to 17.26 percent, with an average of 16.69 percent. Because SYSCO's corporate philosophy is strongly oriented toward reinvestment for future growth, average payout of dividends from earnings was a low 15.3 percent.

Inspection of the year-to-year PE's, EPS data, growth rates, and the present price of $23 per share in late December 1992 leads one to suspect that the shares' price could well reach about $55 within five years. It all adds up to a highly attractive growth potential.

A similar company is George A. Hormel and Co., a mature company that produces many products such as Spam, Little Sizzlers, Dinty Moore, and others bearing its corporate name. The leading competitors against which Hormel is frequently measured include firms such as ConAgra; IBP, Inc.; Tyson Foods; Cagles, Inc.; and Arctic Alaska (see Figure 9-2 on page 162).

According to Value Line, Hormel's latest PE was 19, close to the average on the New York Stock Exchange, with an average over the past five years of 16.5. Over the past ten years sales have grown at 9 percent per year, the average EPS has grown by 15 percent per year, and the dividend increases have been 11 percent per year. The consistent increases in EPS qualify this company as a conservative yet strong growth candidate. Operating margin never fell below 4.20 percent or exceeded 7.20 percent and averaged 5.84 percent over the last ten years. Its return to the stockholders for their investment was 11.54 percent at its low, 15.67 percent at its high, and averaged 14.85 percent. The ROI from its recent 1991 performance was high.

In mid-December 1992 Hormel had a price of $23 per share. Judging by inspection of the indicators and particularly the growth rate of shares, it is expected that the price for Hormel could well climb to at least $52 per share by the end of the next five years. It all seems quite reminiscent of SYSCO, and reassures us that SYSCO is an appealing investment possibility, since it exhibits the same growth characteristics.

Growth companies can be spotted in every industry through a little careful searching and comparing. The first thing that catches your eye is superb sales growth, usually with price per share climbing rapidly with it due to other investors watching the pattern and jumping on the wagon. There is almost always a cyclical pattern of growth, stabilization, then growth, and the canny investor attempts to buy early in a growth spurt rather than when a period of stability seems to be coming up next. See Table 9-2 on page 160 for a few other typical growth companies with outstanding records.

CHARACTERISTICS OF INCOME COMPANIES

If you want your equity to pump immediate profits to you, by now you realize that bank passbook savings accounts and certificates of deposit are no way to go. They produce only a fraction of what can be obtained through securities investments and hover near the rate of inflation.

A moderately higher rate of return is available to you through two broad categories of investments. National governments issue fixed-income securities, bonds that pay back at various defined terms. Short-range instruments of one year or less generate about a fourth higher return than passbook savings accounts. Intermediate-range bonds, with terms of half-a-dozen years, provide more than double the passbook rates of interest, and long-range bonds of twenty years or so yield a little bit more than that. There are United States agency bonds, such as from the Tennessee Valley Authority—less well known than the United States Treasury's but still protected as agencies of the United States government—and even issuances from the World Bank. These issuances pay nearly three times passbook interest rates. The only problem, you realize, is that fixed-income instruments give no protection at all from inflation, and currency devaluation is almost as predictable as death and taxes. Deriving income from bonds works fine when inflation fluctuates under 3 percent per year; otherwise, erosion of your principal is inevitable.

The other relatively nonspeculative security investment is in public utility stocks. Utilities, whether electric, gas, or telephone, are capitalism's curious oxymoron: a legal monopoly. As such they are inherently very defended securities, protected from the exigencies of the business cycle. The preferred stock returns in utilities commonly yield two and a half times the rate of passbook interest rates each year, with common stocks not far behind. The common-stock issuances also provide the added attraction of a likely building in value as their issuing companies slowly grow. The best utilities have been more noteworthy for increases rather than reductions in share equity and dividends. In the mid-1990s, for example, good utility common and preferred stocks showed annual yields of from 5 to 10 percent.

Next we come to the corporations that invest in investments, the mutual funds. Some work with combinations of stodgy, low-return bonds and higher-yield corporate bonds, mortgage-backed securities, collateralized mortgage securities, and preferred stock shares. The yield can attain more than three and a half times passbook

interest rates each year, usually quite a secure position past inflation. Zenix Income Fund and Merrill Lynch's Corporate High Income Fund have paid nearly four times passbook rates. The
commission on brokerage firm–organized mutual fund purchases
is graduated downward from 4 or 5 percent if you hold them for at
least one year, 3.5 percent after two years, and so on to zero after
four years.

A final venue to mention here is mortgage-backed securities.
These can be obtained by trading either on or off the exchanges,
frequently in the limited partnership form where the basic investment unit is $2,000, $5,000, or $10,000. Firms such as JMB, Car-
lyle, Fox and Carskadon, and others assemble portfolios of real
estate mortgages or equities. The mortgages are for multifamily
dwellings, hotels, shopping centers, office buildings, and other re-
alty forms. Sad to say, most real estate limited partnerships have
had a poor to bad rate of profitability, consequently with a rather
disappointing record for later salability in the "after market."

Having said this, let it be pointed out that some of the exchange-
traded mortgage packages have held their own fairly well. These
include America's First Prep Fund 2 (PF), traded on the American
Stock Exchange in certificates of beneficial interest (BCI) rather
than shares, but for most practical purposes act very much the
same as shares. America's First Prep invests in federally insured
mortgages for multifamily housing and in preferred real estate
partnerships (PREPs), which enable it to participate in the net cash
flow and net sales or refinancing proceeds of the projects securing
the mortgage loans. PF holds active positions in the financing of
projects from Colorado to Maryland, as well as a position in GNMA
("Ginnie Mae") bonds. Returns to PF owners have typically been
over 10 percent per year.

RECOVERY INVESTMENTS

On occasion a candidate for investment turns up that seems about
to recover from a seriously depressed position. This is a security
that has enjoyed better times but has tumbled in profitability and

share price. Something intruded to bid down share price—short-term bad publicity, a very short-lived earnings and revenue drop, an embezzlement, a one-day crash. Yet basic financial structure and indicators are positive, and a rally must be coming.

But when? That's the speculator's main concern. If the company takes too long to turn around, an investment in it will tie up equity without hoped-for returns. This risk factor depends upon so many variables that the novice investor is wise not to wager too much on it. A small investment, however, is valid.

Consider the case of Bruno's Inc., headquartered in Alabama but with its business concentrated in the surrounding states. It once had an excellent record for growth but was a fallen angel in 1992. What happened? Earnings per share dropped from $.82 in 1991 to $.69 in 1992, bringing on a rush to unload shares. These had traded for $31.88 in 1991, a high reached after many years of upward mobility. By late 1992 share price had bid down to an astonishing $10.50, at which point canny onlookers saw a late December jiggle up to $13.00. The smart money boys knew that Bruno's basics were sound, since the current ratio was 1.6 and the PE was 26, and they came out in a rush. Sure enough, earnings turned around in 1993, share prices shot up, and those who got in at the low end made major capital gains.

Bottoming candidates should be considered in several lights. Is the company in a very competitive sector? Is it shielded from imports and foreign activities? Is it involved in products or services for which demand is stable? Mainly, how quickly did the price depress? In Bruno's case, it dove by 40 percent in one year despite being healthy. Through this sort of careful inspection, what seems to be a high-risk investment actually may turn out simply to be an artful tracking of recent history.

Here are some guidelines. Candidates with a PE wildly low (3 or 4) or high (over 25) have a pretty good chance of serious underlying financial or other structural defects. Another quality to consider is the trend in the candidate's performance before it plunged. If earnings were erratic, with many cycles including periods with deficits, avoid it like the plague. Also consider the current ratio, because this relates to the candidate's working capital. A current ratio in the neighborhood of 2 is acceptable. If it is anything over 4 or 5, this is a warning signal concerning management competence; a current ratio near or under 1 has insufficient working capital to sustain itself against adverse financial problems.

Another thing to watch for is the niche of the candidate's market or product line. Be wary of any and all companies subject to the vagaries of Japanese or other foreign influences, as well as companies dealing in technology that faces obsolescence on a daily basis.

INTERNATIONAL DIVERSIFICATION

Even prior to the collapse of the Soviet Union in 1989, most of the die-hard socialist national regimes were permitting some degree of capitalist activity. The calming of tensions between the major powers promoted other highly important political changes, particularly in the realm of support for international trade. Despite these changes, the world is still a pretty big place and regional economies retain a notable degree of individuality. Periods of economic expansion in one may or may not influence another, and currencies stabilize or decline at different rates in different places. Therefore it is prudent for a portfolio to include representative investment in more than one region.

The world has commonly been divided into several economic segments, each defined according to economic development. Until recently the preferred system was: the First World, meaning North America, Western Europe, Japan, Australia, and New Zealand; the Second World, meaning the Iron Curtain nations with socialist economies tied to that of the Soviet Union; the Third World, meaning most of Asia, Africa, and South America; and the Fourth World, meaning basket-case economies such as those of Haiti and Bangladesh. As the developed world surges ahead, drawing into itself more of the planet's resources, some economists are speaking of a North that is in excellent shape and booming, and a South wherein population growth and other forces are holding prosperity at bay.

The novice investor should focus on securities issued in nations within the First World, or North, roughly North America, Europe, and Australia. Here is where securities investment is buffered by stable governments and protected currencies. Investment elsewhere is purely speculative, in unstable environments with alien legal and judicial systems. This harsh admonition may be hard on struggling nations attempting to broaden their capital base, but the point here is for the beginning investor to stay away from pure trouble.

Probably the safest foreign securities investments are the American Depository Receipts (ADRs). These are foreign securities held in branch offices of American banks abroad, and therefore fairly protected from seizure by foreign states should any international unpleasantness occur. Some of these foreign issues are listed and traded on United States exchanges and are valued in dollars, and many send periodic reports to their stockholders just like our domestic corporations.

Some of the better "offshore" corporations have very familiar names. Nestlé, South America, is a major manufacturer of food and grocery products in Europe, the Americas, Africa, and Asia. Sony, based in Japan, is a leading producer of electronic devices with worldwide distribution. Canadian Pacific holds vast North American timber resources and manufactures paper products. There are outstanding utilities such as Telmex (Mexico), Telefonos de España (Spain), and British Telecommunications. Grand Metropolitan, a company headquartered in London, has far-reaching food product interests in the United Kingdom and the Americas, with subsidiaries such as Pillsbury and Banquet Foods, a frozen-food leader.

For an extensive list of foreign investment opportunities, ask an informed broker. The best alternatives can be determined in the same way that domestic corporations are analyzed.

CONCLUSION

Nurturing a new portfolio involves becoming familiar with the possibilities at hand and the tools with which securities are evaluated. This chapter gives an idea of how one sorts through alternatives.

Before long, it becomes so ordinary a process that one wonders how it ever seemed difficult. How long does it take to reach that point? Not very. Most novices pick up a large part of the jargon alone within a couple of years, just by talking to brokers and friends with portfolios. Getting the basics straight past that returns us to an invocation of study and practice.

TABLE 9-1:
SYSCO AND HORMEL COMPARISON

YEAR	SYSCO		Hormel	
	% OPERATING PROFIT MARGIN	% ROI	% OPERATING PROFIT MARGIN	% ROI
1982			4.20	11.56
1983	4.80	16.96	6.20	10.50
1984	4.80	15.56	6.20	10.30
1985	4.90	15.01	7.20	12.35
1986	4.30	14.89	5.40	11.54
1987	4.40	13.73	5.20	12.35
1988	4.30	15.78	5.90	14.47
1989	4.50	16.83	6.30	14.98
1990	4.60	17.26	5.80	15.07
1991	4.70	16.83	6.00	14.85
1992	4.80	16.69		
Average Last 5 yrs	4.58	16.69	5.84	14.34
Max Dif from Average	−0.28	−2.96	−1.36	−4.04

TABLE 9-2:
LIST OF OTHER STRONG GROWTH SITUATIONS

Company	Sales (%)	EPS (%)	Price (%)
American Barrick	45	53	51
Archer Daniels Midland	10	18	18
Bruno's, Inc.	21	17	20
ConAgra, Inc.	30	17	25
Cooper Industries	12	15	12
Dreyer's Grand	22	13	11
Forest Labs	35	30	21
Gillette	12	20	28
Good Guys (The)	36	39	34
Great Lakes Chemical	25	28	25
McDonalds	11	14	18
Pacific Health Care	54	38	31
Pentech	81	101	72
Rubbermaid	17	17	23
Stride Rite	15	37	44
Wausau Paper	10	17	29

FIGURE 9-1:
SALES, EARNINGS, AND PRICE TRENDS FOR SYSCO CORPORATION

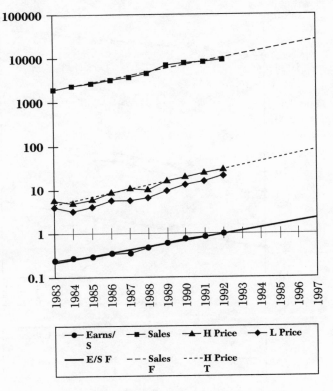

Courtesy Bob Bradford

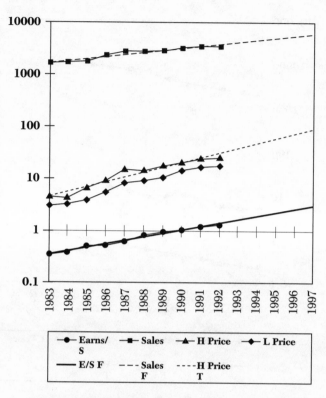

Courtesy Bob Bradford

10
LISTED STOCK OPTIONS

LAWRENCE LYNN

INTRODUCTION

Wasting assets" have a value that may decrease over the passing of time. At a specified future date they cease to have any value at all— they become worthless. What are they, and why does this precarious, time-related destruction of value exist? They are rights, warrants, or options to buy or sell stocks at a future date for a future price.

Trading in such assets goes back over two millennia to the days when traders waited on the docks of Ostia, a Roman seaport. There they impatiently paced the waterfront in the expectation of the arrival of grain ships from Alexandria in far-off Egypt, in those days the granary of the Roman Empire. Profits depended largely on the prices commanded by incoming shipments, and merchants bid on the right to buy early cargos. In effect, Roman traders were speculating on prices for future cereal grain markets on which they had bought or sold option contracts.

This form of speculation languished during the Dark Ages, after the collapse of the Roman Empire, then gradually returned as business conditions became more organized several centuries later. Trading in options on real estate and other valuables was common in medieval Florence during the time of the Medicis and Borgias. Financial experts of that era were also involved with the rise and fall of debt instruments dependent on interest rates, akin to today's bond markets. Trading in commodity futures reached a frantic pace in the Netherlands during the tulip craze. Fortunes were made and lost based on the bidding of prices for tulip bulbs and other goods. Today's trading on agricultural products is a lasting emulation of this practice.

It was probably inevitable that after the initial joint-stock companies started operating using the old practices, associated with trade in real estate and agricultural products, such trading would spread into stock buying and selling. This did occur, but trading in futures and options on common stock developed much more slowly than trading in common stock itself. Initially it was managed through small specialist option shops, boutiques of sorts, most of which dealt only in options of a select group of widely held stock.

RIGHTS, WARRANTS, AND OPTIONS

A "rights offering" is similar to the presentation of a public equity by a corporation. It is a corporate decision to allow its existing stockholders the opportunity to avoid any dilution of their overall ownership portion by receiving certain "stock rights." These rights enable the stockholder to buy additional shares at a preferential price below the present trading value of the stock. For example, a corporation may offer the stockholder one right for each existing share of stock he or she owns. The corporation could then stipulate that ten rights could be used to purchase a new share at a $10 discount on the trading value by that stockholder or others. Consequently, because ten rights save $10, each right is worth $1. Rights have value for only a fixed, fairly brief period of time, typically forty-five days. At that point the rights expire and become worthless.

Rights are commonly traded—they can be bought and sold just like stocks, should the actual rights holder not wish to use them. For example, if you receive 1,000 rights you could probably sell them for nearly $1,000 to someone who does wish to exercise them, or hold them for speculation in the hope that they will quickly be bid up in value. The value of a right depends upon "intrinsic value" (IV) and "time value" (TV), the time left until the right's expiration, assuming that the underlying stock shares remain unchanged in price. The shorter the time left before expiration, the lower the time value, meaning "wasting" of the asset.

A "warrant," on the other hand, is commonly associated with bonds. Consider a situation in which a corporation determines, in consultation with investment bankers, that a bond issue is necessary and desirable to increase long-term capitalization. Because of current American interest rates and the company's earnings and prospects, assume that they would have to pay 8.5 percent interest on a $100 million issue. At that rate it would cost the company $8.5 million per year for thirty years, a total expense of $255 million for the right to use investors' money.

The company's stock is selling for $40 per share and has an excellent record for growth of earnings, price, and dividends. Furthermore, it has a sound base of stockholders. Considering the apparent strength of the company's stock, their advisers suggest a bond with attached warrants. Each warrant will allow the bondholder the right to buy one common share for $40 at any time during the next five years. If the stock were to keep rising, say to $80 per share, taking advantage of each warrant at that point would enable the stockholder to realize an immediate profit of $40.

This makes the bonds much more attractive, enabling the firm to place the bonds with an investor at a reduced interest rate under 8.5 percent, perhaps 8 or even 7.5 percent. By reducing the rate on its bonds by a single percent, the company would save about $850,000 per year on the thirty-year bonds, a total of $25.5 million, not a bad way to cut corporate expenses. The company saves money on the deal, and the investors get a great discount on stock shares if they rise as anticipated.

Just as rights have a finite life, so do warrants. Warrants may be traded separately from their associated bonds. Until expiration, they also have an intrinsic value and a time value. The intrinsic value, as shown earlier, is dependent upon the difference between the market price for the stock and the price at which the warrant is exercisable—$40 in our example. If the price of the stock does not rise significantly, or stagnates near $40, intrinsic value becomes moot.

Similarly, if the time to expiration is short, say a few days or weeks for a five-year warrant, the time value would be minuscule because the warrant is so close to expiration. However, if the market provides a healthy intrinsic value and the time left is reasonable or lengthy, the time value could be substantial. For example, if the market price went to $70 and there were 18 months left in the life of the warrants, one could trade a warrant for, say, $35. This would be roughly $30 for the intrinsic value and $5 for the time value.

This brings us to the third form of wasting asset, the option. In the old days, options bought or sold through the specialty shops were called "market options" in which the future price of the option bought or sold was the current price of the underlying commodity involved. It made it possible for investors to nail down current prices for a part of the action, when there was the chance that prices might well rise or sink later through competitive bidding. If an option holder became disillusioned with the options purchased, there was only a haphazard market in which they could be sold, for there were no formal exchanges.

A modern listed common stock option, which we will hereafter refer to as simply an "option," has some of the characteristics of rights and warrants. It too is a "wasting asset" with a finite life span, intrinsic value, and time value. The option price, called the "premium," reflects both of these values. In the United States, listed options are traded on all the major exchanges. Some market options are still traded by small specialist over-the-counter (OTC) option "boutiques" or shops, but these outlets are relatively minor.

By convention, on the listed exchanges, a "call" option is defined as the right for the purchaser to *buy* units of 100 shares of a given stock at a preordained price up to a predetermined date. That preordained price is called the "strike price," the date is termed the "expiration date," and the cost of the option is termed the "premium." The value of the premium is established by supply and demand, and as a practical matter the financial community's convention defines it as the sum of the intrinsic and the time values. Thus, if you buy a call option on a company's stock share holding a strike price of $50, and the present market value is $52, the intrinsic value of the option is $2. Slang for this situation is that the call optioner is "in the money" by $2. Saying that there is a premium of ¼ means that the cost of the option is one-fourth of a dollar, or twenty-five cents per share. Since options come in 100 share lots, the cost of this option is $25. If the premium had been $2, the cost would have been $200. Time values vary from ¹⁄₁₆ to 2, depending on the apparent underlying strength and recent momentum of the stock.

An option may be said to have a first, middle, and last name, each of which is an indispensable element of its description. For example, at the close of business on February 17 in a recent year, the newspapers showed the listed option data for Pfizer (PFE), which was being trading on the American Stock Exchange (AM). The shorthand notation read as:

59⅞   Pfizer   Jun 65 C   1⅞

Translated, this means that the stock shares last traded at 59⅞; the rest of the notation has to do with options. The first name is Pfizer, the middle name is Jun 65 C (a call at $65 by a date in June, then its strike price), and the last name is 1⅞, the premium price. If you had bought this call option it would have cost you $187.50 (1⅞ × 100). In effect, if you had bought this option in February you would have believed that the price of Pfizer could reach well past $65 by the June expiration date. If your analysis turned out to be correct and the price made it, say, to $68 by early June, the premium would be $3 (68 − 65) and the time value might work out to another $2, for a total of $5. If it did, you could now make a handsome profit by selling the option. If you bought the option for 1⅞ (meaning $187.50) and sold it for 5 (meaning $500), you would have made a profit of well over 150 percent.

If that sort of accuracy happened all the time, everyone in the United States would quit their jobs and become full-time option buyers. Naturally it doesn't, and there is no danger of a helter-skelter stampede into the options game.

The price might only remain the same or even decrease, missing an early June price of $65 by a mile. If that happened, you would take a beating on the $187.50 that you paid for each option. The attraction here was that you believed, due to some careful research, that there was a good chance of a charging price increase.

By working the options alternative, you used the leverage of not having to put out $5,987.50 for each 100 shares of Pfizer in order to speculate on its hoped-for share price rise. It was a matter of operating with much less capital to seek a high percentage gain, but with options, if you were wrong you could lose all or most of your invested equity—all if you rode it out the whole way and lost, part if you were able to sell to a greater optimist as things progressed prior to the deadline and missed target. If you had purchased the actual 100 shares of Pfizer stock, you would still own the stock whether or not it changed. You could, with patience, see it climb to a profit at a later date. The option buyer's opportunity ends with the expiration date, but the stock buyer's opportunity continues until the sale of the stock.

For options, the date of expiration is always defined as the Friday preceding the third Saturday of the assigned month. The floor trader can do last-minute trading or exercising of option positions on that last Saturday. As a practical matter, a non-exchange person must enter a trade by noon on the last day of the option cycle to be sure that it can be traded in time to beat the deadline.

This has been a "call" option; there is also the converse, called a "put" option. Consider the "put" to be the flip side of a call. You buy a call because you think a given stock is about to *increase* in value and think you can make a reasonable guess about how long it will take to reach this new level. You are the buyer of a put when you foresee a *decline* in the price of a stock. When you buy a put, you purchase the right to sell a stock at a given strike price by a given date.

Suppose you are interested in and follow the pharmaceutical industry. In a time of dropping share values you are convinced that the decline has not ended. Perhaps new federal regulations are pounding everybody. Although Pfizer, a well-run drug company with a good track record, has dropped like a stone over the past two months, you believe it will drop still farther. You think the present price of 59⅞ is still *above* where it will be after the full effect of the regulations have been felt. You think it could easily fall to $50 per share or lower. In the newspaper you see in the put section:

Pfizer   Sep 60 P   5¼

This means that if you buy this put you have the right to sell PFE at $60 per share until the third Friday of September, when the option expires. Your monetary risk for this transaction is $525 (100 × 5¼).

Now suppose that it is near the September deadline and PFE has indeed dropped to $45 per share. The put will have an intrinsic value of $15 (60 − 45). With the time value added in, the put may be worth a total of $16 per put option. The premium value moves from $5.25 to $16.00, a three-fold increase during a down market. The stockholders may be jumping out of windows, but you just cleaned up.

Again, what if you are wrong? Therein lies the risk. It's great when it works; otherwise, you lose part or all of your investment.

KEY DEVELOPMENTS IN OPTIONS TRADING

In the early 1970s, after the establishment of the Chicago Board Options Exchange (CBOE), it spearheaded the creation of a number of changes in the rules through which options are traded. The board began publishing daily listings of completed trades in options on a small number of widely held underlying common-stock issues. Regular preestablished strike prices such as $10, $15, $20, $25, and $30 were set for the common issues. Greater gaps of $10 between strike prices were established for shares trading over $100 and smaller strike price gaps of $2½ to $5 for those selling under $25. Some options would have dates of expiration regularized to occur on a quarterly basis, in January, April, July, and October; others would be available in three-month cycles beginning in either February or March.

The financial community wondered how the investing and trading public would react to these "listed options." The response was immediate and gratifying. A high volume of trading rapidly developed. Soon other exchanges set up options-trading departments and began to feature options trading in securities not traded on the CBOE.

After a period of rapid growth in options trading on the five major American option exchanges, several spin-off options-trading vehicles were begun, also with great success. These include "market options" in which you can speculate on how a "basket" of different stocks will perform, for example, on the Standard & Poor 500 Stock Average, or the Chicago Board 100 index.

TRADING OPTIONS
ON INDIVIDUALLY LISTED STOCKS

Because it is much less complicated, the beginning investor interested in tackling options should stay away from market options and concentrate on those of individually listed stocks. And since getting much out of it is problematic, wisdom suggests prudence in how much equity to risk.

The rights and obligations of buyers and sellers of option calls and puts are very different. We'll take the call situation first.

As explained earlier, the call buyer purchases the right to buy units of 100 shares of a stock at the strike price, up to an expiration date. The investor hopes for a dramatic rise in value due to bidding, and looks for modest option costs for the purchase. If the estimated jump in value occurs, the investor makes money on a relatively small purchase cost. If it doesn't . . . that's the way it goes.

Here's a dramatic example of why options tickle some investors' imaginations.

In 1980 the price of gold ran up enormously (and precipitously, since it came back down with quite a crash). ASA Ltd. was a foreign company investing in South African gold, and on August 5, 1980, when the price of ASA was at 22½, it cost ⅛ in U.S. dollars to buy ASA November 30 calls. In other words, an investor's option cost was $12.50 (cost less broker commission), and units of 100 shares cost $1,250.

When the price of gold suddenly took off like a rocket from $300 per ounce to over $850 per ounce—possibly as a result of new rules permitting U.S. citizens to own bullion—the price of ASA followed. It *tripled* to over $60 per share! As a result, by October 15 the option's value had leaped as well, with an intrinsic value of over $30 (the price of ASA less the strike price) plus a time value of $3.50, for a total value of $33.50.

At this point the merry investor had choices. He could either exercise his call and sell his newly acquired ASA stock at $60 per share, using the option to profit from share price increase. If he traded the option alternative, he could simply sell off the call option itself for a premium of $3,350 per call. The short-term capital gain per call would have been $3,350 − 12.50, or $3,337.50 per call. Since the original purchase was 100 options, the total profit would have been an astronomical gain of $333,750 on a risk capital of only $1,250!

Stories like this are what keep the options market going. Amazing profits, however, are extremely rare. Most call or put options are never exercised on the underlying stock or are sold off with any gain, let alone that kind of gain. Most options expire as worthless or are sold at a pittance. But the reality of the situation does not prevent speculators from trying again and again. Presumably they alternate playing with options with betting on the ponies or cranking a slot machine in Las Vegas. The allure of making a financial killing without having to pony up much up-front money will always attract a certain type of speculator.

Similarly, the put buyer has the opportunity, on occasion, to reap a handsome gain if the underlying stock declines extensively and abruptly. A perfect example is what happened with International Business Machines (IBM) stock in late 1992 and early 1993. Under assault from very aggressive competing computer companies, IBM abruptly plummeted from over $100 to below $50 per share in just a few days' time. Those put-options traders who through wit or sheer luck were speculating that it would happen walked away with a pile.

If you are an option buyer, you have two ways in which to gain. If the option is a call, you can buy the stock shares at the favorable strike price as the market soars above that level. Alternatively, you can sell the call option and, taking commissions into account for the transaction, come out ahead without ever having traded the stock itself. If you are a put buyer, you have the alternative of not dealing directly with the underlying stock at all. You can simply sell the put at its higher premium and avoid having to do transactions with the underlying stock.

Where do your connections come from during this dealing? The first law of options is that for each option bought there must be an equal and opposite option sold. The second is that there is always someone foolish or naive enough to buy or sell at the moment you want to trade, no matter what the market looks like.

In general, severe drops in price are as uncommon as moon-shot rises, and the most put buyers usually accomplish is the experience of watching the premium they paid dwindle to worthlessness as the option's expiration date approaches. As with calls, put buyers continue to be attracted by potential large profits while putting up a relatively small amount of capital. It's great if it works.

So much for buying options. But where do they come from? For each option bought there must be an option sold. Let's now turn our attention to the fate of the option *seller.*

The people who sell options accept much more responsibility than do the buyers of options. They do, however, receive certain compensation for it—the value of the premiums (less commissions) paid by the buyers.

The buyer of a call, as we pointed out earlier, receives the right to buy 100 shares of the optionable stock at the strike price. If the underlying stock price rises above the strike price before the expiration date, as promised, the writer of the option may have to sell 100 shares for each option purchased. For instance, it is March and the following option is sold on Sumerian Bitumen, a mythical marine-fastener company:

SUM   Apr 40   1⅞

The price of the stock later rises to $50 per share and the option is exercised—the seller is obligated to sell 100 shares at $40 instead of $50 per share. The seller incurs the opportunity cost of the $10 separating the agreed-upon price from the new price while the buyer receives the commensurate gain.

This would be an even more painful situation if the seller did not actually own the stock before the option sale. In chapter 6 the peculiar convention of permitting individuals to promise the sale of stock shares not yet owned was briefly discussed. It warrants a few more emphatic words.

NAKED VERSUS COVERED OPTIONS

If the seller of an option (who is said to either "make," "write," or "sell" the option, each term meaning the same thing) already owns enough of that stock to be able to sell the full volume for which an option sale was made, he is a "covered option writer," or "long." If the sale of a call is made on stock that is not owned, the seller is said to be writing a "naked" or "uncovered" option, a "short" position. If the price is reached within the defined time period and the option is exercised, the seller must "cover" the sale through selling enough of the promised stock. Both covered and naked option types are permitted by law and are closely supervised by federal securities examiners.

If the seller purchased the underlying stock at, say, $30 over a year ago, therefore being covered, it might be no big deal to release it now to some buyer at $40. He has received the option premium and has also made a long-term capital gain. The stock that went up to the specified option price level could well dive again after the transaction, in which case he is well out of it. That sort of fluctuation in price does occur.

On the other hand, here might be a steadily rising stock that the seller bought at $30, held to $45, but was required through an ill-advised option to sell at $40. Then he might glumly watch his former stock climb farther, to, say, $60. There was no actual loss due to the transaction, but the forfeited opportunity for further gain was galling. This is the risk one takes when selling covered options.

That's covered options. How about uncovered options?

When you sell an option without being covered—the naked-option situation—you are potentially short some or all of the number of promised shares of the stock. The normal procedure for the short-option seller is to watch the stock share price closely. If it swings toward the price where an obligation is owed, prudence dictates picking up enough stock to be covered. The purchaser is buying in to cover the short position, just in case. If he waits too long, he could find himself in the awkward position of being obligated to sell stocks to an option buyer at a price lower than that he himself had to pay for that stock when the option was exercised in order to honor the sale. In that case, paying the broker's commission is obviously salt on the wound.

Here are some numbers from a typical case of an option writer waiting too long before covering. He sells an option on some stock at a premium of 1½, or $150 per call. Later he has to buy stock to cover the obligation at 3⅛, or $313. The loss is $163 ($313 − $150) on each option sold. The option sale could simply have been unwise, or perhaps the seller panicked and bought back his cover too soon, before the stock's short-lived rally collapsed. In any case, it was a relief to close the position before it could be exercised.

When to buy in and cover a naked option is a sometimes tricky matter, especially in an up market. The seller wants to nip trouble prudently, but it is easy to get caught either buying to cover when the option price isn't actually reached, or when it passes the option point and the seller covers, after which it maddeningly dips back below the option price before the option holder can wake up and exercise his right.

Now what about the put traders, who sell naked options to investors who can sell stock shares if the price declines to a certain price within a certain time period? The premium, as usual, is a composite of the intrinsic value and the time value of the option. The put buyer has purchased the right or privilege, but not the obligation, to sell the seller's optioned stock shares if the defined low price is reached or passed. The put seller receives a premium in return for obligating himself.

Follow this scenario. You write a put on a stock whose market price was above the strike price and are paid a premium by the option buyer. The option is said to be "out of the money" by the difference between current market price and the lower strike price. If the stock declines significantly, you may see the put premium bid well above the premium you received on your deal, as investors spot the dropping stock and compete for some of the action. Should the stock fall below the strike price, the put buyer may (shall we say) literally put the stock to you at the strike price.

To give an example, suppose you sold a put option on Dragline Coastal when it stood at 35, the option being:

DLC June 30 P

To your horror, the price of DLC falls to $25. If the option holder then puts his stock shares to you, you will have to buy the stock at $30, then either hold the stock or sell it for $25 a share in order to meet any maintenance obligation. That's a $5 per share real or paper loss. It is tempered somewhat by the earning from the premium you were originally paid, but your long face hardly changes because of that.

For this reason, it is axiomatic that you should never sell puts on stock that you consider likely to dip significantly. Writing naked option puts on stock you wouldn't be caught dead owning is a good way to find yourself wiped out in no time. And, naturally, naked-option put writers should never write obligations for more stock than they can quite comfortably pick up at a substantial loss. If you remember nothing else about options writing, always remember that on October 19, 1987, the market dropped 508 points in a *single day*. This spike wrought havoc among the put sellers. Those who had badly overwritten were crushed by having stock put to them faster than they had ever expected and in quantities they could not possibly absorb. It was not pretty.

The reader might want to review the chapter on margins, to examine Regulation T calls, which must be met within three business days. If an investor's account is suddenly "put" much more than can be paid in to satisfy Regulation T of the Federal Reserve, that account can literally be wiped off the books, with total devastation for the unhappy put writer.

It is a sound strategy to write puts well below the market for longer expiration periods, since it offers the chance to buy stock shares at unusually low prices. Disastrous collapses can work to your good fortune, as when the pharmaceuticals fell on their respective faces in the early 1990s. Glaxo's stock, for example, performed as if it had been blown away by Dirty Harry. Within twelve months of trading it went from $33 per share down to $18 per share, then it went down even farther, to $15 per share. This was in spite of an optimistic earnings situation. The moment was favorable at $18 to make a good-til-canceled (GTC) order, perhaps for 500 shares at $15, or to sell puts at $15. When your highest hopes were achieved—the rock-bottom price for a healthy corporation—you picked up your shares with the virtual assurance that in a short time the stock would come back and you would double your equity situation.

One last thing. A hybrid of selling covered and uncovered positions is "ratio writing," where you do both at once. Suppose you own 300 shares of Eastman Kodak (EK) and decide to write option calls as follows:

EK April 70 C

Your ownership of 300 shares makes this a covered position up through three calls. In a ratio-writing program, you sell more options than already covered. If you feel strongly that an increase in price of EK to $70 was most unlikely, you might sell five calls instead of three. You are 60 percent covered, or in other words, have a covered to uncovered ratio of 3:2. You are more than half covered, and can fill the breach if need be. If you have good reason to believe the stock will not make a sudden significant up move, it is a reasonable way to earn more from your account.

RESTRICTIONS ON OPTION WRITING

Because from time to time options investors make a killing after starting with small or moderate equity, writing options attracts speculators the way honey attracts bees. To protect the naive, ignorant, and hasty, the Federal Reserve, SEC, and the options exchanges have deloped a series of limitations and restrictions placed on option writing. These terms can be reviewed along with Reg T in chapter 6. Some limitations are enforced by the individual brokerage firms simply to protect their clients from overdoing it, particularly neophytes who have never experienced a disaster.

Another group of limitations are those practical considerations that involve account statistics. Uncovered option writing through a brokerage firm requires adequate equity in your credit line, often known as your special memorandum account (SMA). When you write an option you are paid a premium, but you are also voluntarily giving up the use of some of your loan value. In effect, you agree not to use this loan value while your option remains outstanding.

How much slack do you need? The regulations governing this amount for calls have varied over the years, but most recently the size of immobilized SMA has been set as the greater of these two equations. Where CMV = Current Market Value, O/M is the out-of-money difference between value and strike price, and Pm is the premium:

$$SMA = 0.3\,CMV + O/M + Pm$$

or

$$SMA = 0.15\,CMV + Pm$$

Say we relate this to Eastman Kodak (EK)—$50 July calls at a present price of $45 per share. CMV is $4,500, O/M is $5,000, and Pm is $75. If you write an EK April 50 call in March with the premium at ¾, the calculation would be:

$$SMA = 0.3(\$4,500) + (\$4,500 - \$5,000) + \$75 = \$925$$

or

$$SMA = 0.15(\$4,500) + \$75 = \$750$$

The results of the first calculation, being the larger of the two, is the SMA tied up. In this case the restriction will last for three months. Note that the return on the encumbered SMA is calculated by dividing the premium by the SMA—$75/$925, or 8.11 percent for the couple of months involved. This converts to an annual rate of 48.65 percent (6 × 8.11), a substantial return without having to lay out a single dime! As ever, you would be bearing the "opportunity" risk, possibly substantial, should the price of EK unexpectedly soar during the next two months.

There are strategies by which to limit your losses in the event of a wrong decision. If, after taking the option plunge, EK began to show signs of a steady rise, you might quickly buy the options back at a small loss. If, for example, by the time you realized your error and bought the option back the premium had reached $1.50, your loss would be 100 (1.5 − 0.75), or $75.

Pragmatism in admitting a mistake doesn't come easily for some people. Others would decide to stick it out just in case EK turns around. These are the sort of people who should not get involved in options trading.

The SMA requirements for a put are the same as for a call, and the "out-of-money" (O/M) portion of the equation is again calculated as the difference between strike price and current market value.

Consider the situation of EK again, this time when it is at $45. You decide it would be a good buy at $40. What you are saying, in effect, is that if you sold a $40 put on EK you would not object to taking possession of the stock at $40. If the premium were $1, the SMA tied up would be:

$$SMA = 0.3(4,500) + (4,000-4,500) + 100 = \$950$$

or

$$SMA = 0.15(4,500) + 100 = \$775$$

In this case the SMA is $950, the higher of the two values.

Restrictive rules other than this may be imposed and enforced by a brokerage firm. At one major firm, for example, the brokerage requires a minimal equity of $10,000 present in the account for the first uncovered option. Each naked option after that one requires $1,000 in equity; thus an account with $50,000 in equity would be allowed a total of 41 positions.

Another firm insists on puts being limited to 60 percent of the net equity in the account. Under these limitations, an account with $50,000 of equity could write options with up to 0.6 × $50,000, or $30,000 worth of option exposure. In that case, an option with a $60 strike price would support $6,000 per 100 shares of exposure, in other words, the writing of 30,000/6,000, or 5 positions. On the other hand, if an option had a strike price of $30, the account could handle up to 30,000/3,000, or 10 positions.

These are wise restrictions, imposed to prevent you from ruining yourself with foolish speculation. If you overwrite, you could be victimized by Reg T margin requirements in excess of what you can handle. Some firms invoke no restrictions, and in effect are willing to give you all the rope you need to hang yourself within federal and SEC requirements involving FME and SMA. It is best for the novice to find a brokerage firm that cares enough to impose "tough love" restraints.

Within this armature of protection, another restriction on the number of options an investor writes is psychological: the writer's background, proclivities, and pure self-confidence.

Among the questions a new investor should ask himself are:

1. How successful have you been with your program?

2. What is the orientation of your investment portfolio? Is it long-term capital gains, total account return, tax-exempt return, or something else?

3. What funds do you have available outside your margin account to back up option activities? Do you have replenishing income in case of a loss, or are you retired?

When it comes right down to it, are you comfortable with options? If not, don't even get started. There are plenty of other outlets for your investment energy.

STRADDLES AND COMBINATIONS

If you write both a call and a put with an identical strike price on the same stock, your transaction would be termed a "straddle." The SMA to write a straddle is not the sum of the SMA for the individual transactions. Instead, it is the SMA for the higher of either the put or call. The reason for this is that when you write a straddle, it is highly unlikely that the put and the call would both be exercised in the same time frame. Theoretically, it could happen if the stock surged, then sharply reversed, but this is highly improbable.

Many option writers use a quasi-straddle called a combination. In this case an uncovered call is written with a strike price much higher than the strike price for the put. For example, you might write an EK April 60 call along with an EK April 40 put. This strategy assumes that it is highly unlikely that the stock will rise above

$60 and fall below $40 in the same time period. It is much more likely that at least one of your options will prove correct and expire as worthless.

Either a straddle or a combination usually proves safer than either the put or call alone, and for this reason there is a lower SMA requirement. If more than one option is written, it should be fairly obvious that the SMA needed is a combination of those required for each of the options. Thus, if ten of the EK April 60 calls described above were written, the SMA used would be $9,250 (10 × 925).

Also, option offers like this have the advantage of economies of scale, because broker commissions for small trade volumes can amount to a high percentage cost of doing business, especially when the premium is below $1. With straddles or combinations, you use one naked-option vacancy when you are actually carrying out two transactions and getting premiums from both.

ADVANTAGES AND DISADVANTAGES

Writing covered calls, or even a small degree of ratio writing, involves the risk that the stock you already own might be called. If you write calls with a strike price above your purchase price, you might give up an opportunity for added profit but you certainly risk no loss. In fact, you guarantee a profit. This requires no buying power, and brokerage firms place no restrictions on this activity because of its inherently low risk. If anything, it acts as a protective move, or insurance, against a market or stock decrease. The premiums for covered calls are often quite low, but a small amount of added income for very little risk may be well worth it. Brokers, understandably, are usually not too thrilled about this practice because the commissions involved are so small.

In the case of uncovered calls, you ask yourself if there is much chance that the stock price will exceed the strike price for a call, or drop below it for a put. It should be underlined that here is where the risk lies. If the earnings of a company suddenly look bright, and the price shows signs of a sudden gain, you face a serious loss on a call option.

Let's consider the case of an individual who insisted on selling calls of Wells Fargo and Co. (WFC), a banking firm, because of the juicy premiums. He thought he saw a golden opportunity when Wells Fargo showed this listing:

Wells Fargo   Jul 70   2¼

He sold 12 of these options when the price of the stock was in the mid $60s. Sure enough, not long after he made the trade, the stock began to climb. In mid-1992 interest rates started to fall again, and as they continued to fall, banks became more profitable enterprises because business picked up. As soon as the price of Wells Fargo stock started to approach $70 he should have closed the calls by buying them back. He didn't, nor did he when bidding pushed the price well past $70, either because he couldn't admit to a blunder or because of the misguided hope that Wells Fargo would suddenly turn around. As the stock approached $80, and with time to expiration running short, the option was exercised against his account and he had to sell 1,200 shares short at $70 per share, taking a hit of $10 a share, less the premium he received for selling the options in the beginning.

It was a parable on the theory and practice of options trading, from which we derive the obvious conclusion. If a stock tends to be volatile, has significant potential of momentum and growth power, and the premium is "too good to be true," don't write it. Furthermore, don't write more than you would feel comfortable selling short.

The same common sense applies when selling naked puts. If an account is medium-sized, it is foolhardy to write so many puts that the buying power of the account would be destroyed if the puts were exercised. For example, a $50,000 account should not run the risk of having $40,000 of some stock put to it, for a drop in equity like that would unbalance the account and render future trading precarious. A good rule of thumb is never to go out on a limb for more than one-fifth the account's equity.

It should be abundantly apparent by now that the option buyer or seller must use every means possible to keep track of what is going on. Watching the key indicators is essential, and avoiding stocks with a history of dramatic, sudden motion is almost obligatory for the beginner. A stock's history, as expressed in its relative volatility and beta coefficient, is highly important. The beta coefficient, similar to a coefficient of coordination, shows how closely the stock mirrors the S & P 500. There is quite a range among corporations (see Table 10-1). In general, the lowest volatility is found among the largest corporations and public utilities, and newer, smaller corporations have the highest volatility.

If a beta is 1.000, it follows the S & P 500 exactly. If it's 2.0, it moves up and down twice as fast as the Dow. Gold stocks are typically below 1.00; they tend to stagnate and lag behind the S & P 500 or Dow.

CONCLUSION

It should be apparent by now that the option trader must closely monitor the underlying stocks at all times. The more closely you follow them, and the better your "gut feeling" becomes for the security under consideration, the better off you are. Buying or selling options on a stock that is unfamiliar to you is like steering a car blindfolded. The thrill is not worth it.

The safest way for the beginner to get into options is to monitor the behavior of stocks in the securities publications. You could follow the trends published in chart books such as *Options Guide,* printed by William O'Neill & Company, or *Daily Graphs,* published by Daily Graphs, Inc., of Los Angeles. Such publications provide up-to-date bar charts and key indicators of many stocks, providing helpful revelations about stocks' fluctuations.

Then, avoid stocks with the potential to make major sudden moves. If you are a call buyer, don't touch a security with a history of periodic severe drops in price. If you are a put buyer, the same thing goes for securities that have suddenly surged dramatically in price. A conservative options writer should select issues that tend to be stodgy, lag the market, or languish phlegmatically when the market surges or plunges.

TABLE 10-1:
KEY INDICATORS FOR SELECTED ISSUES

Company	Relative Volatility	Beta Coefficient
Blockbuster Enter.	32	0.86
Bruno's Inc.	47	0.63
Caterpillar	12	0.59
Chiron	49	1.41
Compaq Computer	37	1.37
Carnival Cruise	34	1.52
Duke Power	13	0.46
Exxon	17	0.44
General Motors	33	0.85
Hanson Trust	24	1.06
IBM	48	0.65
McDonnell Douglas	56	0.36
Philip Morris	25	0.98
Southern Co.	16	0.50

11

INVESTMENT COMPANIES

LAWRENCE LYNN AND
GEORGE S. ECKHARDT JR.

INTRODUCTION

There are several types of investment companies, of which the mutual fund has become the most common today. In the early part of the twentieth century, investment companies were a minor factor in the total world of investments; by 1941, mutual funds totalled an equity of over 500 million dollars and in the 1980s their equity surpassed 250 billion dollars. Controlled equity in the 1990s had reached about two trillion dollars, equal to about 85 percent of all bank deposits. Mutual funds are so vast that they are both a prop and a major risk to the world trade in securities.

FACE-AMOUNT CERTIFICATE COMPANY

The face-amount certificate company issues face-amount certificates that will pay out a stated sum (the "face amount") after a certain installment period, never less than twenty-four months, in return for a deposited amount. Both the interest and principal are guaranteed, and the payout may either be in a lump sum or in installments. The face amounts are frequently backed by specific property, major equipment, or real estate. They are becoming rarer now because more attractive investment company options are available. Most brokers today are unfamiliar with, and seldom recommend, them.

UNIT INVESTMENT TRUSTS

A much more frequently recommended type of investment company is the unit investment trust. One reason for its endorsement by brokers is because the trusts are commonly organized, planned, supervised, and sold by investment brokers such as Smith Barney Shearson, Dean Witter, Merrill Lynch, and others.

This trust consists of a pool of bonds of differing types selected by a professional management group. A typical tax-exempt municipal bond fund may hold from 10 to 50 different bond issues. They are bought in large quantities to build a portfolio of, say, $50 million. This pool is split into individual trust certificates, typically $1,000 each. In this case, there would be 50,000 certificates. These are sold to clients at par plus a fee. The fee is required to organize the trust and defray the cost of sales.

Once formed, the contents of the trust cannot be bought or sold. As the bonds mature, the trust returns the capital it collects as "return of principal" to its holders. Some of these trusts are so designed as to pay the interest collected on a monthly basis. They could be set up to include corporate, municipal, or federal bonds. Except for the municipal bonds, earnings are taxable.

These units provide the benefits of professional management for investigation and selection, as well as pre-investment knowledge of their liquidation dates. On the downside, while the investor knows exactly what securities the unit investment trust is using, there the trust management lacks the tactical flexibility of other types of investment companies. These have the ability to work their way out of issues that turn weak, or to invest in alternative issues as replacements shortly before they move up in rating or value. It's a trade-off of sorts, but the record of unit investment trusts suffers from this aspect. Also, they rarely afford the investor the potential or the results of well-managed closed- or open-end investment companies, and typically lack the attraction of inflation against currency devaluation. They are vulnerable to inflation because they are not allowed to manage and upgrade their holdings or get rid of "losers."

CLOSED-END INVESTMENT COMPANIES

The closed-end investment company groups several investors' funds so that economies of scale on brokers' commissions can be obtained. Each person might contribute from $1,000 to $3,000, amassing a total of several tens of thousands in equity. Papers are drawn up to formalize the arrangement, and a professional manager is retained for guidance. The manager subdivides the pool into shares, each individual receiving a proportion commensurate with his contribution. After the trust company is formally established, no new participants are admitted, but each shareholder has the right to sell shares as desired.

If, in the course of a year, the manager does well and the cumulative value of the pool enlarges substantially, share value increases by that proportion. Each shareholder has the option of selling his or her shares to net the accrued profit or to wait in the hope of further increases in value. Shares have a value in the secondary market that depends upon people's estimate of how well the company will do in the future. They are frequently listed on either the New York or American Stock Exchange, and are traded on the exchange just like any other stock. Supply and demand will determine the price, although attention will be paid to the prevailing "net asset value" (NAV). The NAV is the value of the fund's total portfolio divided by the number of fund shares outstanding at the end of the day. Some appear in Tables 11-1 and 11-2 on pages 194–95.

Some closed-end investment companies have grown quite large, yet many were being traded at a price *below* NAV by the 1990s, hence at a discount. An example is Adams Express (ADX) on the New York Stock Exchange. It closed 1993 with an NAV of $19.62 per share, with 34.027 million shares. This yields a total investment package of nearly $670 million, trading like any industrial or utility. This company, however, trades at a price below its NAV, hence at a discount.

Despite their favorable history of capital gains, excellence of management capability demonstrated by consistency, ample diversification, and other favorable attributes, closed-end funds were considered stodgy. Sometimes there is a strange sense of "fashion" in investment selection—fashion sense, not common sense.

In the past, such funds were primarily designed for group investments within a given field of interest, such as high-grade bonds, government bonds, preferred or convertible stock, common growth equities, securities within a defined industry or trade class, emerging growth firms, or new corporations. Examples of a defined industry include chemical companies, gold companies, electronics firms, and high-technology industries. More recently, closed-end funds proliferated by region, notably in countries where investment in individual corporations by foreign investors was very difficult.

Trading at a discount to NAV or book value suggests a bargain, yet many old and excellent closed-end funds offer this advantageous pricing. Despite their histories of good capital gains, excellence of management, ample diversification, and other solid attributes, many investors simply don't care to invest in stodgy alternatives. Don't let fashion delude you. Discounted closed-end funds often prove an excellent investment over the long haul. The funds are sometimes the only way to get into certain investment areas. For example, if you want to invest within the context of the Indian subcontinent today, the only selections around are the closed-end funds.

OPEN-END INVESTMENT COMPANIES (MUTUAL FUNDS)

The open-end investment company, the true mutual fund, has proliferated to become the most common type of investment company. Imagine a closed-end fund in which each original investor contributes $1,000 to $3,000, then afterward no new investors are turned away. Mutual funds accept new investors with any equity input over an initially agreed-upon minimum, say $250 to $1,000.

The added investment revenue flowing into the fund is invested along with dividends and capital gains from the equity of earlier investors. The orientation is toward size since, through growth in assets, mutual funds can obtain higher administrative fees and offer top dollar to the best market and stock analysts. As a general rule, the bigger the mutual fund, the better the management, since higher-priced experts can be afforded. Greater size improves economies of scale in operations as well. Sometimes, however, a rapidly growing new mutual fund can outgrow its management and research capabilities, leading to poorer results, so be aware of this risk.

Mutual funds had a squirrelly reputation early in the twentieth century. Fund managers were unencumbered by restrictions regarding what were or were not prudent investments, and in the 1920s wild speculation was commonplace. Managers used margin recklessly, secured control of corporations that they mismanaged ridiculously, and pyramided profits on super-thin incoming investment levels. And they went down by the dozens in the Crash of 1929. This inspired Congressional intervention, first with the Investment Act of 1940. Margin activity became restricted, and management of mutual funds was tightly circumscribed. The ballyhooing of funds was forbidden, and public notifications became limited to what could be said in a sedate "tombstone" ad.

The results of all these new encumbrances upon the industry were dramatic and saved the industry from itself. Further reform, instituted in the Investment Act of 1970, concentrated on aspects such as commissions and the right of shareholders to bring suit for oversights in fiduciary duties. Finally, starting during the years of the Reagan administration, rampant inflation was brought under control and interest rates on passbook saving accounts and certificates of deposit dropped. This produced an outpouring of money from banks, credit unions, and savings and loans into alternative higher-yielding investments, including mutual funds.

Mutual funds are tracked and rated by several good review organizations such as Lipper, Morningstar, and Weissenberger, whose publications are available in most public libraries. The task is made difficult by the large number of mutual funds that exist and form during surging market cycles. There are several hundreds of mutual funds followed by these reviewers, but they cannot keep up with all the bank pool trusts that function like mutual funds, the number of which reaches into the thousands.

Mutual funds typically sell at a price equal to the NAV plus an upcharge that incorporates a selling fee. These are the "bid and ask" prices determined at the close of each business day and quoted in the mutual-fund section of most big-city newspapers and business dailies like the *Wall Street Journal*.

There is a bewildering array of mutual funds from which to choose. Find one whose activities reflect your own objectives and interests, or select from the fund "families" in which a set of funds are managed by the same group. At no charge, many fund groups provide the option of switching from one fund to another within the group. That can be handy. For example, if you had invested in a go-go common stock fund in high-tech issues and felt they were topping out, you could, with one phone call, switch to a bond fund or a fund specializing in metals.

A common favorite of many investors is the "balanced fund." This fund splits its portfolio between bonds or other fixed-income vehicles and common stock. Balanced funds keep a certain percentage of assets in government or corporate bonds at all times. They are the least volatile of the equity-based funds.

The Bond Fund of America, part of the American Funds Group, is a good example. It dates back to 1974, and has always provided a decent yield but a limited growth potential. Within the same family, Investment Company of America (ICA) has a record dating back to 1933. It is primarily a common-stock fund, but of a relatively conservative cast. It has the objectives of a combination of growth of principal with moderate current income. Within the Franklin-Templeton group you might consider Templeton World Fund. This, as the name implies, diversifies its investment activities on a global basis. Within the same group is Templeton Growth, which concentrates its efforts on American corporations.

The Pioneer group includes Pioneer Europe, Pioneer U.S. Government Trust, which holds only government securities, Pioneer Municipal with its tax-exempt municipal investments, and, finally, Pioneer Gold with its investments in gold-mining corporations. By a like token, Merrill Lynch has offered Capital Fund, a broad-gauge fund focused on growth of principal from corporations that are well situated in terms of size and basic market position. The group also offers the Corporate High Income Fund. This spins out its monthly payments in cash or reinvests them. Reinvesting permits a monthly compounding of an already high yield level.

For the more aggressive investor, Merrill Lynch provides Global Allocation Fund. This is worldwide, and uses both stocks and bonds. Lord Abbett Developing Growth Fund, another fund worth mentioning, provides investment specializing in smaller growth companies. Then there are the "hedge funds," offering highly speculative activity, trading on margin, going short as well as long, trading in warrants and options, and taking positions in corporations so small or new that there is nearly no market for their shares. These are probably not for the green investor and require a $100,000 minimum investment.

Your basis for deciding whether or not to invest in a given mutual fund depends on an evaluation of the nature of the fund, fund management, and consistency of performance level over time. How the fund has done recently may be misleading. What matters is the long haul. And avoid investing on banker or insurance salesman recommendations. They tend to lack the expertise necessary for making sound recommendations. More important, they lack the resources to do so.

CLOSED-END VERSUS OPEN-END FUNDS

Closed-end funds have certain definite advantages over open-end funds. Because the number of shares outstanding is fixed, the manager of a closed-end fund always knows how much money there is to work with. There is no need to keep a large cash reserve on hand for fund redemptions, particularly in a down market. The fund can remain fully invested if conditions are favorable.

Table 11-1 on page 194 lists some typical foreign closed-end funds in the mid-1990s. Note that the price for such funds usually trades at a premium over NAV. Contrast these funds with the sample of domestic or worldwide funds in Table 11-2 on page 195. Here we see a number of funds trading at discounts from NAV.

The open-end fund manager must be aware of possible redemptions and keep that cash reserve handy. Furthermore, when interest rates fall, new money flows into the open-end bond funds from bank passbooks and certificates of deposit, forcing the fund manager to constantly make new commitments. The influx of new funds when interest rates are dropping can be substantial and can cause a dilution of the high yields secured for earlier investors. This sort of problem is not going to occur with a closed-end fund.

Another possible advantage with closed-end funds is that share price is determined on the auction market. On occasion the price of the fund will show an attractive discount to the NAV; at other times there will be a premium. This can be disconcerting over the short term. You must determine what the NAV is before you buy or sell a closed-end fund so that you don't get stuck buying a fund with a steep premium or selling one at a steep discount. The NAV of closed-end funds is published weekly in the *Wall Street Journal* and other financial publications, or your financial consultant can find out for you.

With open-end funds you pay the NAV plus any load for the new shares. A minor secondary disadvantage is that they cannot be margined when you first buy the new shares, on the convention that they resemble shares coming off an IPO (initial public offering on prospectus). They must remain "long" in the account for at least thirty days before they enjoy any loan value.

How a mutual fund has done recently may be misleading, so always look for long-term performance. An example of a fund that did well one year and poorly the next is the Janus Fund. In 1991 it had a spectacular year and was praised to the stars by analysts, and of course its own management. A huge amount of money flowed into the fund as a result—just as the growth cycle flattened out. In 1992 the plateau inspired fund jockeys to bail out into cash positions, taking some losses and undoubtedly rushing onward into the next hot fund they heard about.

In 1992, Terry Edgerton published the results of a study on mutual fund performance from 1978 to 1992. He identified a group of nine mutual funds that had *never* lost money, the top five of which all yielded an annual return of over 17 percent (see Table 11-3 on page 195). Further research by Edgerton in 1993 reviewed fund performance for seventeen three-year periods (see Table 11-4 on page 195). Note that the average equity mutual fund revealed an increase more than doubling in seven years. One fund studied—Fidelity Contrafund—tripled over the period. On the risk rating side, only AIM Weingarten shows a high risk factor of 1.3. Most funds were well below 1.0. The average annual total return was 10.3 percent, with the star, Fidelity Contrafund, returning no less than 19.9 percent for the preceding seventeen three-year periods!

You see why mutual funds are considered so attractive.

LOAD VERSUS NO-LOAD FUNDS

Turning to mutual fund commissions, there are several alternatives.

The spread between the bid and ask price is called the "load." For some funds the load is zero. These are termed the "no-load" funds, but beware: there is no free lunch. Someone has to pay for all the advertising and management fees, and in this case it is done by passing on costs to the investor through deductions from earnings.

In many cases there is an initial load of from 4 to 6.5 percent of the purchase price, with discounts for larger investments, such as $50,000 or more. The commission is charged up front when you buy, and there is no commission when you sell. It's not that different from your experience in investing in any single stock you might choose.

A variation on this is to back-load, meaning that you pay when you sell. This is common among leading brokerage firms today, which offer A and B shares to buyers. The A shares carry the full 4.5 to 6.5 percent initial fee, but the B shares carry no front-end load. If you sell within a year of purchase, you pay the full commission at the time of sale. If you retain your position for one year, the commission drops by at least 1 percent, and thereafter commissions continue to decrease yearly until no commission cost remains. These funds also have 12B-1 charges, a "maintenance" charge of varying amounts, which are charged to the fund on a monthly basis. Today the 12B-1 fees in many cases disappear in about seven years.

Perhaps it is no accident that the top funds happen to be funds with commissions. Like many other aspects of life, you seem to get what you pay for. Some of the large funds manage to hire and retain the best analysts and stock selectors for prolonged periods with a due payoff for investors. However, this said, it must also be admitted that there are some excellent no-load funds around. The choice is therefore not a simple one.

MUTUAL FUNDS AND THE SMALL INVESTOR

Because of performance, mutual funds are highly attractive investment alternatives to the new investor. Let's see how our several small investors from back in chapter 1 might get involved with their choice of a fund.

Retired Colonel Robert Richardson has a secured, if nominal, pension from the army, plus Social Security benefits. He would probably be best off with something like Merrill Lynch Corporate High Yield Bond Fund B, where good management has produced both high yield and gradual growth.

Dr. William Malone, the successful surgeon, learned a lot from his unfortunate initial forays into investment, namely that he ought to concentrate on being a surgeon and leave his equity to work with as little hassle as possible. He and his wife decided to set up a custodianship for each of their three children, using half their investment equity. The balance of their equity now goes into one of the great tax-exempt mutual funds in the Nuveen Series.

Our young engineer, Edward Elkins, now in early middle age and having found fairly secure employment, decided with his wife that Capital Fund B and a closed-end high-income fund such as ACM Managed High Income Fund, trading on the New York Stock Exchange, were right for them. The young nurse, Nancy MacAshan, wound up splitting her investments between sound long-range growth and income. She selected Investment Company of America, with its long and enviable record of performance, for half her equity. The rest she put into Zenix Income Fund, a closed-end fund carefully using junk bonds to achieve quite high interest rates.

CONCLUSION

Recent studies of mutual fund performance have documented excellent performance in general. At comparatively low risk, average annual total returns have recently been above 10 percent and stars have weighed in with returns of nearly 20 percent over long periods of time. In short, for the beginning investor—and for that matter, part of nearly anyone's equity—using the services of an investment company makes obvious good sense.

TABLE 11-1:
CLOSED-END FOREIGN COUNTRY FUNDS PROFILE
(IN U.S. DOLLARS, TO 1992)

Fund	Last Share Price	Net Asset Value	Price (Two Decade Period)
Argentina Fund	17.13	14.09	12.00–17.38
China Fund	28.25	20.04	11.25–28.75
India Growth Fund	28.50	19.33	8.13–30.50
Japan Equity Fund	15.00	12.30	8.13–15.13
Japan OTC Equity Fund	9.88	9.05	7.13–10.88
Mexico Fund	39.00	35.71	1.81–40.38
Portugal Fund	14.13	12.42	8.50–20.25
Spain Fund	11.00	10.45	9.00–39.00

TABLE 11-2:
SELECTED DOMESTIC CLOSED-END FUNDS
(IN U.S. DOLLARS, TO 1994)

Fund	Last Share Price	Net Asset Value	Discount or Premium	Current Yield %
America's All Season	4.31	5.24	(17.70)	1.8
Clemente Global Growth	11.25	12.36	(9.00)	5.0
Gemini II Income	11.63	9.44	23.10	16.4
MFS Special Value	17.63	15.67	12.50	3.1
Pacific American Income	16.38	16.45	(0.50)	7.6
Pilgrim Prime Rate	9.13	10.01	(8.80)	6.5
Templeton Emerg. Markets	27.75	22.90	20.70	1.0
Templeton Global Util.	17.00	15.57	9.20	3.4
USLife Income	10.50	10.54	(0.40)	8.6
Worldwide Value	16.63	18.46	(9.80)	0.6

TABLE 11-3:
THE "FAB FIVE" MUTUAL FUNDS (%)

Fund	Compound Annual Gain to 4/1/92				
	1978–1992	10 Yrs. %	5 Yrs. %	3 Yrs. %	Load %
CGM Mutual	15.0	17.9	10.3	17.0	None
Invest. Co. of Amer.	16.6	18.5	10.5	14.8	5.75
John Hancock Sovereign	15.6	17.2	10.2	16.6	5.00
Merrill Lynch Cap. A	16.9	17.3	10.6	14.1	6.50
Phoenix Growth	20.2	20.3	11.5	17.6	4.75

TABLE 11-4:
SELECTED FUNDS SHOWING CONSISTENT PERFORMANCE (%)

Fund	Avg. Ret. 17 3-Yr. Periods	Ret. Last 12 Months	$10,000 After 7 Yrs.	Risk Rating	Load %
AIM Weingarten	16.8	1.0	$30,021	1.3	5.5
Fidelity Contrafund	19.9	16.3	$34,860	0.7	3.0
IDEX	19.6	4.5	$31,682	0.9	8.5
IDS New Dimensions	16.9	9.3	$31,075	0.9	5.0
Janus	18.2	9.4	$29,943	0.7	None
Olympus Stock	15.9	5.6	$28,201	0.9	4.8
Average Fund	10.3	9.3	$23,468	1.0	N.A.

12
COMMON INVESTOR MISTAKES

CHARLES L. FAHY AND LAWRENCE LYNN

CHANGING OBJECTIVES

Get a coherent plan, implement it, stay with it, and it will work just fine.

What plan? Just about any regular, cautious program will do. The main thing is to not change directions all the time, starting with one objective and shifting to another at irregular intervals. Yet that is exactly what most investors do. Investors repeatedly jump ship on a good strategy just because it hasn't worked so well lately. They almost invariably abandon it at precisely the wrong time.

John Templeton, one of the greatest value investment managers of all time, has had occasions when his stocks underperformed the averages for up to four years before surging ahead. Investors who deserted him during the down periods, ignoring his wisdom about long-term results, have lived to regret their decisions. A solid, consistent plan will almost always serve you well.

UNREALISTIC EXPECTATIONS

The simple truth is that success in investment usually requires more than a modicum of patience and the passage of time. It is the cumulative effect of constant investment, the correction of bad moves, and reinvestment of capital gains, dividends, and interest.

Investors can, and novices frequently do, have unrealistic expectations from their investments. No small part of this may be the contribution of unscrupulous vendors of investments—brokers, insurance salesmen, and financial advisers. They talk up their wares in extravagant fashion because they want you to put down your money, earning them commissions. The stock exchanges and other responsible agencies try to restrain such practices, with mixed success.

One gimmick these folks use to make your blood race is the compound interest factor. A single dollar, if invested in a stock earning 12 percent annually, will over a period of 15 years increase in value by 5.474 times. At 18 percent, the dollar will increase by 11.974 times. That's great, but only the very best investments pay at this range. That little fact may be overlooked when a sales pitch is being made.

The "rule of 72" is another exciting invocation. The rule is a mathematical generalization used to estimate the amount of time it will take for an investment equity to double in value. Find the answer by dividing the number 72 by the interest rate in question. For example, at a 12 percent rate of return it will take about six years (72/12) for an investment to double. Wow! Where do I sign, and what stock was that again . . . ? As ever, learn to distinguish between a smoke-and-mirrors pitch and a solid discussion of pros and cons.

In the early stages of investing your goal is to keep equity abreast of currency devaluation; later you will begin maximizing profits. A mature investment portfolio is one in which there is modest personal use of profits and maximum reinvestment. The guiding *principle* is to continually enlarge *principal.*

Let me make a pronouncement on the idea of getting rich quick through investment. Although this is not impossible, it just won't happen to most people, and they should understand this up front. Even with a well-planned and logical program, the best way to look at investment is as a way to salt equity away in the face of inevitable currency slippage. If things work out, and you get moderately or seriously financially healthy, it's the cherry on top of the sundae.

A lot of people don't want to hear that, and when investment doesn't make them millions from peanuts, they give up and quit. Some terminate their efforts at the very moment when they should have redoubled them. They wind up spending their money on transitory, ephemeral pleasures and late in life have to trust in the dubious promises of Social Security, corporate annuities, or relatives for support, getting much less enjoyment in their golden years. Patience is a prerequisite for financial success, and success means maintaining or increasing equity, not the attainment of vast, shameless ostentation.

LOOKING WHERE YOU ARE GOING

The most common error investors of all types and with all types of equity make is to not plan coherently. No, I take that back. The most common error is to not plan at all.

It has nothing to do with intelligence. It has to do with being preoccupied, living life to the fullest, and wandering into investment haphazardly. Moreover, most of the tomes on the subject are so formidably boring that they might better be used by anesthesiologists rather than as a means of transmitting information. As a result, investors wanting to protect their equity, and maybe see it grow some, tend to bet their marbles with unstudied and almost utter incompetence.

The profile averages out like this hypothetical example.

Dr. Leon Martin was born in San Antonio to a poor blue-collar family. Early on he found that he loved to read, and this along with his family's belief in the value of hard work led to success in school. He won a National Merit Scholarship, shot through the University of Texas in three and a half years, got grant support to study at Baylor Medical School, and became a skilled surgeon with a splendid practice in Houston. Along the way he married his high-school sweetheart. Their home in a suburb was animated by their three young children.

Dr. Martin knew plenty about biology, and both he and his wife are quick studies in general, but when his practice suddenly kicked off in the first wash of money they had ever known, what to do with it became a big question mark. They cautiously bought a home well within their income, intending to pay it off early. They bought smaller, less expensive vehicles. One vacation a year to the Caribbean or closer was enough to satisfy them. That left a lot of money lying around waiting for use.

Perhaps it tied back in to his roots,when he would visit relatives on a small ranch near Corpus Christi, but when Dr. Martin heard that raising Arabian stallions was a good tax shelter, he found the idea quite appealing. He and his wife found a spread for sale about one hour's drive north of Houston in the rolling country of Washington County and bought some Arabian mares. They expected to raise fine Arabians for sale to racing people, and because they knew nothing about raising horses the day-to-day supervision of the place was turned over to a young man in the neighborhood who had experience as a cowboy. The Martins would come up to see what was going on once in a while, as their increasingly hectic schedule permitted.

Within a few years, it seemed reasonable to start putting money into securities. They first invested in a group of biogenetic research and development companies in the United States and Europe. Being bilingual led Dr. Martin to buy stocks on the Bolsa de Valores in Mexico City, but information was hard to get on how they were doing. When they heard about the astronomic rise in the Nikkei Dow Jones averages in Tokyo, they got in on many Japanese securities. After all, the price/earnings ratio (PE) had reached over 50 for many of them and this seemed to show that they had no place to go except up.

After a few more years they branched out farther, first into real estate. They bought three town homes in a spiffy section of Houston, intending to rent them out for a good profit and benefit from the boom in real estate prices. And they bought a good sized group of municipal bonds and several municipal bond monthly payment trust certificates. Dr. Martin made this type of investment because he wanted to avoid additional taxable earnings.

It was like the federal government throwing money at programs. For a while all was well, then some big problems began to develop. The Arabian horse ranch provided solid, continuous losses, as planned. The only trouble was that the federal tax regulations don't permit continual losses to be written off forever. The Internal Revenue Service people want to see a profit every few years, the Martin's new tax adviser cautioned them, otherwise they don't consider a venture to be a serious business enterprise. Since the ranch could not be made profitable, it transformed on the spot into a nondeductible hobby and a flat, unsheltered loss.

Bad news comes in clusters. On the heels of the word about the ranch, the Mexican stocks inexplicably plunged to an all-time low. Well, that was a business loss at least, to report and deduct on a Schedule D at tax time. Not exactly, the tax adviser informed them. Allowable deductions stop at $3,000 per year! It didn't begin to match Dr. Martin's lost equity.

The cloud forming overhead darkened. The purchases on the Tokyo market were made just before the snorting Nikkei Dow Jones got the vapors and dropped to and through the floor. "Precipitous decline" doesn't begin to describe it. The PEs of the 50 vanished like smoke in a cyclone and along with them most of the Martins' Oriental equity.

Well, things were bad, but the town homes would help make up the losses. They had spent a fortune on decorating and outfitting, making them outstandingly attractive. Beauty and charm don't mean a thing, however, if your rentals stand empty! The real estate market had been booming; now, overbuilt, it stopped climbing, plateaued, and hit the slides. Trying to cut their losses here, they finally dropped their monthlies to prices that got renters to sign on. What a relief, except for the fact that the rental payments didn't cover mortgage, taxes, and maintenance fees. To get out from under, they sold the town homes for far less than they had paid for them, losing both there and on the decoration expenses.

The one bright glimmer was from the mutual funds. These plodded on as if part of a propagation service, not investments subject to influence from economic fluctuations.

It was fortunate that Dr. Martin was a good surgeon. He never reached the point of disaster from his investment fiascos, something which might easily have struck someone without the same direct income. But it was somewhere between maddening and frightening to realize on his fortieth birthday that, after a decade of working at a high income, all he and his family had left were their home, their vehicles, and a few mutual fund shares.

This story has been repeated endlessly. Let us out of charity draw the curtain on the hapless Martins and get on with this chapter. They still have time to build up college funds for their children, to set up a retirement program, to set growth of principal as a key objective, and to hire the professional help required to guide them. Others have not been so lucky.

POORLY TIMED SELLING

If sheer disorganization and ignorance define the classic investment bozo, the next most common type of blunderer is the individual who panics and sells at the worst possible moment. Securities start to tumble when the market takes a dip, and out of fear the investor bails out in order to preserve equity.

But a rule of life in the stock market is: what goes down must come up. Usually. If you have checked your key indicators, then watched the charts to see the best time to buy, you ought to have investments that will ride out most storms. You shouldn't sell securities just because at the moment bidding has knocked them down in value. It is better in the long run to endure short-term opportunity costs than to lose equity.

Of course, sometimes you get trapped. You might find yourself holding on to an investment that you should unload because no one wants it. Poor liquidity can get you, too, particularly in real estate.

Limited partnerships can put you in a similar situation. This happened a lot during the 1980s. Presumably, partners were warned that no regular secondary market existed for their $5,000 or $10,000 units of partnership in such investments as shopping centers, hotels, and apartment complexes. Or maybe they weren't told. There are brokers around who, assuming it is general knowledge, forget to discuss the full array of possible risks when closing a sale. And some who know just don't tell you. The fact remains that a lot of partners lost their shirts on nose-diving partnerships that couldn't be given away.

It is also true that many investors trap themselves psychologically into poor timing with more liquid investments such as bonds and stocks. There are two main ways in which investors have done this to themselves: holding on to a souring position, and exiting too early from a sound investment. In either case the results are the same—bad.

The first timing folly is the easiest to understand, if usually after the fact. You purchase a security, say, 300 shares at $68 per share based on supposedly sound reasoning. After the purchase the stock begins to drop, suggesting that perhaps your analysis was not so hot after all. Then some bad news comes out concerning the stock's corporation and it decreases again, more steeply. Many people have the tendency to be dogmatic about their decision making and do not easily admit to having made a mistake. Despite the trajectory downward, which indicates an unusually deep plunge and a possibly long time to recover, you hold on to the stock, perhaps deluding yourself that the data lies and the stock will defy reason and come back quickly.

If it declined from $68 to $62, then quickly to $55, a stock is intensifying its decline. A canny, watchful investor would get out somewhere between $60 and $55; you, on the other hand, decide to wait at least until it recovers to $60 before selling. But once underway, the forces causing the drop persist and down, down the price goes. It reaches $40 and you tell yourself that you might as well hold on because it must be close to a turning point. Naturally, that's not the case; it then declines to $25 and plateaus. Only when totally defeated do you finally sell—at which point it begins to rise.

This sort of error could have been avoided by close monitoring and unambiguous damage control. The best thing to do when a stock goes over the waterfall is to admit error and to take your medicine at a small loss. Any poker player will tell you that wishful thinking will never turn a bad hand into a good one. Toss it in and try again next time.

Perhaps the situation is an option position in which a group of naked calls have been written. The underlying common stock is rising with momentum, evidenced by good volume in trading. It approaches the strike price for which the call was sold early in the holding period. The smart thing to do is to admit error and close the position by buying the option to cover, or buying the underlying stock, converting to a covered position. By doing either trade you are guaranteed a loss, but a sting instead of the coming body blow if the strike price is surpassed.

Doggedly holding on to a souring investment is mirrored by selling a good position too early. You pick up 300 shares of a stock at $68, which then promptly rises to $70, then $75, a strong upward trend. You sell the stock at $75, in mid-rise, because you will realize a profit of $8 per share. This is thinking like a speculator, a gambler: get yours and get out quickly with some pocket money before the blasted stock tumbles. It isn't even intelligent gambling, because the stock is increasing its velocity upward, not tapering at the peak.

Always remember that major gains are rarely made through in-and-out trading. Long-range maintenance of positions is where the fortunes are created, through equity enlargement. The only one who usually gains from in-and-out trading is the broker, not the individual, because the broker gets commissions up or down. It is a rare broker who energetically will caution clients about jumping around, and not just because of the commissions. If the client turns out to be right and the broker argued against a trade, he looks incompetent, perhaps endangering his relationship with the client. If the trade bombs, the broker can cluck sympathetically, but not as a responsible party.

The general rule in all this is to study a potential move carefully, then let profits compound—but keep a wary eye out for signs of severe drops and take steps to cut losses early.

OVERDIVERSIFICATION

When persons of moderate means find a lump sum in hand, perhaps inherited or as the result of a job change, many of them dive into investment only aware that a wise man spreads his risks. This negativist investing is possessed of several hazards, particularly if the investments aren't watched closely.

Say you are a crackerjack young engineer whose designs are so good that you are interviewed and profiled in a national journal. Several firms immediately contact you with offers, and your own

company counters with a big promotion, a free vacation, and a sign-
ing bonus of $10,000. After the paid-for celebration trip on a cruise
ship through the Leeward Islands, you decide to invest the bonus
in solid stocks.

You are a systematic type of person and spend several evenings
in your public library learning the rudiments of investment theory
and how to pick healthy securities. You read Standard & Poor's,
Value Line sheets, and Moody's reports, and wind up picking 20
corporations whose earnings look good and whose key indicators
are all one might want to see. Since they all look good, you buy
$500 worth of each and get back to work being a crackerjack en-
gineer.

The $500 plunked down for twenty shares of Carnival Cruise
Lines (CCL), picked both for its record and because CCL had
hosted your cruise, turns out to have been a good choice. CCL goes
up from $25 per share to $40 per share over the next two years, an
increase of $15. Stated another way, that's 30 percent per year, a
most satisfying equity gain.

Unhappily, elsewhere all is not well. Because you are very busy
and don't trouble to monitor all twenty stock issues, when you learn
the good news about CCL you learn the bad news overall. Some of
your stocks have decreased slightly in value over the same time
period, enough to erase the CCL gain. At the end of the two years
your equity is essentially what you started with. Since currency devaluation has skipped along to a two-year total of 8 percent, you
have lost 8 percent of your equity.

That's no way to run a railroad.

What were your errors? There were several. You purchased issues in such small quantities that you could not buy in "round lots"
of 100 shares each. The small quantities were also subject to the
minimum commission charges brokers charge to discourage minimal purchases, amounting to an exorbitant commission percentage
(most brokerage houses have a minimum fee of $35 to $65 per
transaction). If you had wanted to, you couldn't possibly have written covered options on your tiny blocks of securities, meaning the
elimination of collecting covered option premiums on them, a potential 15 to 20 percent profit per year. And because you were too
busy to keep track of all the stocks, you didn't prune out weaklings

when earnings reports and price changes dictated early on that you should do so.

It would have been a lot better to buy more of fewer stocks, or just to have your broker put the $10,000 into a few mutual funds until you had the time and interest to think about investments in a bit more detail. Think: If your purchase in CCL had been 100 shares instead of 20, an outlay of $2,500, the $15 per share profit would have translated into a portfolio gain of $1,500 even if the mutuals just kept even. Your gross being 15 percent profit on the $10,000 less 8 percent currency devaluation, your net equity profit would have been 7 percent. And that's before you pulled in profits from options, if you got into them.

Don't feel too bad. Now you know better, and at least you broke even during your learning experience. Under similar circumstances, many a novice investor winds up with a solid loss.

UNDERDIVERSIFICATION

The polar opposite of overdiversification is underdiversification.

You are a young flight attendant based in Chicago, flying domestic turns as you wait for the seniority that will give you a shot at the glamour runs to Japan and Europe. Your fiancé is an exploration geologist who relocated to Houston after college, where the two of you will live when you marry next year. The free airline passes mean that you are able to spend plenty of time together as you plan your married life.

The surprise death of your unmarried great-aunt brings you a bequest of $10,000. What do you do with it?

Your fiancé has been involved in the recent crude oil discoveries near Lake Maracaibo in Venezuela and has access to news about the high petroleum production potential of fields in several parts of South America. You use his tips, a sort of insider information, as the basis for investing the $10,000 in an oil company with drilling rights to good fields in Colombia. The stock trades at $60 per share. Alert vaguely to the advantages of buying stock in round lots of 100 shares each, you understand that a round lot here will cost you some $6,000. Your inheritance leaves you short by $2,000 from having enough money for two round lots. What to do? Use $6,000 here, and use the remaining $4,000 for something else?

You have found out a little about the oil company before buying in. It paid a dividend of $3.95 during the past year, a percentage rate of 6.6 percent. And you have also learned the tantalizing entrancements of buying on margin. You reason that if last year's dividend returns are repeated, and why shouldn't they be, the dividend will cover borrowing $2,000 to buy that much more stock on margin. Paying $160 for the use of $2,000 so that extra shares can be obtained, contributing their part to an expected profit next year of $790, seems magical. Why, the profit itself will pay off the $160, leaving a net profit for the year of $630. According to your calculator, that net is 5.25 percent, more than passbook savings or certificates of deposit could get you. So you set up a margin account based on your $10,000, acquire $12,000 in this equity (200 × $60), use margin to pay for $2,000 to fill out buying two round lots, and you and your fiancé congratulate each other on the sophistication with which you are entering investments. How can you lose?

Here's how. The oil company had been earning over $7.00 per share a few years ago, then dropped to $1.70 at the start of the oil crunch, and staggered up to $2.20 a year later. Despite holding good drilling rights abroad, the plateauing demand for petroleum-diluted benefits from potential exploration hurt the company. It managed to divest and downsize enough to jink the dividend up to the $3.95 you heard about. Your first payout after your purchase makes only $1.40 per share! And a management shake-up during the reorganization process caused stock prices to free-fall to $46 per share by year's end.

The unappealing consequences are several. Your investment equity on the 200 shares has dropped in value from $12,000 at $60 per share to $9,200 at $46 per share; moreover, you have the unpaid $2,000 margin debt hanging over you. That means an actual equity of only $7,200. Your net loss has been 28 percent in less than six months. In addition, you are having sleepless nights agonizing over the further decline that can be expected, not to mention the instability of the oil company's dividend.

Your most serious error was to put everything into a single investment. You should have selected two to four different issues, ideally in different, unconnected industries. You made your investment decision on a tip from your fiancé, based on unchecked "insider" information. Because you used a discount broker, you got no advice to the contrary. You get what you pay for with the discounts, which is the bare-bones trade, period. The discount broker probably couldn't have given any coherent advice anyway, since discount brokers tend to be young, underpaid, and underinformed. A broker in a conventional firm might have cautioned you about the impending problems of that oil company, and, for that matter, throughout the oil industry in general.

OVERREACHING

Whether new trader or old, on occasion the allure of profit can get one's blood up and pulsing. Imagine it: You can make money simply by ordering securities trades! Why, it's better than chocolate! So you fall into the trap of madly trading, trading, trading—past the point of common sense.

This commonplace error comes in several forms. One is hyperactivity in and of itself. You spot great securities and want to jump aboard, but because of equity limitations you have to get rid of something you already have in order to buy. You make changes in your portfolio before earlier investments have fully achieved their potential. You rush and rush until "frenetic" doesn't begin to describe the situation. It's a great way to earn yourself a stroke along with millionaire status, assuming that all goes well with that hair-trigger whipping about.

This can also come about without direct involvement. Some wealthy individuals with large accounts and nil interest in securities, perhaps with a fascination for the arts, assign discretionary power to a broker about handling their equity affairs. The broker, wielding the vast power of a large portfolio, may either simply get caught up in the matter of maximizing profits or unwittingly (or wittingly) wander into maximizing commissions for himself by moving equity around for no good reason. Excessive discretionary trading—"churning"—has resulted in angry altercations when discovered by clients.

Since the time a half century ago when the Supreme Court relieved the federal docket of securities litigation, such cases are heard by an arbitration panel, and justice usually boils down to an agreed-upon fine. The safe bet is to not assign discretionary powers to your broker unless you know him extremely well or he is a close family member. Maybe not even then.

Another form of overreaching is the excessive use of margin for your account. This is not to damn or condemn the use of margin accounts; margin may be a worthwhile and powerful tool with which to augment income. Yet it can cause disasters if used imprudently. A useful rule of thumb is to use margin very conservatively, only to the extent that it can be covered from other resources without undue stress. If the entire market craters, as it did in 1929 and in 1987, high degrees of margin can bring in painful maintenance calls. The novice investor should probably never extend himself past 10 percent of a margin account's potential. Also, use margin for defined time periods and periodically clear it out entirely. A dormant margin account makes for better sleeping patterns.

Another type of overreaching is in the use of options, particularly naked ones. Admittedly, a sound program of covered option writing can actually be a conservative way to increase income, and a cautious naked option program can produce exciting results. However, writing naked options is fraught with peril for beginners and pros alike. Such programs can easily lead to catastrophic results if the investor doesn't pay close attention to what is going on. Many a charging optimist has overwritten calls in a fast, upwardly moving market and gotten caught by a load of short sales that abruptly had to be covered. Also, an excessive position in sold puts in a severely downtrending market can create rushing put assignments and dread Reg T calls, maintenance calls, or both, beyond someone's liquidity. Either scenario can lead to the total vaporization of an estate.

You might wonder if your broker will try to make sure you don't overwrite options or don't use margin excessively. Alas, usually they won't. Brokers are human and out for themselves first and foremost, meaning an interest in commissions overrides any notions of warning off the foolhardy. This is true even in a full-service broker-age firm. If you want to cut your own throat, few brokers will try to stop you.

TRADING ON IMPULSE

An amazing amount of stock trading is carried on based upon noth-ing more than sheer whim. People see a stock going up in price and buy; they see a stock going down and sell. The mindlessness of responses never ceases to dumbfound investment professionals, and it causes no end of hardship to the ignorant, worried people behind the buying and selling.

The typical story goes like this.

A bull market is raging with speculators in and out of the market, snapping up their money and running. Many more cautious long-term investors are being swept along by the furious trading, taking advantage of the abounding opportunities. Everyone seems to be making money on the upswing and the fabulous profits are making the newspapers.

Without telling his wife, Jerry decides to make his family some money in the stock market. When he and Catherine arrive home from work one day he tells her that he has just bought 500 shares of a new, rising corporation selling at $10 a share. Just a couple of days ago it was at $7; in a couple of more days they can sell and reap a quick profit.

Catherine first wants to know where the tip came from, and sec-ond, where the money to invest surfaced. Jerry explains that his golfing buddy's stockbroker got him in at $2 six months ago and was predicting that it would go to $15 a share inside a year. The money came from the savings account into which they had for sev-eral years been putting away a nest egg to pay for their two chil-dren's college educations.

Catherine is nervous about the whole business, but the plunge has been made and everything seems secure. If the stock behaves as predicted, their saved equity will soon have jumped by 50 per-cent, after which they can pull out and open a passbook account again.

Now what's the first thing that happens when you buy stock? Inevitably, the price dips. Sure enough, Jerry's great $10 stock immediately drops to $8 and the spouses have some words, mostly Catherine's impressions of how insightful Jerry was to risk their money in the stock market.

So the next day Jerry sells the stock. What happens when you sell a stock? It goes up. Sure enough, within forty-eight hours the unloaded stock reinvigorates and leaps up to $12 a share. Jerry and Catherine have more words, the subject this time being what you can guess.

In order to retrieve their losses, and because the stock clearly was on the rise after all, the next day Jerry and Catherine buy 500 shares back at $12 a share. They use the equity of the college savings plus every last cent available to make the distance on the shares.

With the inevitability of a law of thermodynamics, the stock immediately goes down to $11 a share. Jerry and Catherine wait anxiously for it to rise again, but it doesn't. Over the next few months it plateaus, then drops back to $10 a share. The couple decides to sell the stock at $10 a share—what do they know about securities, anyway?—and bite the bullet on losses. They do so, and as if awaiting the opportunity to mock them, the stock finally does as predicted in the first place and leaps to $15 a share.

That's the way it goes. Jerry and Catherine bought and sold hastily and without guidance, and the only person who made money on their foray into the stock market was the broker who handled their action.

They would have been better off in Joe's unwitting shoes. Joe is a forty-year veteran dockworker foreman with a major oil corporation. When, as a young man, he signed papers to begin work, he rushed through the process and didn't pay close attention to what verbiage he was acknowledging. He had never been much at reading, anyway. Imagine his total surprise four decades later when he found that he had agreed to a benefits program wherein the company automatically deducted 15 percent of his net income and salted it away for him. He had now amassed some $565,000! Joe was able to retire at sixty-five. He handed over his equity to a sea-

soned stockbroker, who used it to create a carefully planned investment program for him. Not counting Social Security benefits, Joe
now has a retirement income of at least $50,000 a year.

You see that haste does indeed make waste, and a long-term,
systematic, tax-deferred, compounding, dollar-cost averaging, accumulating stock account can make up for a lot of ignorance.

MISINTERPRETING THE ROLE OF BONDS

You see them advertised on television. You read about them in re-
spectable magazines and newspapers. Your next-door neighbor
owns some, and so does your doctor and your second cousin. What
are they?

Government bonds.

You might say that everyone is jumping on the "bond wagon."
They're touted as safe and high-yielding; some are tax-free; some
are low in commission. What more could you ask for?

A better return to investment, for one thing. Repeated studies
of relative performance among securities over a considerable period show that the returns on corporate stocks and bonds have exceeded inflation about two-thirds of the time, whereas treasury
bills exceeded inflation only about one-third of the time. A $100
investment in stocks at the end of 1925 would have been worth
more than $50,000 in 1990; a $100 investment in Treasury bills
would have brought in a paltry $942.

Tax-free municipal bonds seem charming because of the break
on taxation. Tax-planning accountants like them for that reason;
after all, their whole existence is devoted to keeping as much
money out of government hands as possible. But here's the caveat:
you have to be fairly well-off for the tax angle to do you much good.

When you read a prospectus on a tax-exempt bond fund you
commonly see the bland assertion that a 7 percent tax-free municipal has the same earning power as a 10 percent rate of return elsewhere. The trick here is that the calculation assumes that you are
in the 30 percent tax bracket; most of us are actually in the 20
percent bracket, meaning that the bond's yield is only 8.75, not 10

percent. The tax-equivalent charts that accompany municipal bond information sheets are irrelevant to all but the wealthy.

New investors should therefore recognize government bonds for what they are: convenient temporary parking places for equity. When inflation tapers for a while, they will yield a moderate return. When inflation takes off, the bondholder inevitably loses ground.

THE PROSPECTUS

Remember that stockbrokers vary in education, intelligence, and scruples. They make money by moving product, just like any other salesman. The broker is not your pal. He's in business. Whether a security is healthy or ill, the broker earns a commission by carrying out the transaction of buying or selling for you. So it is up to you to bear the responsibility for determining what to do with your equity.

Never be satisfied with short-term performance data sheets on a stock. If a broker tries to get you to buy something based upon very recent history, this is not full disclosure. You need ten-, twenty-, even thirty-year performance histories. These data are readily available in advisory reports commonly accessible to brokers in their own offices.

Many investors are persuaded to buy securities based upon flashy sales "slicks" oozing patriotic symbolism by featuring full-color photos of American flags and eagles. The actual prospectus is a small, dull booklet filled with microscopic print written as taxingly as possible. Here is where everything must be spelled out by law, but the law doesn't guarantee that the text should be jargonless or easily understood. Take it home and read it anyway.

CONCLUSION

You're going to make mistakes as you learn the ropes in investing. Just don't repeat the ones discussed here, however, and you will find the way a lot easier.

As to other blunders? There are as many possibilities as there are investment opportunities, so take conservative steps, pay attention, and learn from your own mistakes. Trust what you understand, not what someone asserts. Make no snap decisions, and play for the long haul. There will be bumps here and there, but you can ride them out.

13

RETIREMENT PLANNING

KENNETH G. ALTVATER

Everyone knows that he or she should put aside savings for retirement, but only a few individuals actually do so with any regularity, or at all. Current needs and wants seem pressing, and after all, retirement is way off there somewhere in the distant future. That future begins to loom menacingly around the time the last offspring leaves home, at which point most people have a remaining work life of only ten to fifteen years. The sprint to do something about the gap almost always develops into a lot less attractive retirement situation than would be preferred—but by then it's too late.

The worst case is to count on Social Security as a fallback alternative. Those who find themselves relying totally on Social Security in retirement wind up living in poverty, nothing less. Social Security is not, nor was it ever intended to be, a retirement program. It was designed during the Great Depression to help out the worst-hit aged, and later evolved into a sacred cow that would supplement income from individual retirement savings and company-sponsored retirement plans.

Another thing: Social Security is on the verge of receivership. Total payments have risen to an extraordinary degree as people live longer and elders have lobbied for greater support. Unless something dramatic happens, Social Security won't even be available shortly after the turn of the twenty-first century. All the more reason to take charge of one's own affairs instead of trusting them to Uncle Sam.

ADVANTAGES OF BENEFIT PLANS

For several decades, corporate retirement planning has spread as one attraction to get and hold good employees. We may be poorly equipped with the resolve to save and invest by ourselves, but paying into a managed plan is a different matter. It's just like paying bills, or a mortgage; after a while, you expect the payment and build your personal budget around it. The good part is watching the numbers go up and up, and knowing that there will indeed be something for you when you retire.

Tax legislation has helped make employee benefit plans quite attractive. For one thing, plans are protected from creditors. Plan participants may not pledge, collateralize, assign, loan, or offer their balances as security for any reason. As a result, Federal law protects those balances from creditors. If the company goes broke, the plan funds will still be there.

Deposits and earnings accumulate tax-free until the time retirement payments are actually received by the employee. When distributions are received at retirement, you may have no taxable income from another source, meaning that the benefit payments should be taxed at a low rate. You also have the potential of rolling the dollars over into a tax-deferred individual retirement account (IRA) or, if available, choosing some type of income-averaging if you prefer to get the entire distribution.

If you own a company, you probably play two roles: you are both the employer and the highest-paid employee. As an employer, you may receive a tax deduction on the plan contribution you regularly make; as an employee, and the one with the highest salary, you should receive back the largest share of the contribution. And you will receive a tax-deferred accumulation on the contribution you made in your role as the employer. Frequently, in smaller companies (under twenty-five employees) the tax savings alone will take care of the cost of covering the rank-and-file employees. It sounds almost dishonest that all these benefits accrue. It isn't.

In order for a company's plan to be qualified under Section 401(a) of the Internal Revenue Code, it must be recorded in a document that contains all the Internal Revenue Service rules and regulations concerning plans of its type. The plan must be permanent and must be for the exclusive benefit of all the employees—not just the highly compensated employees. The employers must keep their plans sound. In the case of a profit-sharing plan, contributions must be both "substantial and recurring."

The United States Supreme Court has verified that corporate plan balances are protected from creditors. This protection, however, has not yet been clarified in the case of plans covering owners exclusively, self-employed individuals with employees, and partners. These and individual retirement accounts (IRAs), simplified employee pensions (SEPs), and salary reduction simplified employee pensions (SARSEPs) must currently rely on state laws for protection from creditors. Since not all states offer this reliably, the qualified corporate plan approach offers the best overall security for retirement planners.

PERSONAL RETIREMENT PLANS

The simplest retirement plan is the individual retirement account. Under this plan you may deduct up to $2,000 per year, tax-free, unless you or your spouse is covered by an employer-sponsored plan. In that case, the ceiling of deduction may be smaller. Also, the higher your gross income, the lower the deduction from income at tax time. At some level of income, variable depending on family status and adjusted periodically by Congress, the contribution becomes nondeductible, making it necessary for the participant to weigh whether there is a sufficient benefit from future tax-deferred income to warrant making the contribution right now.

Along the lines of the IRA is the "403(b) annuity." This plan is generally available to tax-exempt organizations, school teachers, college professors, and others in similar fields. In the 403(b) plan you may enter into an agreement with the employer to deposit part of your salary into the 403(b) annuity. The employer has the option of matching part of this contribution. The dollars that are contributed are "before tax" dollars and the income earned on the dollars accumulates on a tax-deferred basis.

DEFINED BENEFIT PLANS

With the passage of the Tax Equity and Fiscal Responsibility Act (TEFRA) in 1982, and additional supporting legislation, plans for sole proprietors and partnerships were afforded substantially the same scope as plans for corporations. All Employee Retirement Income Security Act plans are now under uniform rules and regulations, and are classified according to their funding approach.

The standard of the employee benefit plan industry is the "defined benefit plan." This type of plan remains popular among larger companies; smaller companies tend to avoid it because of the complex rules, regulations, and administrative costs surrounding plan design and maintenance.

There are four basic types of defined benefit plans. The first is a "fixed benefit plan." Here all participants receive the same size of retirement benefits, for example, $500 per month. The second type is a "flat benefit plan" in which the return is based on salary. All participants receive the same percentage of former salary as a monthly retirement benefit, meaning a range. Then there is the "unit benefit plan" based on some combination of salary and service. An employee may receive 1 percent of former salary multiplied by the number of years of service with the employer.

The last defined benefit plan type is the "integrated defined benefit plan." In this case, the plan is integrated with Social Security. A typical formula would be one in which the employee receives 55 percent of salary less 50 percent of the Social Security benefit payable at retirement. You can mix and match variables to satisfy almost any philosophy, but these formulas are best left to plan designers. Although the Internal Revenue Service has set up certain requirements for defined benefit plans, actuarial firms can usually determine a benefit formula that favors the older, higher-paid participants.

Defined benefit plans are serious, long-term commitments, and the employer must be fully aware of all the responsibilities involved. First, minimum contributions are mandatory. If a contribution is not made, a funding deficiency occurs and the employer becomes responsible for both the contribution and an excise tax. Second, both an actuarial firm and an administration firm must be hired to perform services for the plan. This is quite a drawback because costs tend to run as much as three times as high as for alternative plans.

Third, the federal Pension Benefit Guarantee Corporation (PBGC) insures pension benefits. Although the PBGC was never intended to be a problem, it has recently become so. It was established to ensure minimum benefits for defined benefit plans in the case of a company's bankruptcy. When the agency was first started, the overhead cost per plan participant was $1 per year; now it is $19 per year. Weaker companies are being bailed out by stronger ones. Additionally, if a company goes bankrupt, the PBGC may go back and attach the assets of the company declaring bankruptcy. In that case, the valuation of the company is based on assets in existence 210 days before the date of bankruptcy.

DEFINED CONTRIBUTION PLANS

Most medium- to small-sized companies prefer to offer a defined contribution plan. These plans are easier to understand, easier to explain to employees, and do not saddle the employer with significant administrative responsibility or expenses.

The "profit-sharing plan" is by far today's most common and preferred plan of this type. The employer need not make a contribution to the plan if there are no profits, nor if the decision is made to skip a year. The requirements are that the contribution be "recurring" and "substantial," but the IRS has not defined either of those terms. We know from experience that if contributions are made in very early years and then stop for several years, there is a possibility that the IRS will disqualify the plan as a tax sham. A company failing to pay in had better be able to document that no profits were available for contributions.

Normally, in these plans an employee is required to wait for one year before starting up as a plan participant. The size of the contribution after the trial period is normally left to the discretion of the management and is declared annually by the board of directors. In most cases the tax deductible contribution made by the employer may not exceed 15 percent of the participating payroll.

Smaller plans tend to be "top-heavy," meaning that the key employees of the company account for more than 60 percent of the balances held in the plan. When a plan is top-heavy, graded vesting must begin at two years of service and employees must be fully vested within six years of service. Vesting refers to the amount of assets, usually money, payable to a given employee upon separation from any qualified plan, e.g. pension or profit-sharing, in accordance with the existing vesting schedule contained in the plan. Thus, a person might be 10 percent vested, 50 percent vested, or fully (100 percent) vested. If the plan is not top-heavy, then employees must vest 100 percent in their balances within seven years of service. An additional option is "cliff" vesting. Under this type of vesting schedule an employee is either 0 or 100 percent vested. When cliff vesting is used, a top-heavy plan must vest employees 100 percent within three years. A plan that is not top-heavy may delay 100 percent vesting for five years.

Once a contribution is deposited by the employer, it may be allocated among the participants in various ways. The first and easiest is a pro-rata allocation. The employer contributes to the plan some percentage of participating salaries. Each participant receives a contribution equal to the same percentage of salary. Usually, there is a formula that allocates contributions by integrating the plan with Social Security. Determination of the best allocation formula is complex and is saddled with IRS rules and regulations. Nevertheless, it is usually well worth the exercise if you are trying to determine the fairest contribution of those earning salaries.

Profit-sharing plans that contain "401(k) provisions" retain all the good attributes of profit-sharing plans, and in addition an employee may elect to contribute some part of his or her unattached net salary to the 401(k) plan if the employer is unable to maximize contributions to 15 percent of employee salary. The employee enters into an agreement with the employer to reduce salary by a particular percentage, as defined by the employee. In turn, the employer agrees to take those funds and contribute them as an employer contribution to the employer's 401(k) profit sharing plan. This is considered an employer contribution by the Internal Revenue Service.

Many, many rules and regulations govern how much can be contributed by an employee through salary reduction. First, if the plan is top-heavy, a special top-heavy minimum contribution must be made by the employer for all non-key employees before the key employees are eligible to defer any funds in the 401(k) plan. The maximum employee 401(k) contribution is indexed annually for inflation; in 1994 this ceiling was $9,240. The absolute dollar maximum contribution is determined through a series of complicated IRS tests that must be applied to all the participants in the plan.

All employees must be counted, whether or not they contribute, so as to meet the discrimination testing requirements of the federal government. For purposes of testing, the company is divided into two groups. The first group is comprised of the highly compensated. Generally, in order to be a part of the highly compensated group (for 1994), the participant must fit into one or more of the following categories: owns 5 percent or more of the employing company; earns over $99,000 a year; earns over $66,000 and is one of the highest paid 20 percent of all employees of the company; or is an officer of the employer with a salary greater than 50 percent of the defined benefit limit ($59,400 in 1994). The highly compensated group is usually limited to owners and officers except in companies where specialists earn more than $66,000 per year.

The second group is made up of those who are not part of the highly compensated group.

Once the groups have been determined, an average contribution rate is calculated for the highly compensated group and an average contribution rate is determined for the non-highly compensated group. The maximum spread between those two rates is governed by current IRS regulations. As long as the contribution rate differential fits Internal Revenue Service parameters, it satisfies the requirement that there shall be no discrimination in favor of the highly compensated group.

Frequently, an employer will match employee contributions by some percentage in order to entice the employees to enter the 401(k) plan. If employer matching is used, the percentage differential between the highly compensated group and the non-highly compensated group is also governed by Internal Revenue Service regulations. These tests are cumbersome to perform and require knowledge and experience for their application. It is strongly suggested, because rules and regulations change frequently, that these tests be provided by an administrative company hired to handle the plan, not by the employer.

If both tests are passed, the nondiscrimination requirements in the 401(k) plan are satisfied. If not, then there are various ways in which to make them work. For example, the employer may make a qualified nonelective employer contribution (QNEC) on behalf of employees in the non-highly compensated group.

Another approach is an "age-weighted" profit-sharing plan. Under this plan, a formula is based on the factors of age and salary, with the contribution allocated on the basis of a ratio between each person's credits and the total plan credits. This is subject to certain minimum requirements for top-heavy plans. This type of plan, which offers maximized rewards to the same group of workers who usually hold the top-paying jobs, is still relatively new. Individual legal documents must be used, and administration charges are higher than in a regular profit-sharing plan.

This section would not be complete without mention of employee stock ownership plans (ESOP). Under these plans, the employer funds the entire trust with employer stock. Cash contributions or secured loans may be used, and both are used to buy company stock now or in the future. There are usually no general investments except investment in employer stock. This alternative offers the employer the opportunity of transferring stock in the corporation to the employees via a profit-sharing device. Again, there are complex rules governing the value of the shares sold and the qualification of the appraiser who determines the value of the company. Significant liabilities may result for both the trustees and the employer if proper procedures are not followed, or if proper stock valuations are not made.

Then there are defined contribution plans requiring obligatory contributions, particularly "money purchase" pension plans. This plan has been avoided for years because an annual contribution is required. Most employers refuse to consider it for this reason. The strength of the plan lies in the fact that the plan document holds the option of a contribution rate of up to 25 percent of the participating payroll, in comparison with the subjective maximum 15 percent of the participating payroll under the conventional profit-sharing plan.

Another defined contribution plan that requires an annual contribution is the "target benefit" pension plan. Here the amount of retirement benefit you will attempt to fund is determined by a formula. The benefit is calculated exactly like a defined benefit plan. Government-sanctioned interest tables are used to determine the level annual deposit needed to fund the benefit at retirement age. If the investments perform as expected, then the target will be reached and there will be sufficient funds to pay for the target benefit. By the same token, if performance is better than expected, the participant will receive a benefit greater than the target, but if performance is substandard, the benefit will be less. This plan is particularly appropriate for smaller companies with few employees and older, highly compensated participants. A skilled plan designer can achieve a large contribution for the highly compensated participants with a low benefit formula. The disadvantage of the plan is that the same benefit formula must be applied to the salaries of all rank-and-file employees once they vest in the system.

THE SEP AND THE SARSEP

The simplified employee pension (SEP) was established in 1974 as an easy way to install a pension plan for employees. Under this program an employer may contribute up to 15 percent of a participant's salary, funding an IRA for the participant. Blessedly, no legal document must be filed by the adopting employer with the Internal Revenue Service. When the plan begins, a simple one-page adoption agreement is all that is needed. There are virtually no administration charges involved because little administration is involved.

Unfortunately, the simplified employee pension has become significantly less than simple. First, the employer must contribute for all employees who have satisfied the eligibility requirements. At this writing, a contribution must be made for an eligible employee as long as the employee has been paid more than $396 in the year. Once the contribution is made, it is automatically 100 percent vested in the employee and may not be returned to the company. The participant has the right to cash in the IRA, pay taxes and penalties, or just blow the money. This defeats the retirement-planning process. Furthermore, contributions deposited and accounts held under a SEP may not have protection from creditors, because an IRA is being used instead of a corporate plan.

A recent twist to the SEP is a plan with a salary reduction feature. The salary reduction simplified employee pension (SARSEP) has the same strengths and weaknesses as in the standard SEP, the major difference being that under a SARSEP an employee may elect to reduce salary with tax-deferred dollars, just like in a 401(k) plan. Similar highly compensated/non-highly compensated employee ratio tests must be made in the SARSEP. In case you wonder, this means that the administration costs for the SARSEP are significant.

A MAJOR CHANGE

In 1993 an amendment to the Internal Revenue Code reduced the amount of compensation that may be covered by a retirement plan to $150,000 annually, effective in January 1994. This was a 36 percent reduction in the salary amount that could formerly be counted for plan purposes. Uninformed employers confronted with this change are likely to be paying significant plan cost increases. The law still allows a $30,000 annual allocation, which can be obtained through a single plan, or a combination of plans. In both cases it is likely to cost the employer more money. Some will pay more; others will accept lower benefits for themselves in order to keep employee contributions level.

RETIREMENT PLAN INVESTMENT

Employee benefit plans have been invested idiosyncratically, to say the least, in everything from securities to tapestries to racehorses. Trustees of some plans found it engaging to put down plan assets for the utilitarian—equipment for their companies—and the flagrantly questionable—trustee limousines and beach houses for personal use.

Responding to this, government watchdogs have felt obliged to impose controls. In 1974, the Employees Retirement Investment Securities Act was passed in an attempt to stop abuses in both defined benefit and defined contribution plans. Regulations were established concerning the quality of investments, and safeguards were introduced to protect benefits and investments.

Today, various plan investments are allowed. Cash equivalents, stocks, and bonds are the most common and comprise the vast majority of plan investments. Real estate investments increase and decrease in popularity as real estate cycles change. The courts frown on real estate as an investment for benefit plans. Mortgages, second lien notes, business loans, car loans, non-income-producing property, and similar investments have also been defined as risky and are to be avoided. Valuable (legal) substances have been allowed in rare cases, such as gold depository receipts of a broker.

Overall, the orientation is now toward the conservative investment portfolio. Stock options are a preferred investment for benefit plans. Only options can be sold on the owned stocks, but any such extra income may add significantly to the total plan income. Life insurance is another perfectly acceptable investment, except for the self-employed individual. Many large estates have been created by life insurance proceeds. Years ago, plan insurance proceeds were estate tax-free. Today there is no such special treatment; insurance in a plan is just like insurance outside a plan.

The most popular investments today are mutual funds and investment funds offered by trust companies and insurance companies. These investments offer diversified, quality portfolios at low investment management costs.

Whatever the choice, there are two standards that must be met by those investing dollars in employee benefit plans. The first is the "prudent man rule"; the second is to diversify assets so as to minimize the risk of large losses from one particular asset.

Because the accumulation on retirement plan money is tax-deferred, the casual onlooker might at first think that investments with the greatest potential return should be purchased. The reasoning is that it is much better to tax-shelter a 15 percent annual rate of return than a 5 percent annual rate of return. What is frequently overlooked is that 15 percent annual rates of return are the exception, not the rule, and that potential big winners are also potential big losers. Instead of the touted 15 percent rate of return, the speculative asset might easily lose money or default completely. If an individual takes a loss, it is deductible against current gains and/or current income over this or future years. Employee benefit plans don't have this cushion. If the company offering the speculative stock goes bankrupt, there is no tax deduction permitted by the Internal Revenue Service. Moreover, the tax-deferred earnings base is reduced and can only be replenished with new contributions. Bad investing may severely damage the contributing power required by the company, not to mention having the potential for Department of Labor fines and/or penalties. Trustees may be held personally liable to make up plan losses, and prison sentences may be imposed for what is considered to be criminal conduct.

The recent movement of an asset's price, up or down, does not solely determine whether investing in it is prudent or imprudent. One must look to the quality of the corporation, its history of dividend payments, the strength of its management team, its growth and earnings through the years, and a host of alternative factors. Generally, the best bet is to keep the plan invested in different economic sectors and different companies within the economic sectors.

PLAN DISTRIBUTIONS

When you are ready to receive a distribution from your retirement plan due to termination of employment or retirement, different rules and regulations apply depending upon your age at the time you receive the distribution. For example, if you are under age 59½ when the benefit is paid, you normally have the option to either place the benefit in a tax-deferred IRA rollover or pay taxes and penalties on the benefit and do whatever you please with the money. If you elect to take the benefit in cash, the IRS now requires a 20 percent mandatory withholding tax. Additionally, there is a 10 percent penalty assessed for distributions to those under age 59½ that are not rolled over to an IRA, and there may be additional penalties if the distribution exceeds a certain threshold amount.

If you are over age 59½ and receive a lump-sum benefit, you will generally have the option of rolling the dollars over to your own IRA or electing some type of income tax averaging. In order to be able to elect income tax averaging, the benefit must be paid as a lump-sum distribution. A lump-sum distribution is defined as: an entire amount credited to the participant's account at the time of the distribution and that must be distributed within one calendar year; distribution if the participant has been an active participant in the plan for five or more years; or distribution because of death, disability, separation of service, or attainment of age 59½.

There is no point in exploring the endless rules and regulations concerning current taxation of benefit plan distributions. What is "current" now may be cast aside in six months. Participants are required to receive many disclosures before benefits are paid, but the language used and the complications of the regulations themselves make even those "easy to understand" notices less than easy. Always consult a tax adviser, or ask the plan administrator, if you are unsure about the taxability of your benefit.

Remember, the advice you receive about your distribution is only as good as the source providing the advice. Try to find a professional who specializes in employee benefit plans and in distributions from those plans.

THE IRA ROLLOVER ACCOUNT

Say that a participant has received a retirement distribution, that the participant is over age 59½, and that the participant has decided to place the money in an IRA rollover. In this case, tax-free

rollovers are available for most plan distributions in the case of termination of service, attainment of age 59½, disability, death, or termination of the plan itself.

The main advantage of a tax-free rollover is that the dollars deposited to the rollover continue to accumulate earnings on a tax-
deferred basis until they are paid to the participant in the form of
a retirement benefit. Prior to 1993, a participant could be paid a
lump sum in cash, elect to have no income taxes withheld, and then
roll the dollars over to an IRA custodian within sixty days. As of
January 1993, the participant is required to decide upon termination of service whether dollars would be transferred directly to an
IRA custodian or first to the participant. Although the participant
still has the right to roll the dollars over to an IRA rollover account
within sixty days, now he is saddled with a 20 percent income tax
withholding requirement if he gets the money in person first. Most
participants have seen the merits of rolling over dollars directly
to an IRA custodian. All noncash property received must also be
transferred to the rollover if deferred taxation for that value is
wanted.

Once the assets are rolled over, the participant, unless an investment management team has been retained, has the responsibility
for investing the assets. This is called a "self-directed plan." If the
participant wishes, assets may be left in the IRA rollover until age
70½. At that point, the Internal Revenue Service requires that at
least a minimum distribution be made. Minimum distributions are
made based on IRS actuarial tables.

At the time of the first distribution, the participant must decide
whether future distributions will be based on annual recalculation
of life expectancies or will be based on the original calculation of
life expectancies, less one year for each year of distribution. This
election can have a significant impact on future distribution if the
participant dies. For example, if the participant elects to have life
expectancies recalculated annually, and then dies two years later,
the total account may be continued by the spouse in the form of a
widow's benefit IRA rollover. Upon the establishment of a widow's
benefit IRA, the only alternative is to take distributions over the
life expectancy of the surviving spouse, rather than over the *joint*
life expectancy of the deceased participant and the surviving

spouse. If the initial benefit is taken over the life expectancy of the participant and spouse, reduced by one for each year of payment, then the surviving spouse may continue that liquidation rate even after the joint annuitant's death.

Most participants, well aware of their own mortality, begin distributions as early as age 60 or 65, depending upon needs or optimism. Benefits for highly paid persons are often delayed to age 70½, because these individuals are usually in a lower tax bracket at that time.

A participant turning 70½ has the right to take the first distribution in the same calendar year that that age is attained or by April 1 of the next calendar year. If that postponement is decided upon, two distributions must be paid during the second year.

CONCLUSION

Retirement planning has taken on all kinds of new dimensions. The last decade has witnessed so many new alternatives for accumulating wealth on a tax-deferred basis that one can only guess what sort of retirement plans will be available in a few more years.

Investment in employee benefit plans form the vast majority of all investments in our country, and will continue to compound exponentially as they have in the past. That's good for everyone, because it means both regularized investment and regularized security for elders. All one has to do is participate, keep working, and wait for the time when all that managed investment comes back to you.

14

INVESTMENT CLUBS

JAMES GALBRAITH

ORIGINS

The burgeoning world economy that emerged in the latter part of the nineteenth century produced unprecedented opportunities for investment. Then, as now, the general trend on the stock exchanges was upward, but not without the jolts of sudden "adjustments" when busts succeeded booms. Each time a major downturn came along—and they did each fifteen to twenty years—many small-time, poorly informed investors lost their shirts during the frenzied selling of the "panics." Unlike some of the big boys, who had the cushion of wide diversity and enormous reserves, small investors were wiped out.

During the four years of deep economic depression that followed the crash of June 1893, bloodied partisans of minor equity began joining together, pooling their resources, and sharing risks and profits. These joint ventures were serious efforts to hold equity and make a profit; perhaps it is because they "played the market" that they became known as investment clubs. However they started, soon there were clubs wherever investors could be found.

Unfortunately, sharing outcomes does not in itself offer protection from the vicissitudes of economic reality. Club members tended toward wild-eyed speculation as much as anyone else in those days. The degree of naiveté among all investors at the time seems amazing today, and of course the minimum equity laws didn't help hold things down. The blue sky optimists of all levels pushed the envelope too hard again in 1907 and then horrendously in 1929. October 24, 1929, known thereafter as "black Thursday," saw the start of a panic on the exchanges the like of which had never before been seen. In two weeks, over $30 billion worth of securities' equity vanished, investors were catastrophically ruined, and the dozen years of the Great Depression were under way.

It was obvious to nearly everyone that if recovery ever occurred, the unbridled pattern of investment pyramiding had to be brought under control. Partly this was accomplished by much tighter federal regulation of securities investment, partly it was the result of better data becoming more widely distributed and analyzed.

THE NATIONAL ASSOCIATION OF INVESTORS CORPORATION

On the investment club front, a major improvement came about with the formation of the National Association of Investors Corporation (NAIC). The NAIC started out as a confederation of four investment clubs in the upper Midwest, which first joined forces in 1951. The objective: to create a nationwide securities information system so that club members could more wisely use their resources. This was so attractive an idea that clubs joined in droves. There were thousands of participating clubs within just a few years.

But why stop there? In no time at all the NAIC had become a leading advocate of internationalized securities education. In 1960 it was an important player behind the formation of the World Federation of Investment Clubs, currently based in London, England. The next year the NAIC backed the formation of the Investment Education Institute at Wayne State University to foster cooperation in investment education by government, industry, and the financial community.

An ongoing program provides pointers on how to set up a new investment club. Written materials may be obtained by writing the NAIC (the address is 1515 East Eleven Mile Road, Royal Oak, Michigan 48067) or phoning ([313] 543-0612). Most clubs are formed as a partnership, but some incorporate. In a partnership, members are ordinarily not responsible for the personal debts of the partners but are responsible for the acts of the partnership. The club partnership does business with only the broker, so liability risk should be limited to this one source. The NAIC recommends consultation with legal council in this matter because state regulations may vary.

The NAIC encouraged the adoption of rule 13-03 by the Transfer Agents Association. This provides that club securities can be transferred directly into and out of the club's name with the signature of only one member without supporting papers if it is a true partnership. Individual clubs devise their own controls on how their pooled resources should be allocated.

NAIC member clubs are usually associated with local volunteer councils that conduct classes on securities, invite investment professionals to give talks, and invite corporation officers to discuss their companies. The NAIC sponsors, for a fee, an advisory service providing investment information and recommendations on specific companies. For the individual who does not want to join a club there is the individual accumulation program, in which any individual can make modest monthly payments toward the accumulation of a portfolio. In NAIC's dividend reinvestment program, participating corporations help employees become securities investors by covering brokers' commission costs even when the members can only afford to buy just one share of stock. This support continues until a large enough holding has been accumulated for the investor to make transactions through a regular broker independently.

Other subsidiary NAIC programs include a group life insurance plan, a national congress held once a year, the 21 and 40 program, and the factory-office-town program. New investors can get involved as little or as much as they want.

The NAIC hews to several basic tenets in investment:

1. Invest regularly. Make investments each month without regard to the overall outlook of the stock exchanges, maintaining a spirit of cautious optimism but avoiding speculation. Club members should approach investment with the perspective that they are

buying an interest in a business that they expect to own as long as
that business operates successfully.

2. Reinvest most or all securities' earnings. Living modestly
while securities' equity grows is a long-term approach to investment that is generally best for small and new investors. The idea is
to build up an estate, not to squander fairly small current earnings
on frivolities.

3. Invest in "growth" companies. These are companies that grow
faster than at the rate of the economy overall. By seeking out such
opportunities, the investor will be best able to protect gained equity against inflation and see portfolio size expand in real terms.

4. Diversify. Rather than putting all hopes into only a single
company or a few companies, or one industry, branch out in several
directions. By spreading out risk, no single downturn can seriously
damage a portfolio.

The NAIC recommends a big company/small company orientation in investing. It suggests a balance of about 25 percent in major
companies in major industries, about 25 percent in smaller, possibly younger companies, and the remainder of a portfolio in diversified, mid-grade securities. This is hardest during a down market,
when it is tempting to off-load the more volatile stocks. Restraint
is the rule, since over the long haul basically solid companies will
nearly always flow with the cycle and will return. Patient investors
who have the equity during a downturn can pick up securities at
a bargain from those who are naive, hasty, or without a sense of
historical continuity.

THE NAIC MAGAZINE

Financial information from the NAIC is disseminated to investors
through the magazine *Better Investing,* now the largest investments education magazine in the world. This is a monthly periodi-
cal with three primary sections: focus, stocks, and learn and earn.
In the focus section the concentration is on general stories of interest and special reports. It includes letters, editorials, notices, and
the like. In the stock section a particular company is profiled for
study, usually because analysts feel that its stock is undervalued or

that the company is about to surge, making it a good candidate for investment. In the stock section is also a discussion of NAIC's model purchase portfolio—a group of twelve stocks that are attractive in price and have a reasonable potential to double in value in the next five years or by the next market peak.

The learn and earn section has useful essays on different contexts of investment, for example market timing. A section entitled "Repair Shop" is reserved for answering common investment questions, such as details on how to monitor a company or how to go beyond the NAIC's stock selection guide (SSG) to measure a company's growth rate and growth potential. This section also reviews the portfolios of various clubs to show how well they have done and where they could make improvements in their investment strategy.

THE NAIC STUDY TOOLS

The NAIC has developed a number of study tools for the evaluation of individual companies, the comparison of several companies, and record-keeping. The stock check list is designed for the beginning investor and is a cursory analysis of securities. More seasoned investors move on to the stock selection guide (SSG), more advanced tools for organizing securities comparisons (see Table 14-1 on pages 235–36 and Figure 9-1 on page 161).

The portfolio management guide helps to review holdings so that decisions can be made about buying more, continuing to hold, or selling securities. Once each month you record the price of the stock on a graph where you have prerecorded the bottom of the sell zone and the top of the buy zone as derived from the SSG. It also requires recording of the current PE as well as the PE buy and sell guidelines. Thinking here is helped by the portfolio evaluation review technique, useful for making buy, hold, and sell decisions for individual stocks. This is a more time-consuming and professional way of monitoring securities, involving the tracking of fundamentals such as the earnings growth, sales growth, pre-tax profit growth and margins, current PE relative to historic PE, percent yield, and actual growth compared to expected growth of sales, pretax profits, and earnings per share.

A particularly helpful analytical tool provided by the NAIC is its stock selection guide (SSG), in use for over thirty years by professional investors and amateurs alike. The guide is used to spot companies that are growing faster than their industry average. It shows how companies have grown in the past and therefore gives some insight into anticipated future growth. The NAIC gives guidelines for generating projections, evaluating management performance, and evaluating risks and rewards.

There are a number of places in the guide where judgment is required, for example on what trend lines reveal. The NAIC gives certain axiomatic guidelines about this. For examples, projecting a company's sales and earnings per share at more than 20 percent for longer than five years is unrealistic, since high rates are difficult to maintain. If present management has had a record of producing growth in the business, it is reasonable to assume that it will continue, but with fluctuations. Earnings growth ought to be at least equal to or greater than sales growth, since this demonstrates that management is at least maintaining its profit margin. For another thing, the trend line for earnings per share should generally be drawn parallel to the sales trend line or at the earnings per share trend, whichever is lower. The profit margin would have to be increasing before you would consider otherwise. In general, use the profit margin trend as a guide to place the other trend lines above or below their latest year's values. Study the changes in the percent payout over the last five years to make a judgment about management's expectations for growth. If these values are decreasing, then you might think that management is optimistic about future growth.

CONCLUSION

Joining an investment club can be a very rewarding and educational experience. You will find that the club can be a sturdy support group, especially in those vulnerable first years of investment when you fear the stock market the most. Involvement in NAIC support is an excellent idea because it is strongly inclined toward education of the small and inexperienced investor, and can keep you out of trouble at low expense.

TABLE 14-1:
EVALUATION OF SYSCO WITH THE STOCK SELECTION GUIDE

1. Analysis of Sales, Earnings, Price

Latest Qtr. Results =   2QTR 93   20.05%

	Sales	E/S
Latest Qtr.	2392	0.26
Year Ago	2181	0.24
% Change	9.67%	8.33%

Current Price = 24.25

10 Years of Historical Data
Sales Growth = 20.05%
Earnings/Sh. Growth = 17.60%
Share Price Growth = 22.45%
Dividends Growth = 17.77%

10 Years Used to Forecast 5-Yr. Trend
Sales Growth = 20.05%
Earnings/Sh. Growth = 17.60%

2. Evaluating Management

Years	1983	1984	1985	1986	1987	1988	1989	1990	1991	1992	Avg. 5 yr.
A) Operating Margin	4.80%	4.80%	4.90%	4.30%	4.40%	4.30%	4.50%	4.60%	4.70%	4.70%	4.56%
B) % Earned on Inv.	16.67%	15.61%	14.80%	15.11%	13.73%	15.61%	16.95%	17.38%	16.94%	16.34%	16.64%

3. Price-Earnings History as an indicator of the future

Present Price = 24.25   High This Year 27.75   Low This Year 27.75

Year	Price High	Low	E/Sh.	High P/E	Low P/E	Div/Sh	% Payout	% High Yield
1988	9.70	6.50	0.47	20.64	13.83	0.08	17.02	1.23
1989	16.00	9.20	0.60	26.67	15.33	0.09	15.00	0.98
1990	19.20	12.80	0.73	26.30	17.53	0.10	13.70	0.78
1991	23.70	15.00	0.84	28.21	17.86	0.12	14.29	0.80
1992	27.80	20.60	0.93	29.89	22.15	0.20	21.51	0.97
Average	19.28	12.82	0.71	26.34	17.34	0.12	16.30	0.95

Average P/E Ratio 21.84   Current P/E Ratio 26.08

(continued)

TABLE 14-1:

EVALUATION OF SYSCO WITH THE STOCK SELECTION GUIDE (*continued*)

4. Evaluating Risk and Reward over the Next 5 Years

A) High Price - Next 5 Years

Avg. High P/E   26.34 × Est. High E/Sh. of 2.11 = Forecast High Price   55.61

B) Low Price - Next 5 Years

    17.34 × Est. Low E/Sh. of 0.93 =

a) Avg. Low P/E	16.13
b) Avg. Low Price of Last 5 Years	12.82
c) Recent Severe Market Low Price	6.50
d) Price Dividend Will Support Div./High	
Yield =	21.00
Selected Estimated Low Price	21.00

C) Zoning

       55.61 Est. High Price =   21.00 Est. L. Price   34.61 Range ⅓ of = 11.54

Lower ⅓ =	21.00 to	32.54 Buy
Middle ⅓ =	32.54 to	44.07 Maybe
Upper ⅓ =	44.07 to	55.61 Sell
Present Market Price of	24.25 Is in the Buy Range	

D) Up-Side, Down-Side Ratio (Potential Gain vs. Risk of Loss)

(High P - Present P) / (Present P - Low P)   9.65 to 1

5. 5-Year Potential

A) Present Dividend / Present Price = Present Yield or % Return on Purchase Price   0.82%

B) Average Yield over Next 5 Years

    Avg. E/Sh. Next 5 Yrs. × Avg. % Payout/Present Price   1.57 × 0.16 / 24.25 =   1.05%

Courtesy Bob Bradford

15
MONITORING AND CONTROL

OTTO GLASER

INTRODUCTION

The new investor, having read this far, understands the need for discipline, organization, and planning. This chapter provides a basic, noncomputer-driven system that anyone can use successfully when starting out. Many investors will be satisfied with using it indefinitely.

Start by getting a loose-leaf notebook in a size you find convenient. Using tabs, separate the notebook into four sections with these headings: Market Outlook, Money Management, Investments, Things to Do and Not to Do. Between each section insert paper; grid paper or columnar pads are particularly helpful in keeping it neat and organized.

In the front of the notebook, so that you will always remember them, write these questions:

1. How much potential is there in this investment?
2. How much risk do I face?
3. How much time is needed to accomplish my goals?
4. Why buy or sell?
5. Why buy or sell *now*?

Seeing these five questions every time you open the notebook will drill them into your consciousness.

Have a specific target price for each of your investments—a price at which you will buy and a price for which you will sell. Try always to muster a clear understanding of the risk a particular investment represents. It is important to gauge your personal risk tolerance and select only those investments that fit into your comfort zone. How long do you anticipate holding (owning) your investment before reaching your goal? Are you looking at this as a short-term, medium-term, or long-term investment? Have specific reasons for buying a particular security as well as for selling it. Then, what are the compelling reasons for buying or selling a security at this time?

Ask yourself each one of these questions every time you consider buying or selling an investment, and be honest. Accept nothing less than a thorough and satisfactory answer. By doing so you will learn to define your investment strategy and focus on investments most suitable for you.

MARKET OUTLOOK

This first section is a journal of your investment progress. Keeping a record is a good habit because before you can chart a course you must know where you have been.

For each recorded date, write summary figures on how stocks and bonds are doing. For your stocks, track one of the three major stock exchange indexes: the Dow Jones Industrial Average, the Standard & Poor's Index, or the New York Stock Exchange Index. There are others, but these are easily accessible to most investors because they are published in most daily newspapers' business sections. For your bonds you need two indexes, one which deals with short-term lender interest rates (applicable for such securities as six-month certificates of deposit or three-month Treasury bills) and one for long-term rates (applicable for such securities as ten- or thirty-year United States Treasury bonds. Banks and brokerage firms make these figures, called "yields," readily available.

Next to the stocks and bonds indexes, predict their trends for the

short term, the intermediate term, and the long term. Shorthand
abbreviations can be used here, such as:

ST	(short term)	↑	(trend is up)
IT	(intermediate term)	↓	(trend is down)
LT	(long term)	→	(trend is horizontal)

Here's an example. Let's assume that you've selected the Dow
Jones Industrial Averages for your stock index. A typical daily Dow
entry might look like this:

11/24/94   DJIA @ 3248.70   ST↑   IT→   LT→

Your bond average might look like this:

11/24/93   6mo CD 3.08%; 30yr T Bond 102, 7.72%; ST↑   IT↓   LT↓

To one side you write remarks if you need to underline and remember some peculiarity or distinction of what is going on.

The visually oriented individual, particularly the chartist, will
very likely also want to maintain a graph of the several numbers.
Others will be satisfied with the simple log.

MONEY MANAGEMENT

Here is where you keep track of your investment net worth, using
Table 15-1 on page 244. Be careful not to mix in personal assets.
The real estate section, for example, should exclude the value of
your residence.

How often you update this section depends on your personality.
Some people keep a monthly record, others are satisfied to tally
up quarterly, semiannually, or annually. Pick the periodicity most
comfortable for you.

Under the general heading "Short Term," list subheadings for
savings and checking accounts, certificates of deposit, money market funds, and fixed-income investments maturing in less than one
year. At the bottom here, and for each other general heading, total
the value of all your listed assets.

Bonds are listed in two sections, according to quality. The general heading "Long Term Bond/Investment Quality" is for fixed-income investments of investment grade quality (BBB and better from the Standard & Poor's rating or Baa and better from the Moody's rating) with maturities longer than one year. Under the heading "Below Investment Quality," list fixed-income bonds with more than one year maturities and ratings less than investment grade (less than BBB from the Standard & Poor's rating or less than Baa from the Moody's rating).

The stocks section is also broken out according to quality. The listings from a rating service such as Standard & Poor's identify common stocks as "investment quality," "good quality," and "speculative quality." Charitably, and for fear of lawsuits, no stocks are described as "awful" or "losers," sad to say, despite the great help such designations would be for the novice investor.

After listing all the raw data, make a calculation of the percentage of assets found in each investment category and note them down beside the data. This makes it possible to understand at a glance how balanced your portfolio is. The data itself describes enlargement or deflation of value, meaning profit or loss.

Naturally, each time you make a new purchase it is noted by date and size of equity. Some investors cross-reference to the next section, which lists all investments and their specific records. And again, the chartists will want to make graphs that visually describe what is going on.

Regular review of investment holdings determines what changes need to be made. Bring them into compliance with your market strategy.

INVESTMENTS

This section is for specific records of all the investments you buy and sell. Whenever you buy any type of investment, record the date you purchased it, the type of investment, the price and quantity purchased, and the dollar amount spent on the item. Record these data using Table 15-2 on page 245. Record sales in the same fashion, and place the tally of net profit or loss.

As you record your buys and sells, continually review the array of the portfolio. Do all your investments still fit with your objectives, your current "market outlook"? If not, sell the errant investment.

You've heard this before, but let me say it again: It is important to be as unemotional and analytical as possible in reviewing your portfolio. Do not make the mistake of holding onto an investment that has turned sour and gone past the degree of risk you *originally* were willing to assume. Few of us like to admit a mistake, but denial or procrastination only worsens things. It is better to take a small loss now than a major hit later.

THINGS TO DO, AND THINGS NOT TO DO

History repeats itself, negatively for the ignorant, hasty, and foolish, positively for the informed, considered, and wise. The latter group learns from experience, preferably someone else's disasters, but also from personal achievement or a lack thereof.

This section is where you record your personal investment epiphanies. One page holds the heading "Things to Do"; a second holds the heading "Things Not to Do." Decisions that turned out most agreeably are summarized on the "Things to Do" page, and poor to catastrophic decisions are summarized on the "Things Not to Do" page. Looking back at triumphs and failures gives you insight about what to do in future.

SOME GENERAL SUGGESTIONS

When you invest, use a big enough part of your total equity to keep your attention. That way you are more likely to carefully study and follow the investment. A solid rule of thumb is to make purchases using from 5 to 15 percent of your total equity, but never with more than 15 percent. If best expectations go awry and the investment loses money, you can bear the loss without too much pain. Your careful record-keeping makes it possible to know what the percentage means in your unique case.

It is better to "average up" than "average down." Averaging up occurs when you purchase an equal amount of a security that is going up in price. For example, you buy 100 shares of Dravidian Combustibles at $50, another 100 at $52, and another at $54. The average cost for the whole 300 shares is $52. Averaging down works the same way with multiple purchases of a stock at prices progressively lower than the original purchase price. The cautionary perspective here is that a stock on the downward trend may have no bottom. Records show you what is going on here, too.

And, of course, good records make it much easier to do your taxes. You keep up with "open" positions (stocks or options you bought or wrote) and "closed" positions (stocks sold or options closed). The United States government requires that your broker send you a year-end statement listing all purchases and sales of securities made during the year. This form lists the transactions but may not provide the results in terms of net profit or loss.

CONCLUSION

The main thing to emphasize to yourself about all this is that you need to stay organized and abreast of what is going on. That is, do so if you want to be an active participant in what happens to your equity. For lighthearted souls who are happy to drift wherever the wind carries them, none of what was discussed in this chapter applies. For the rest of you, get systematic and stay systematic.

It is inevitable, now that personal computers have become so ubiquitous and inexpensive, that the maturing investor will eventually want to turn over the dirty work of keeping track to a faithful machine. A first venture will no doubt be application of a word-processing program, where the ease of editing and filing will be useful to enhance the format proposed here. But eventually, as your portfolio grows, you will start wondering about how subscription information services and portfolio organization systems work. Remember that computers are wonderful aids in saving time, but are only as good as the program driving them and the diligence with which even the new, reduced workload of surveillance is carried on.

Oh yes, one last thing here. When you buy that computer, contract a computer pro for a fee to help you get started. All the books in the world are not as useful as some hands-on aid both in the purchase and in learning how to operate things. And hold on to your receipts, both for the equipment and for the fee. They are tax deductible.

TABLE 15-1:
INVESTMENT ASSETS

Category	DATE _____		DATE _____		DATE _____	
	Amount	Percent	Amount	Percent	Amount	Percent
SHORT TERM						
Savings and Checking						
CDs (under 1 year)						
Money Market Funds						
TOTAL						
LONG-TERM BONDS Investment Quality CDs and Bonds						
1–4 year						
5–8 year						
9–12 year						
13 year and larger						
TOTAL						
Below Investment Quality						
1–4 year						
5–8 year						
9–12 year						
13 year and larger						
TOTAL						
TOTAL SHORT-TERM AND LONG-TERM BONDS						
STOCKS						
Investment Quality						
Good Quality						
Speculative Quality						
TOTAL						
REAL ESTATE Property 1						
Property 2						
TOTAL						
TOTAL ALL CATEGORIES						

TABLE 15-2:
INDIVIDUAL INVESTMENT MONITOR

	NAME ————————————————————————
	IF BOND, INTEREST RATE AND MATURITY ————————————
	NEWSPAPER ABBREVIATION ———————— TICKER SYMBOL —————
	PURCHASE AND SALE, SPLIT AND STOCK DIVIDEND RECORD
DATE	Number of shares, price per share, total cost including commissions, and costs adjusted for splits
	Dividend and Interest Records—Keep track of dates to be paid and amount per share, just for checking receipt, not for income tax
	1st Qtr.
	2nd Qtr.
	3rd Qtr.
	4th Qtr.
DATE	Answers to 5 investment questions and continuous review

INDEX